Christine Noelle-Karimi / Conrad Schetter / Reinhard Schlagintweit (Eds.)

Afghanistan – A Country without a State?

Mediothek für Afghanistan e.V.
Im Bondorf 33
53545 Linz
Tel./Fax: + 49 - 2644-5813

In der *Schriftenreihe der Mediothek für Afghanistan* werden Beiträge über Afghanistan aus allen Wissenschaftsdisziplinen publiziert.
Jedes Jahr ist mindestens eine Veröffentlichung geplant, die die Ergebnisse des jährlichen Symposiums der *Mediothek für Afghanistan e.V.* dokumentiert. Darüber hinaus ist die Schriftenreihe offen für weitere wissenschaftliche Arbeiten zum Thema Afghanistan.

Christine Noelle-Karimi / Conrad Schetter /
Reinhard Schlagintweit
(Eds.)

Afghanistan –
A Country without a State?

Schriftenreihe der Mediothek für Afghanistan, Band 2
IKO – Verlag für Interkulturelle Kommunikation

Die Deutsche Bibliothek – CIP-Einheitsaufnahme:

Ein Titeldatensatz für diese Publikation ist bei der Deutschen Bibliothek erhältlich.

©   IKO-Verlag für Interkulturelle Kommunikation
        Frankfurt am Main • London, 2002

Frankfurt am Main	London
Postfach 90 04 21	4 T Leroy House
D - 60444 Frankfurt	436 Essex Road
	London N1 3QP, UK

e-mail: ikoverlag@t-online.de • Internet: www.iko-verlag.de

ISBN: 3-88939-628-3
(Schriftenreihe der Mediothek für Afghanistan, Band 2)

Umschlaggestaltung: Volker Loschek, 61184 Karben
Herstellung: Verlagsdruckerei Spengler, 60488 Frankfurt a.M.

Table of Contents

        page

Prefaces   IX
Siegmar-W. Breckle
Sultan A. Karimi

Introduction   1
Christine Noelle-Karimi, Conrad Schetter,
Reinhard Schlagintweit

Part I
National Ideologies and Their Manifestations

Afghanistan – Land of the Afghans?   17
On the Genesis of a Problematic State Denomination
Angela Parvanta

The View of the State by Afghans Abroad   27
Rameen Moshref

The Loya Jirga – An Effective Political Tool?   37
A Historical Overview
Christine Noelle-Karimi

Table of Contents

Part II
Regional and Cultural Development

A Tense Autonomy 53
The Present Situation in Nuristan
Max Klimburg

Finding a Balance between Religious Orthodoxy and the 65
Maintenance of Afghanistan's Performative Traditions
Bruce Koepke

Hazara Research and Hazara Nationalism 1978-89 77
Rolf Bindemann

Part III
The Role of NGOs

About the School System under the Taliban Government 89
Peter Schwittek

Country without a State 97
Does It Really Make a Difference for the Women?
Heike Bill

Part IV
Aspects of a War Economy

The 'Bazaar Economy' of Afghanistan 109
A Comprehensive Approach
Conrad Schetter

Table of Contents

Illicit Opium Production in Afghanistan *Michael von der Schulenburg*	129
From Holy War to Opium War? A Case-Study of the Opium Economy in North-Eastern Afghanistan *Jonathan Goodhand*	139

Part V
Political Formation

Afghanistan's Road to Failure *Reinhard Schlagintweit*	163
Tribe and State in Afghanistan after 1992 *Ahmed Rashid*	175
Perceptions of State and Organisation of the Northern Alliance *Michael Pohly*	179
The Taliban and International Standards of Governance *Citha D. Maass*	191

Part VI
International Dimensions

Afghanistan – The Perspective of International Law *Hermann-Josef Blanke*	205
The Role of Outside Actors in the Afghanistan Conflict *Amin Saikal*	217

Table of Contents

The Failure of UN Mediation in Afghanistan 229
Anwar-ul-Haq Ahady

Biographical Notes 239

Prefaces

Prefaces

Preface of the Chairman
of the Arbeitsgemeinschaft für Afghanistan

The conference on 'Afghanistan – A Country without a State?', the papers from which we present in this volume, was the result of a close cooperation between the two research organizations in German-speaking countries which concern themselves with Afghanistan – the 'Arbeitsgemeinschaft Afghanistan' and 'Mediothek für Afghanistan' – and the 'Museum für Völkerkunde' in Munich, which hosted the conference and was also the venue for the accompanying exhibition on present-day Afghanistan.

This cooperation and the generous support of the German Federal Foreign Office, the Fritz-Thyssen-Stiftung and the Deutsche Forschungsgemeinschaft enabled us not only to attract a large number of prominent researchers from the English-speaking world and from France, among them many Afghans, as speakers, but also representatives of the responsible organs of the United Nations, including the former and current Special Envoys of the Secretary-General of the United Nations, Lakhdar Brahimi and Francesc Vendrell, as well as experts working for non-governmental organizations. Almost all the speakers were able to base their papers on personal, recent experience in the country.

The 'Arbeitsgemeinschaft Afghanistan' (AGA) was founded in 1966 in Heidelberg by a group of researchers from various fields, all of whom were involved in different aspects of research concerning the geographical and cultural region of Afghanistan. Their aim was and still is academic research on Afghanistan, the dissemination of knowledge about the country through publications and conferences, and the provision of expert knowledge. The AGA is an extensive network of competence and expertise on Afghanistan in Central Europe. It is proud to continue this tradition in a time when field work is practically impossible, when research funding is ever more scarce and when Afghanistan as a friend and partner threatens to disappear from our consciousness. We are working to avert this danger – and the Munich conference is an initiative in this direction.

Prefaces

Many observers expected we would map out firm proposals for peace. We have done much analysis, but created few syntheses. We have exchanged personal experience and advice, listened to many opinions and views, and we have tried to arrive at conclusions. We have also collected much new information and many new perspectives. More could not have been expected. Political decisions will be made elsewhere. Yet we can all act as multipliers and make our pleas for reason and against irrationality and inhumanity. If these papers can make a contribution in this direction, the conference will have achieved its aim.

Bielefeld, June 2001   *Siegmar-W. Breckle*

Prefaces

**Preface of the Chairman
of the Mediothek für Afghanistan e.V.**

The conference on 'Afghanistan – A Country without a State?' has met with a wide response. It was the first successful discussion of the issue of the *failed state* in relation to Afghanistan with a large group of international experts. Not only did it include researchers currently working on questions concerning Afghanistan but also representatives of German and international politics as well as non-governmental organizations, all of whom came together to approach the problem of 'Afghanistan – A Country without a State?' from of his or her own perspective. We are glad that we were able to bring together so many well-known experts and friends – amongst them many leading figures in the field – to tackle this difficult task. The group also included the former and the current UN Special Envoys to Afghanistan, Lakhdar Brahimi and Francesc Vendrell.

The aim of this conference was to help find a possible way out of the apparent hopelessness of the situation in which Afghanistan finds itself. It is very important that conditions should become more secure and stable. The conference and the contributions published in this volume are intended as stepping stones along this path – helping us understand and analyse the problems of Afghanistan in its current situation in order to get closer to a non-military solution of the conflict. Mr Vendrell, head of the United Nations Special Mission for Afghanistan (UNSMA), said that this conference had given him new ideas which might serve as a basis for new approaches in the field of conflict mediation.

As a member of the community of nations, Afghanistan signed the Charter of the United Nations at the time that organization was founded. It is not only the task of the Afghans themselves to implement measures of conflict mediation, to strive towards a lasting peaceful solution, and then to keep that peace, but it is also the task and the obligation of the international community to do so. By emphasizing that it is a joint task of the community of states to achieve peace in Afghanistan, I assume that all observers of the conflict agree that the war which has now lasted for more than twenty years has its roots in the so-called *Great Game*. What is being played in Afghanistan was not originally an internal Afghan conflict but

Prefaces

rather an international 'game' held in the arena of Afghanistan, commonly regarded as a buffer state.

As early as ten years ago, many experts believed that if the conflict in Afghanistan could not be solved it would develop into a regional conflict. Today, we have to realize that this was a realistic conclusion, and that the worst pessimism has been proven too modest. The conflict has since taken on a global character spanning drugs, terrorism, illegal trade, and migration.

Allow me to briefly introduce. the organization which I, as co-organizer of the conference, represent and which is also responsible for publishing the series in which this conference documentation appears. 'Mediothek für Afghanistan e. V.' has been dealing with Afghanistan for almost ten years; it is an initiative by Afghans and Germans. We work – on a voluntary basis – at three levels: First, we collect media material on Afghanistan which one day will be made available to the Afghans in their home country. Secondly, we support education projects in Afghanistan. And thirdly, we try to set up a network of experts dealing with this country.

'Mediothek' is committed to peace in Afghanistan and to building bridges: On the one hand a bridge between Afghanistan and Germany, on the other a bridge between the fields of science, politics and international development. Scientists do research on Afghanistan, including on the causes of the conflict. Politicians work out concepts for peace mediation and try to implement them. Humanitarian institutions and institutions in the field of development policy commit themselves to relieving the most pressing needs of the population and to reconstruction. It is very important to interlink these different approaches, experiences, and perspectives in order to benefit from the lessons we have all learned, and thus, to make this work more profound, more effective, and more durable. Mediothek strives to make a success of this double bridge-building or *networking* between the countries on the one hand and the different fields of work on the other. For this purpose, it cooperates with various partners and institutions.

I should like to express my sincere thanks to all those who have actively contributed to the Munich meeting, particularly the Fritz-Thyssen Foundation, the German Federal Foreign Office, and the Deutsche

Prefaces

Forschungsgemeinschaft. Only their financial support made this conference and the publication of the contributions possible.

In conclusion, I would like to summarise my considerations in a little story by the thinker and mystic Jalal al-Din Balkhi, also known as Rumi or Maulana who was born in Afghanistan. Rumi tells us about an elephant that was led into a dark room. Different people then enter the room to find out by touch who or what is in that room. The first one enters and grabs the trunk. He thinks there is a water pipe in the room. The second one touches the elephant's ear and is convinced he is holding a fan in his hand. The third one catches one of the elephant's legs in the darkness and is sure it is a pillar. The last one, finally, touches the elephant's back and thinks it is a rostrum. Each one of them believes he knows the truth about the object in that room. Now, Rumi is of the opinion that if there had been some light in the room or if each one had had a candle there would have been no differences in perception. I hope that in the course of this conference some light was shed on some of the issues and that after having read these conference papers we will be able to no longer think about pillars and fans but about the entire elephant. If this thinking process were to be followed in successful and sustainable steps towards peace and reconstruction in Afghanistan, it would greatly help the people in Afghanistan and the entire region.

Bonn, June 2001   *A. Sultan Karimi*

Introduction

Christine Noelle-Karimi, Conrad Schetter,
Reinhard Schlagintweit

The attacks on the World Trade Center and the Pentagon on 11 September 2001 catapulted Afghanistan into the centre of world events. Until then Afghanistan, a country in a state of war for over twenty years, had all but been forgotten. The Afghan war, which broke out in 1979 and until 1989 was conducted as a Cold War confrontation, kept the world spellbound, yet during the continuing conflict in the 1990s, attention faded against a background of a changed mood in world politics. In spite of the considerable regional consequences of the conflict, it seemed no longer to have any significance for the outside world. It wasn't until the terrorist attacks on the political and economic symbols of the United States of America that Afghanistan once again entered public consciousness. Suddenly everyone was asking: How could social and political conditions have arisen in Afghanistan that are diametrically opposed to all the norms of a modern state and a civil society? Who are the Taliban? Is there still a country or a state called Afghanistan? And: How did Afghanistan turn into a 'black hole' – as it is now called – and become a 'breeding ground for international terrorism'? These questions show that present-day Afghanistan is a political and social phenomenon that we have difficulty in comprehending, but one that requires urgent and careful examination.

In June 2000, an international conference in Munich (15 – 17 June 2000) sought to analyse the latest developments in Afghanistan and their causes, with the focus on state structures and functions. The difficult issue addressed was: Is Afghanistan a 'country without a state'? The present volume, a collection of papers given at this conference, attempts to find answers to questions that now, following the attacks of 11 September 2001, are more pressing than ever.

1. How 'Failing States' Arise

In the second half of the twentieth century, the nuclear stalemate between the two superpowers, the United States and the Soviet Union, had imposed a political system across the globe that was based on the principle of sovereign nation-states – regardless of whether those states were capable of surviving and acting in the political and economic sphere. Many of these states had emerged through the process of decolonization and possessed neither integrating social and historical traditions, nor sufficient political or economic resources. Although representing only a constructed world, and reflecting very inadequately the social realities in the individual states, this system did at least guarantee the First and the Second World a measure of peace, albeit one that was constantly under threat. Conflicts in the Third World were conducted as wars by proxy between the two superpowers, regardless of the fact that they generally had social or economic causes, and took place within national borders. These conflicts released tensions which resulted from the efforts of the superpowers to demonstrate the superiority of their philosophy; this gave them a particularly destructive force.

With the implosion of the Soviet empire in 1989 this system founded on nation-states started to crumble in many places. Yet no new world order emerged. And, with the gradual disappearance of the edifice of a bipolar system of order, the solidity of its building blocks also became doubtful. One of the main characteristics of globalization after the end of the East-West conflict is the disintegration of state structures, a development that can be observed all around the world. Yet the concept of the nation-state still seems to us to be a suprahistorical principle that cannot be called into question. We easily forget that most nation-states are little older than one hundred years. The first states to fit our present understanding of the word, i.e. states with a monopoly on the use of force, an administrative system and a clearly defined state territory, arose following the Treaty of Westphalia of 1648. The principle of *cuius regio eius religio* set up a direct relationship between the power of a sovereign and a clearly defined territory. Hobbes' influential work, *Leviathan* (1651), declared the state to be the only political construct that was able to save humankind from destroying itself. The rise of the people as a power factor, supplanting the aristocracy, a development which started with the French Revolution of 1789, led to the people of a state and the territory of a state becoming

Introduction

constitutive elements of the modern state. This was the birth of a political system in which a homogeneous people, however arbitrarily defined, rules over a clearly fixed territory through the instrument of the state apparatus. Since the French Revolution the concept of the nation-state has spread continuously – mostly with the exercise of force – and in the second half of the nineteenth century, it drastically changed the political order in Europe. As part of the decolonisation, which started in the middle of the twentieth century, the nation-state has become the accepted form of statehood. Until the end of the twentieth century it therefore provided the accepted framework for political thought and political action. However, the success story of the nation-state also represents one of the bloodiest phases of human history. The victory of the nation-state and its ideology led to massive, historic acts of violence (First and Second World Wars) and the most horrific crimes against humanity (mass murder, the Holocaust).

Since the collapse of the bipolar world order, this model has begun to show clear weaknesses. The overall picture differs according to circumstances: in the developed countries state sovereignty is weakening; regional alliances, the growing power of supra-regional corporations and the stronger role of non-governmental organizations are all placing far-reaching restrictions on governments. It is becoming increasingly difficult to define the term 'society' within the framework of the nation; in many areas of society the nation-state is no longer the point of reference for social and political alliances, nor for lines of conflict (Guehenno 1994: 32-34). The transformation countries are characterized by the growing weakness of state direction and control in the face of corruption, economic crime and mafia-like groups. And in the developing countries we witness the collapse of entire state apparatuses through separatist movements, civil wars and economic crises.

However, the internal structure of countries like the former GDR or Yugoslavia cannot be squeezed into a theoretical model which also describes the situation in Sierra Leone or Somalia, although in all these cases the apparatus of state weakened and the capacity for a foreign policy guided by international law dwindled. Too great are the political, social and economic differences between those shocks which prepare the way for a new political order but which have little impact on important parts of the administration and the economy, and those jolts which destroy in the long run the ability of state and non-state institutions to survive.

Developing countries whose governments lose the ability to act or impose their will, are often termed 'failed states' or 'failing states'. Luke & Toal (1998) note that these terms were first used by humanitarian aid organizations, officials of the United Nations and concerned security analysts, i.e. experts who wanted to describe a crisis phenomenon in developing countries that they were worried about; however, these experts did not want to develop scientific models and use them to examine whether and to what extent one could identify changes in the phenomenon of 'state'. As a consequence, but of course also because of the diversity of state weaknesses mentioned above, these terms are used to apply mostly to endangered non-industrial states. The present volume follows this restricted meaning and focuses in particular on the character of the state and its manifestations in the fields of ideology, economy, society, political formation and the relationship between centre and periphery.

We placed a question mark after the title of our conference: 'Afghanistan – A Country without a State?'. For even if the term 'failed state' is only applied to economically or socially less developed states, it does often reveal one-sidedness or prejudice. Upon closer inspection it tends to lose clarity rather than promote understanding. It is used for widely different countries – like India, Myanmar, the Democratic Republic of Congo, Colombia and Sierra Leone – without there being even basic common criteria for defining the weakness of the state. Sometimes it is the limited capability of a government to act in the face of economic misery or a war economy, sometimes it is the fact that the government cannot cope with internal conflict or independence movements, or it is an inability to keep to international agreements and operate in international organizations, above all the United Nations. There are even some states – like Bosnia, Tajikistan and Palestine – which already appear to fail even before they come into being. An analysis of the different cases reveals a common denominator in the infringement of important norms of government quality (governance), including the associated efforts to adduce ethnic and historic reasoning for them.

Introduction

2. 'Failing' or 'Failed'?

In view of the haziness of the termini used in this context, an attempt at clarification is advisable. The term 'failed' state should only be used when both the internal and external signs of decay are not just temporary but prevail over a period defined in years. Among the internal symptoms are the lack of a government accepted or at least tolerated by the population, or which exercises a monopoly of power in the most important parts of the country and which implements a traditional rule of law, even if this be only rudimentary. Governance and legitimacy are determined by the extent of the power actually exercised, not by any reasoning based on Western norms. A state cannot be regarded as 'failed' only because it does not wish or is not in a position to implement democracy, human rights and a market economy; the key issue is the existence of governance. Important external criteria are the inability or absence of a will to be a partner of the international community, and the question of whether the state is accepted in this form by that community. Caution is called for here. Not all regimes that have been outlawed by the international community have failed as states; often they are in a real, delayed or expected state of transition. According to international law it is not governments that are recognized but states; in serious conflicts all that is interrupted is political communication.

It is more difficult to say when a state can be justifiably described as 'failing'. There are many countries – and their number is growing constantly – which have long been predicted to fail, but which still have governance, albeit a poor one, and which are full members of the United Nations. Examples include Angola and Tajikistan. Careful analysis is therefore necessary to determine if the observed process of decline is really progressing permanently in the direction of a failed state. Often it is impossible to say whether we are just facing a long period of weakness or if there is indeed a case of progressive decline. Important indicators are the condition of state and administrative structures, the efficiency of state control and the integrating power of shared political or cultural values and convictions.

3. Characteristics of Failed States

A key indicator of 'failed' states is a replacement of the loyalty previously afforded to an anonymous state apparatus, by tribal, ethnic or religious ties. Such ties are built up on networks which generally correspond to a system of patronage. Often these 'failed' states are led by warlords or charismatic leaders. The competition between state and non-state structures or the replacement of state by non-state structures frequently derives from the lack of a national integrating force such as traditions and myths suitable for overcoming ethnic or religious divisions. Another element in the dynamics of the development from state to tribe (Fanon 1961) is the failure of modernization. For the implementation of the triple paradigm of modernity – democracy, market economy, human rights – only seldom improves the lives of the whole population; generally it gives rise to a widening of socio-economic disparities; this leads to increasing loss of confidence on the part of the population in the capabilities of the state. Perhaps it is one of the great challenges of the 21st century, that the population, above all in former colonies, considers clientelistic links with a high emotional content more suitable than the state for the exercise of power, for providing security and for guaranteeing the basic human needs.

Such patronage networks can be described as the very opposite of the modern state. With no claim to completeness, the differences between both poles can be characterized as follows: 'Failed' states do not possess typical state institutions like a government with ministries which are responsible for particular aspects of public life. Government offices are treated more as a kind of reward or sinecure for outstanding personal loyalty, not as positions with certain incumbent duties. The power of the leader depends on personal networks and a policy of *divide et impera*. Leaders feel responsible only for their followers, not for the whole population. There is no binding legal order; the system of patronage limits the power and the scope of action of the leader.

It is in particular economic processes that make failed states seem irrational or chaotic. Yet as a rule they do follow an inherent logic. In this volume Schetter shows, using the example of Afghanistan, that there are forms of informal, unregulated or illegal economic life in 'failed' states, which the political leaders consciously promote and from which the population – or at least a part of it – benefits. Using the example of African states, Chabal &

Introduction

Daloz (1999) point out that war or chaos economies often follow important traditional patterns and serve to maintain forms of power which are acceptable to the population. Those in power apply widely differing standards to the quality of a state, ranging from 'legitimate monopoly of power' (Max Weber, 1980) to 'postage-stamp, flag and passport' for Palestine.

Such considerations should of course not lead to political or even social relativism. One clearly quantifiable criterion is quality of life. It can be proved that in all 'failed' or 'failing' states minorities are subject to serious discrimination and that the standard of living is at the lowest level of the socio-economic world index. This applies to childhood mortality rates, undernourishment, life expectancy, literacy, forced expulsion, not to mention the absence of political rights – be it in Somalia, Angola, Sierra Leone or Afghanistan. The economic and social wounds which are caused by the lack of public order generally take generations to heal. Many of these regimes deliberately offload the responsibility for primary state functions, mainly in the social field (e.g. education, health), onto humanitarian aid provided by industrialized countries and international organizations. The attacks on the World Trade Centre and the Pentagon have also made clear that failing or failed states are likely to offer international terror organizations the chance of maintaining an infrastructure in the form of bases and training camps.

4. Conditions in Afghanistan

A scientific engagement with the 'failed' state, as is undertaken in this volume with the example of Afghanistan, must first thoroughly analyse the character, phenomena and causes of this condition. Only a knowledge and understanding of the true circumstances can form the basis for effective and accepted aid, and perhaps even prepare possible ways towards a better condition. The papers presented here cast light not only on various facets of the current situation, but also map out the genesis of the Afghan state and its nature before the Soviet invasion.

The events of the last twenty years make peace seem like a distant vision. Even so, a nostalgic memory continues to persist of what Afghanistan was or how it might have developed had it not been for foreign intervention.

The first section of this book gives a historical perspective and sheds light on the odds that beset modern efforts at state-building. Angela Parvanta explores the ideological foundations of the Afghan state. Tracing the development of the term 'Afghanistan' from a denomination for one tribal segment of society to a national frame of reference, she analyses the endeavours of the urban elite to create a corresponding all-encompassing identity on the basis of a common history, culture and religion. The tenuous nature of this process is reflected by the manoeuvring involved in the choice of a national language. Although the imposition of an 'Afghan' identity on the non-Pashtun population met with limited success, Afghanistan ultimately did take shape as a defined political entity in the minds of its citizens.

Arguing from the point of view of a young Afghan who has grown up in the West, Rameen Moshref discusses conceptual deterrents for peace. In his opinion, the Afghan community in exile is caught in a verbal war that tells us more about the political past of its protagonists than present requirements. His contribution illustrates the need to move away from outdated authoritarian conceptions of state-building which equate peace with the forceful silencing of opposition. The solution to the political problems in Afghanistan hinges neither on the advent of a strong man nor on the return to pre-war political institutions but on the cultivation of a 'culture of peace' in which Afghans of all ethnic backgrounds have equal rights before the state.

Among the political traditions that developed in the twentieth century, the *loya jirga* or grand assembly is certainly the most evocative one. This concept is presently being propagated by the former king Muhammad Zahir Shah as the only possible means of creating peace in Afghanistan. Christine Noelle-Karimi discusses the origins of this institution and delineates its growth up to the communist era. Her analysis points to a close correlation between the efficacy of the *loya jirga* and a well-functioning central state, which in turn demonstrates its limitations under the current political circumstances.

In the period from 1964 to 1978, Afghanistan seemed to be on its way to becoming a modern nation state. The country received its first democratic constitution, and its relatively well functioning administration was bolstered by revenues deriving principally from foreign aid and tourism.

Introduction

Even so, the activities of the central government mostly focused on Kabul and the provincial towns. Contact with the rural areas remained limited and administration at the local level was entrusted to intermediaries. Given this structural weakness, it is hardly surprising that many regions reverted to an autonomous state once war began to tear at the foundations of governance. At the same time, the resistance to the communist regime brought about changes in local identity and political discourse. According to Max Klimburg, the region of Nuristan was exposed to the first waves of Islamist preaching as early as the 1960s. During the war against the Soviet occupation, competition between the various resistance parties not only exacerbated local conflicts but eventually resulted in the creation of a Nuristani 'emirate' funded by Saudi Arabia. While the Taliban presently content themselves with nominal authority in this region, Islamist tenets have affected local culture, including architectural styles, in a lasting manner.

In this light, the Taliban may be seen as part of a larger phenomenon: They are not at the root of the Islamist discourse in Afghanistan but rather one of its (admittedly, most powerful) manifestations. This impression is borne out by Bruce Koepke's account of changes in local culture in one of the last regions truly beyond the grip of the Taliban. Badakhshan is presently experiencing a serious decline in non-religious perfomances because both the population and local commanders feel insecure about their appropriateness in the context of Islamic society.

Another region that developed autonomous administrational structures during the 1980s is the Hazarajat in central Afghanistan. In many ways, the Hazaras, who had occupied one of the lower rungs in the social order throughout the twentieth century, came into their own with the political developments subsequent to the Soviet invasion. Rolf Bindemann describes how Hazara intellectuals linked to the government and the resistance reformulated their position vis-à-vis and within the Afghan state by taking the analysis of their ethno-genesis and history into their own hands.

The next section discusses the failed state from the perspective of Europeans working inside Afghanistan and reflects the uneven impact of Taliban policies on everyday life. Highlighting the situation of women, Heike Bill challenges ready-made western assumptions concerning the Taliban agenda. While western media and policy-makers justly point to restrictions imposed on Afghan women, they conveniently forget that these restrictions, albeit now more stringent, are not entirely the making of the Taliban. Here the traditional gap between city and countryside comes into play again. State endeavours – be they modernist or Islamist – have primarily affected the status of women in Kabul, whereas the lives of rural women continue to be determined by the attitudes of their immediate male relatives rather than public policy. Bill also raises the question of whether the current blockade on Afghanistan is justified. Backwardness, she argues, should be an incentive for, rather than an obstacle to, providing developmental aid.

Peter Schwittek's report on the state of education in Kabul allows a glimpse into the mechanisms at work in the Taliban administration. Education forms one cornerstone of the ideology of the Taliban, who emphasize the need for religious instruction and take a restrictive view on girls' education. From the NGO perspective, education in the western sense of the word is not only a human right but a vital prerequisite for the reconstruction of Afghanistan. What happens when these two world views meet? Schwittek's report gives some interesting answers. For one thing, it points to different currents among the Taliban. On the one hand, there are the hardliners who deny women and girls all access to public institutions. On the other hand, there are those who quietly cooperate and get things done. One result of this tug-of-war is that several thousand girls and boys in Kabul receive regular education in so-called mosque schools administered by the Ministry of Hajj and Islamic Affairs rather than the Ministry of Education. Another effect is that the circumstances in Kabul are not applicable elsewhere in Afghanistan. Each region displays a unique mix of local attitudes and the temperament of the Taliban commander in charge.

Failed states are characterized by their own economic logic, the growth of a new entrepreneurial elite and a huge underclass of young men who know no other means of livelihood than warfare. This development is delineated in three articles dealing with the war economy. Conrad Schetter traces the transition from a rentier state in the 1970s to the present bazaar economy, in which war parties and traders benefit from a transnational network of smuggling and a drugs trade operating unbridled by any state intervention. Michael von der Schulenburg focuses on the dynamics of opium production and elucidates why poppy cultivation 'makes sense',

Introduction

economically speaking, for local farmers. Jonathan Goodhand takes a closer look at changing ecological and social patterns in Badakhshan. In a setting where hardship is brought about not only by war but by a dramatic population growth combined with ecological degradation, the traditional local leadership has given way to a new brand of military commanders, who in turn depend on poppy cultivation for their economic survival.

In the light of the fact that peace would mean a disruption of informal economic networks that function so well within the logic of a war economy, all three authors take a critical view of developmental aid in its present form. Goodhand is of the opinion that policy-makers would benefit from a careful analysis of the mechanisms at work rather than resorting to stop-gap measures which address the symptoms instead of the roots of the problem. Schetter even sees NGO activities as part of the failed state. By rendering assistance in health care, education and agriculture, they absolve the war parties from tasks that would ordinarily form the domain of government, in effect allowing them to devote all their resources to war activities. Schulenburg, on the other hand, stresses that the internal economic logic of opium production and drug trafficking can only be broken up by means of a long-term commitment to developmental aid. A point well taken, considering the fact that the UN Drug Control Program had no funds at its disposal to assist Afghan farmers in the transition to other crops when the Taliban prohibited the production of opium at the beginning of this year.

For the past twenty years, politics in Afghanistan has been a game involving many players and a bewildering succession of changing coalitions. When the Taliban emerged in 1994, they held out the promise of creating a unitary political system in the name of 'true' Islam. While they can point to military successes and a certain degree of territorial unification, their political agenda has turned out to be curiously self-limited. Reinhard Schlagintweit and Ahmed Rashid elucidate some of the inherent contradictions of Taliban conceptions of state-building. There is for instance, a marked tension between their claim of establishing universal Islamic institutions and their inability, or unwillingness, to move beyond their localized power base in southern Afghanistan. Instead of transcending historical ethnic biases in the name of Islam, the Taliban seem to aim at re-establishing Pashtun hegemony, in effect reverting to traditional patterns of state-building familiar to Afghans since the nineteenth century. At the same time, the traditional relationship between centre and periphery is turned around in a way that village values are forced upon the city. Michael Pohly takes an equally critical view of the Northern Alliance. While the groups that have coalesced around the person of Ahmad Shah Massoud represent all the ethnic categories threatened by Taliban advances, they lack a solid political agenda that would mark them as a true alternative to the present regime.

How should the international community deal with failing or failed states? This question has gained added stringency with the events of September 11. Citha Maass points to some of the factors that have made communication with the Taliban utterly cumbersome during the past years. It is not only the human rights abuses and the terrorist links which have turned the Taliban into a pariah regime. Equally important are their internal secretive organization and their dependence on Pakistan which have caused them to remain a quasi-foreign body in Afghanistan.

Hermann-Josef Blanke, on the other hand, analyzes the present regime from the legal perspective. He reaches the conclusion that Afghan statehood continues to be a fully fledged entity under international law despite the erosive effects of the ongoing war.

The involvement of external powers is a major ingredient in the equation of power inside Afghanistan. Amin Saikal links the interests of the countries bordering on Afghanistan with the strategical considerations of Russia and the US. Tracing the topsy-turvy approach to the Taliban that has characterized US policy so far, he emphasizes the need to develop a constructive post-Cold War strategy that would enhance America's standing in the region while avoiding the pitfall of entering a direct military conflict, a fitting warning that has been overtaken by the latest developments. Anwar-ul-Haq Ahady also feels that peace efforts in Afghanistan have been on the back burner for too long. In his opinion, issues like international terrorism and drug trafficking can only be addressed within the framework of a functioning government which enjoys both the support of its citizens and the international community. In a setting where the entire social and political infrastructure have been destroyed by war, such a government can only be established with outside help, specifically a sustained and well-funded UN mandate.

Introduction

The range of articles collected in this volume sheds light on the complex nature of the current conflict in Afghanistan and makes it clear that there are no easy answers. Nonetheless, we hope that the spectrum of views expressed here by scientists, journalists, policy-makers and NGO representatives will help the reader to gain a deeper understanding of present-day Afghanistan and will refocus the discussion on possibilities of addressing the problems there in a constructive manner. Given the diversity of voices presented here, it goes without saying that each contribution reflects the opinion of its author and not necessarily that of the editors.

Bibliography

Fanon, Frantz (1960) *Die Verdammten dieser Erde.* Frankfurt a.M., Suhrkamp.

Guehenno, Jean-Marie (1994*) Das Ende der Demokratie.* München, Artemis und Winkler.

Hobbes, Thomas (1651/1998): *Leviathan.* Stuttgart, Reclam.

Luke, Timothy W. & Toal, Gerard (1998) The Fraying Modern Map: Failed States and Contraband Capitalism. *Geopolitics and Modern Boundaries* 3 (3): pp 14 – 33.

Weber, Max (1980) *Wirtschaft und Gesellschaft.* Tübingen, J.C. B. Mohr.

Part I

National Ideologies and Their Manifestations

Afghanistan – Land of the Afghans?
On the Genesis of a Problematic State Denomination

Angela Parvanta

> Oh children of the fatherland! Recognize religion, state, nation and home as the four main elements of your life! Make the greatest effort for the fulfilment of the religious duties, the protection of the honour of the nation and the love for your fatherland itself! (Tarzi 1976: 347)

1. Introduction

Afghanistan is today unquestionably the 'country of the Afghans'. The year 1747 is regarded as its date of birth and Ahmad Shah Abdali, later Durrani, as its founder. Its history stretches from ancient Aryana to the empire of the Kushans, Bactria, until the Islamic Khurasan, finally reaching its peak with the foundation of Afghanistan, the first Afghan state in history.[1] In fact, the empire of Ahmad Shah was a military and tribal confederation which was not named Afghanistan either by Ahmad Shah or his successors but was known as Kabulistan, Kingdom of Caboul, etc.

But how did Afghanistan acquire its name and who are these Afghans who since the nineteenth century have been known as wild, heroic, freedom-loving, self-reliant and impervious to colonialism? In the following, I will investigate the ideological components contained in the terms 'Afghan' and 'Afghanistan' and their development through time, rather than conceptions of space, such as the drawing and shifting of boundaries. In this context, the central question is if and how the Afghan governments and intellectuals succeeded in constructing a unified nation out of a heterogeneous mix of peoples that originated from diverse cultural and linguistic milieux and in subsuming their members under the category of 'Afghan'.

---

[1] About the state foundation cf. Gregorian (1969: 46–51).

2. Who are the 'Afghans' in the 'Land of the Afghans'?

The earliest mention of the name 'Afghan' (Abgan) is to be found in a Sasanid inscription from the third century AD, and it appears in India in the form of 'Avagana' for the first time in the sixth century AD in *Brhat-samhita* by the Astronomer Varaha Mihira. *Hudud al-'alam* (982 AD) is the first Islamic work that mentions the Afghans (Caroe 1964: 112).

Until the nineteenth century there was still confusion about the exact meaning of this term, as the following remark by the German General-Major Gens shows:

> The caravans coming to Khokand from Badakhshan are accompanied, apart from the inhabitants of the latter, also by Indians, Afghans and Kabulis. Murtasa [informant of Gens] distinguishes between them and denotes as Afghans those inhabitants of Afghanistan who are nomads and have long hair. Kabulis, on the other hand, are the inhabitants of the cities, who shave their heads.[2]

The confusion in terminology prevailing at this time is also reflected in a statement by Elphinstone:

> The origin of the name of Afghaun, now so generally applied to the nation, I am about to describe, is entirely uncertain; but is, probably, modern. It is known to the Afghauns themselves only through the medium of the Persian language. Their own name for their nation is Pooshtoon; in the plural, Pooshtauneh. [...] They have no general name for their own country; but sometimes apply the Persian one of Afghaunistan. Doctor Leyden has mentioned the name of Pooshtoonkhau, as bearing this sense; but I never heard it used. [...] The name most generally applied to the whole country by its inhabitants is *Khorassaun*; but this appellation is obviously incorrect. For, on the one hand, the whole of the Afghaun country is not included within the strict limits of Khorassaun; and, on the other, a considerable part of that province is not inhabited by the Afghauns.[3]

Thus 'Afghanistan' in the original sense denoted the areas where the Pashtuns settled and the word 'Afghan' was used for the Pashtun tribes. Afghanistan as a state was first mentioned by the neighbouring powers in the Anglo-Iranian treaty of 1801: although the Persian text of the treaty speaks of the 'Padshah-i Afghanistan' (Mahmud 1970: i. 34), the English

---

[2] Gens (1968: 105). Many thanks to Michael Friederich who drew my attention to this quotation.

[3] Elphinstone (1969: 151). For Elphinstone Khurasan is a part of Afghanistan, while another part clearly belongs to Persia: 'The remaining part of Khorassaun, (the boundaries of which may be loosely fixed by the Oxus, and the desert, through which that river runs; and the Caspian Sea), belongs to Persia' (p. 93).

translation says 'the King of the Afghans' (Aitchison 1983: 48). In the Anglo-Afghan treaty of 1809, it is the 'King of Cabool' who ratifies the treaty with the British, and in the treaty of 1855, it is 'His Highness Ameer Dost Mohummud Khan, Walee of Cabool and those countries of Afghanistan in his possession' (Aitchison 1983: 233).

Here 'Afghanistan' means a distinct area settled by ethnically defined Afghans and not a state as such. In the treaty of Gandamak of 1879, the ruler is finally mentioned as 'the Amir of Afghanistan and his dependencies' (Aitchison 1983: 240). After the First Anglo-Afghan War the meaning of Afghanistan as a toponym for the tribal area of the Pashtuns shifted among foreign observers to a denomination for the entire area between Persia, Russia and British India.[4] Only at the end of the nineteenth century did Afghanistan become a generally used and accepted name for the Afghan national state, both within the country and abroad.

3. Ideological Foundations

What did a common identity have to offer to the inhabitants of a territory that came to represent the state of Afghanistan and that is characterized by ethnic, linguistic and cultural diversity until today? Belonging to a certain ethnic group, a religion, a language, a tribe or a region is the main feature of identity capable of generating loyalty.[5] In Afghanistan there is no common accepted identity that cuts across the various segments of society. Shahrani primarily views family ties as the basis for interpersonal relationships, collective identities and differences among the Afghan peoples. He adds:

> All other forms of recognised categorical solidarity groups, generally referred to as *qawm* in all major languages of the peoples of Afghanistan – which can mean lineages, clans, tribes, races, linguistic groups, religious–sectarian groups, nationalities and even nation – are similarly conceived, organised and mobilised. (Shahrani 1998: 218).

---

[4] In the correspondence between the British envoy in Tehran Mr Ellis (1835–7) and Lord Palmerston in London 'Affghanistan' [sic] is used in this sense (British Foreign Office 1838: 4).

[5] According to Orywal there are no certain features of a religious, linguistic or regional type in Afghanistan that would be generally accepted by everyone so the identification takes place on a substate level (1986: 82).

At the beginning of the twentieth century, a small section of intellectuals from the capital[6] made first attempts to conceive of the inhabitants of the country as citizens and to offer them, with the concepts 'Afghan' and 'Afghanistan' a common superordinate factor of identity. The aim was to set up an Afghan *millat* (in the sense of a state nation) that would be dependent on the *milliyat* (citizenship). Islam was taken as the sole basis of a common identity to which the majority of the inhabitants could relate. Here the idea of the Islamic *umma* as a community of all Muslims and not that of a single group was decisive. However, Islam by itself did not suffice as an identity-creating factor for the foundation of the nation, since it went beyond territorial boundaries of power.

But why were the terms 'Afghan' and 'Afghanistan' chosen? On the one hand the Afghan state was dominated by Pashtuns until 1978, and the ruling elite consisted mainly of Pashtuns (apart from the short interlude of the Tajik Habib Allah Kalakani in 1929), on the other hand this term was not an emic Pashtun concept and was, moreover, commonly used. Again a short reminder: the term 'Afghan' is ambiguous in meaning. Until the late nineteenth century, this term was exclusively applied to the Pashtuns (also called Pathans) by the non-Pashtu-speaking parts of the population, especially the Persian speakers. Originally denoting an ethnic membership, its meaning expanded to include the entire population of the national state of Afghanistan. Even today it can only be deduced from the context who is meant by the word 'Afghan': not every Afghan is an Afghan in the sense of a Pashtun and not every Pashtun is an Afghan in the sense that he is a citizen of Afghanistan (Pashtuns live on both sides of the border in the Pakistani North West Frontier province).

The foundations of an Afghan nationalism were first formulated in the journal *Siraj al-akhbar-i afghaniya* (Light of Afghan News, Oct. 1911– Dec. 1918). Its editor Mahmud Tarzi (1865–1933) and his comrades prepared the theoretical framework for the unity of the Afghan nation that was further developed in the next decades and partly put into practice. Tarzi tried to define the Afghan nation from a religious, national and

---

[6] The majority of intellectuals of that era were concentrated mainly at the court of Amir Habib Allah Khan. Cf. Ghubar (1980: 716 passim), Kakar (1974: 25), Gankovsky (1985: 196).

cultural perspective. In his opinion, Islam, the history of Afghanistan and the Afghan language Pashtu formed the basis for the building of the nation. Interestingly, he himself wrote his articles exclusively in Persian. Under the heading 'Din, dawlat, watan, millat' (religion, state, home, nation) Tarzi gave the following explanations:

> The word *millat* (nation) is in our opinion the entirety of all peoples and inhabitants that live on the pure soil of our holy fatherland Afghanistan and who are the subjects of a state and a government to which the term Afghan nation can be applied. The term *qawm* (people) does not include the meaning of *millat* (nation). The nation consists of diverse and different tribes (*aqwam*). Just as the word *watan* (home) is not limited to a single city, a settlement or a village the word *millat* (nation) comprises not only one people, one tribe or a family. The entirety of the Durrani, Ghiljai, Tajik, Turk, Uzbek, Hazara, Kohistani, Panjsheri and so on are called the *millat-i afghan* (Afghan nation). They all live in one home and are governed by one state. This is to say that this home is the holy fatherland of Afghanistan, that this state is the independent Afghanistan. (Tarzi 1976: 343).

Tarzi resolutely rejects the identification with just one area, one city or one village. His reason is that abroad only the word 'Afghan' allows a clear identification since it is familiar to everyone – be they Chinese or Americans! (Tarzi 1976: 321).

But how were these terms to be accepted by all inhabitants of the country as a superordinate national identity – an identity that until then had solely been defined by local, regional, ethnic or linguistic ties? For those portions of the population which were non-Pashtun in origin they implied something intrinsically foreign and, moreover, identified with the Pashtuns, as well as their culture and values. This is one of the reasons why these designations are still rejected today by a large part of the non-Pashtun population (Orywal 1986: 82; Pstrusinska 1990: 27). The propagation of national values that built especially on Pashtun cultural elements fed on an idea and an ideal which could only be accepted by a small fraction of the citizens. Instead of distinguishing between its traditional and the modern meaning the term was henceforth applied to all ethnic groups of the country. From then on the denominations were used in parallel in both meanings, not only in Afghan but also in foreign publications.

A continuing reception and development of Tarzi's ideas and those of his companions were found until 1978 in the political and intellectual sphere. The Pashtu academies Da Pashtu maraka (established in 1923 and supported by King Aman Allah) and the Pashtutulana (founded in the

1930s), as well as diverse other organizations like the Anjuman-i Adabi and the Anjuman-i Tarikh (circles for literature and history) aimed at researching Afghan history, culture, language, literature and folklore and, furthermore, developing it. In 1937 Pashtu was promulgated as *the* Afghan language in the constitution. It was to replace Persian, which had been the *lingua franca* until then, as the sole national language. The acceptance of Persian along with Pashtu as the second official language of the country in the constitution of 1964 shows the failure of this venture. The Persian spoken in Afghanistan was designated as 'Dari' in order to stress its local nature. Archaeological findings were interpreted in such a manner as to suggest a common origin of the two languages (Habibi 1966: 738).

Afghan historiography concentrated to a large extent on representing the Afghan history as a continuum. This effort of linking the present statehood to a larger past is by no means limited to Afghan historians and writers. Rather, it is a phenomenon common to all 'newly awakened' nations and inherent in romantic nationalism. Thus a common origin of all inhabitants of the 'Aryan' and a continuity over thousands of years was propagated for the area of Aryana, Bactria and Khurasan, leading to Afghanistan as a historic entity (Ghubar 1980: 9). These ideas were incorporated into the schoolbooks and so passed on to the following generations.

4. The 'Afghan Nation' – Integration or Assimilation?

With the invasion of Soviet troops in Afghanistan in 1979 and the beginning of resistance new élites arose and new political ideas were propagated. Within Afghanistan, the communist régime tried to create new identities based on the model of Soviet nationalities. In addition to Pashtu and Persian – the two official languages of the country – Uzbek, Turkmen, Baluchi, Nuristani and Pashai were introduced as national languages, in order to tie the national minorities to the Afghan state. Noteworthy is that identity in Afghanistan itself was dominated by non-Pashtun elements during the 1980s. Nonetheless the push for linguistic-cultural particularism proved counterproductive. Particularly the non-Pashtun groups perceived and rejected it as an effort to foster the disintegration and fragmentation of Afghanistan.

When coming to power, the communists also questioned the word 'Afghanistan'. In order to break the old Pashtun (=Afghan) hegemony, various name changes were proposed. The country was to assume its 'old' name of Khurasan (this term denotes a landscape and has never been the name of a state!) or to be called Azadistan, 'country of the free', in analogy to Pakistan, 'country of the pure' (Pstrusinska 1990: 48). Attempts to create analogous terms for the inhabitants of the country based on the word 'Afghan' like 'Afghani' (rejected principally because this is the name of the Afghan currency) or 'Afghanistani' (analogous to Türk and Türkiyeli) were also doomed to fail. They neglected historical usage and thus had no chances of replacing the word 'Afghan'.

The resistance against the USSR, along with the experience of war, flight, expulsion and emigration, caused loyalties and identities to be redefined for the first time in Afghan history. They also brought about a process of ethnic and political emancipation inside and outside the country. While ethnic and regional identities were strengthened, the war also nourished a common feeling of 'us Afghans'. In addition, the resistance encouraged a recapitulation and new evaluation of Afghan history. Now the focus was on the Islamic movements and their protagonists, as well as the continuous threat the Soviet Union posed to the people. In critically looking at and questioning the role of Pashtun rule, the new historiography broke a taboo. Henceforth, a common Afghan identity was to be based on the shared qualities of the subjects rather than Pashtun superiority. This concept was called into question soon after with the take-over by the Taliban. In the current Emirate of Afghanistan the Taliban, who have no awareness of Afghan or Islamic history, are oriented towards the Pashtuns (Rashid 2000: 93 and 212). They recruit their administration officials from loyal followers in Kandahar and Pashtu has become the administrative language. The focus is on Pashtu and Islamization, and other ethnic groups are openly discriminated against. The Taliban have apparently started a historic roll-back that calls into question the new Afghan identity which was acquired during the resistance. But even they heed a principle that has been observed by all other war parties: never to question the unity of the territory of Afghanistan and to preserve it.

5. Conclusion

The supposed contradiction between Afghanistan as the land of the Afghans, that is, Pashtuns, and Afghanistan as the home of all Afghans in the sense of citizens is tautological. The meaning has at present become detached from the equation of Afghan with Pashtun. No Afghan would accept the word Pashtunistan instead of Afghanistan as a denomination for his home country. What started as a coincidence of world history, an external process set into motion by the Great Game, has developed an autochthonous dynamic in the last 200 years and has found its expression in the acceptance of the name Afghanistan by its citizens. If the name of Afghanistan were to be abolished today, and replaced by other names like Pashtunistan, Khurasan or even Azadistan, this would mean the decay and dissolution of the entire territorial state.

Bibliography

Aitchison, C. U. (1983) *A Collection of Treaties, Engagements and Sanads Relating to India and Neighbouring Countries,* Vol. XIII *Persia and Afghanistan.* Delhi, Mittal Publications (reprint).

British Foreign Office, ed. (1838) *Correspondence Relating to Persia and Affghanistan. Presented to Both Houses of Parliament by Command of Her Majesty.* London, Harrison.

Caroe, Olaf (1964) *The Pathans 550 B.C.–A.D. 1957.* London, Macmillan.

Elphinstone, Mountstuart (1969) *An Account of The Kingdom of Caubul and Its Dependencies in Persia, Tartary, and India.* Graz, Akademische Druck- und Verlagsanstalt (reprint of London, 1815).

Gankovsky, Yu. V. (1985) *A History of Afghanistan.* Moscow, Progress.

Gens, General-Major (1968) *Nachrichten über Chiwa, Buchara, Chokand und den nordwestlichen Theil des chinesischen Staates.* Osnabrück, Biblio (reprint of St Petersburg, 1839).

Ghubar, Mir Ghulam Muhammad (1980) *Afghanistan dar masir-i tarikh.* 2nd edition. Qom, PayÁm-i Muhajir.

Afghanistan – Land of the Afghans?

Gregorian, Vartan (1969) *The Emergence of Modern Afghanistan*. Stanford, CA, Stanford University Press.

Grevemeyer, Jan-Heeren (1990) *Afghanistan: Sozialer Wandel und Staat im 20. Jahrhundert*. Berlin, Verlag für Wissenschaft und Bildung.

Habibi, 'Abd al-Hayy (1966) *Tarikh-i Afghanistan ba'd az islam*. Kabul, Anjuman-i tarikh.

Kakar, Hasan (1974) Trends in Modern Afghan History. In: Louis Dupree and L Albert (eds.), *Afghanistan in the 1970s*. New York and London, Praeger: 13-33.

Mahmud, Mahmud (1970) *Tarikh-i rawabit-i siyasi-yi Iran wa Inglis dar qarn-i nuzdahum-i miladi*. Vol. I. 4th edition. Tehran, Iqbal.

Orywal, Erwin (1986) Ethnische Identität – Konzept und Methode. in: Erwin Orywal (ed.) *Die ethnischen Gruppen Afghanistans*. Wiesbaden, Reichert: 73-86.

Pstrusinska, Jadwiga (1990) *Afghanistan 1989 in Sociolinguistic Perspective*. London, (Central Asian Survey Incidental Paper Series 7).

Rashid, Ahmed (2000) *Taliban. Islam, Oil and the New Great Game in Central Asia*. London and New York, I. B. Tauris.

Shahrani, Nazif (1998) The Future of the State and the Structure of Community Governance in Afghanistan. In: William Maley (ed.) *Fundamentalism Reborn? Afghanistan and the Taliban*. London, Hurst: 212-42.

Tarzi, Mahmud (1976) Maqalat-i Mahmud Tarzi. In: Ghafur R. Farhadi (ed.) *Maqalat-i Mahmud Tarzi*. Kabul, Intisharat-i Baihaqa.

The View of the State by Afghans Abroad

Rameen Javid Moshref

The Afghan view of the state is a simple one. Generally speaking, the state is viewed as an institution of power that commands its people or subjects. Politics was never seen as the preoccupation of the masses. One reason for this has been an overwhelming lack of education among the Afghans. Some argue that mass ignorance was a plan orchestrated by the former ruling class. While this statement may open some old wounds, it certainly has some consequences in current politics.

Among educated Afghans, power was overwhelmingly viewed as a tool used for forcing 'progress' according to 'party' ideologies. It could be argued that either progress was not desired, or it was not truly understood. This concept has still not changed altogether, even today. For most Afghans abroad and those inside the country, reaching power means the end of opposition to the victor, and the beginning of peace for all segments of Afghanistan. As most Afghans say in the current situation, 'I hope one side wins so there is peace all over Afghanistan'. What they fail to recognize is that this 'peace' would again turn into violence – as it has so often in the past – if those in power eliminate the opposition. Moreover, long-term suppression of one group by the other is impossible today, due to solid patron–client relationship of the various Afghan groups with their foreign patrons. For now, peace in the true sense will only be wishful thinking.

Arguing automatically for the establishment of a broad-based government, many forget the countless failed attempts to that end, due to lack of understanding and/or interest in peace by those involved in the peace process. Put simply, the problem with peace is that it forces fighting men out of business. And in today's booming demand for the religiously inspired, nothing is more appealing than being rewarded cash (hard green) while fighting for the Almighty, and in kind (lush green) when martyred (Rashid 2000). The failure of a broad-based government could be attributed to many things, including lack of trust among the various groups. I am reminded of the story of two people traveling in an airplane low on fuel who both have guns pointed at each other. They both know that to save themselves they must throw their guns out the window. However, in the back of their minds there is a suspicion that when they both throw their guns out, the other may be carrying a knife (Moshref 1999).

There are those who blame the meddling of neighbouring countries for Afghanistan's downfall. While it is true that Afghanistan has become the proxy battleground of regional powers, the lease for those battlegrounds has been obtained from the Afghans themselves. Surely, no interest group could afford to pass up this bargain lease, when landlords greedily displayed their price, in bright colors, all over Afghanistan – and abroad.

Historically, in Afghan politics, I can scarcely recall a professional diplomat. Very few people thought of diplomacy or any other liberal arts careers as a profession. Those who were interested in politics would study medicine first and later take up politics as a full-time profession, while practising medicine on the side. Following twelfth grade in high schools in Afghanistan, there was a general exam. Those students with highest grades would qualify for medical school, the second highest tier would qualify for engineering school. Law and politics were lower and all other schools were last choice or an alternative for those medical school hopefuls. Therefore, it was no coincidence that when, a few years back, one of my father's friends inquired about my academic pursuits, not remembering easily how to describe Near Eastern Studies in Dari, I explained that I was studying for my masters in the history, languages, politics, religion, arts, etc. of the Islamic world at NYU, which has a joint program with Princeton University, which I also attended. After a short pause and reflecting on my future career, with a paternalistic tone he advised me, 'Son, why don't you learn the *tabla* [musical instrument] with master *tabla* player Ustaad Khiyaal?' I was left dangling in amazement, not knowing how to respond.

Scholars argue that Afghanistan never reached statehood in the true sense. Starting as an empire in 1747, Afghanistan was reduced to a small country due to outside political dynamics and constant internal conflict. Depending on foreign aid and run by a fraternity of patrons and clients, and plagued by civil strife Afghanistan stumbled along through history as a country. The slightest change in its geographic integrity upsets the uneasy balance maintained in the region. It is no secret that Afghanistan's population has relatives on the other sides of its borders. Chipped off to its contemporary geographical shape, its people must live together in peace with each other, or risk setting off a chain reaction in the region.

As Amin Saikal of the Australian National University puts it best,

> ... no government since the foundation of modern Afghanistan in the mid-eighteenth century has come into existence on the basis of a direct popular mandate. Legal-rational frameworks and constitutional legitimacy marked Afghan politics only for a short time, from 1964 to 1973, and even then only in a very limited sense. In Afghanistan, political order and governance have always largely rested on a mixture of personalized, clientelistic politics, and elite alliance and elite settlement, legitimate through traditional mechanisms of consensus building and empowerment, such as the *Loya Jirga* (Grand Assembly) – but with the threat of actual use of force frequently deployed as means of rule enforcement and rule maintenance. Given the dearth of legitimized avenues for political expression, regime change and development has often proven arbitrary and violent. (Saikal 1998)

Being among the few Afghan scholars who did not actually study medicine, Saikal sees Afghan politics as being shaped by ethnolinguistic preferences, backed mainly by Pakistan, in the last two decades. Proposing a method of reaching a national peace settlement in the mid-1990s, Saikal placed much confidence on the individual Afghan voter to choose the right candidate based on democratic reasoning. Furthermore he had much faith that the contestants would play 'fair' in such elections. Although a moderate, he is seen as pro-Massoud in the Afghan community. Therefore most of what he writes is disregarded by the self-righteous who consider it tainted. Saikal sees the Afghan voter or constituent as educated and versed in a Western-democratic approach, and willing to de-emphasize tradition and even religion. Although his model may be appealing to a Western-Afghan audience, it is hard to imagine the realization of such theories inside Afghanistan in the foreseeable future.

On the other hand, Nazif Shahrani of Indiana University spares no detail in outlining the Afghan politics as a Pashtun conspiracy (1998). He holds the former ruling class (members of the royal family) responsible for much of the animosity existing between the various Afghan ethnic groups. Following the same line of reasoning as Saikal, Shahrani accuses Pakistan of direct intervention in Afghan affairs in recent decades. They both see Pakistan as the main agitator in the Afghan civil war following the fall of Najibullah's government in 1992. Shahrani endorses a federalist government, where all ethnic groups are semi-autonomous, and where each region determines its own destiny as part of a united confederation. An anthropologist by profession, many of his views stem from a violent reaction to the Taliban.

Hassan Kakar, much like a number of educated Pashtun older Afghans, is a self-styled Taliban supporter. He sees the Northern Alliance as a tool of Russia, Iran and Uzbekistan that disrupts the total peace which the Taliban has already brought to most of Afghanistan (Kakar n.d.). Kakar sees the Taliban's total take-over of the country as the first step towards peace. Attributing most of the Taliban's extremist policies to wartime emergency measures, he predicts that such policies will be reconsidered once the Taliban have total control of the country. Arguing against a broad-based government, he sees the patrons of the Northern Alliance as the main agitators against peace in Afghanistan. Kakar sees no reason to include the warring Northern Alliance leaders in a joint government. He foresees the imminent take-over of the whole country by the Taliban, followed by a reconsideration of their wartime policy, as well as the creation of an inclusive government where other non-allied Afghan ethnic minorities work for a Pashtun-dominated government. He believes that this ideology would naturally meet the approval of the majority of educated Afghans abroad. Subtly, Kakar tries to discredit the former king Muhammad Zahir, whom he views as being seen as a viable alternative to the Taliban by the United States, and some moderate and many traditional Afghans. Arguing that he is old and unable to perform effectively as the head of a deeply shattered country, Kakar advises against the elements that are using Muhammad Zahir as a symbolic leader to replace the Taliban government. Kakar considers those who are rallying around Muhammad Zahir as a legitimate threat and therefore an alternative to the Taliban government, should Washington decide to intervene in Afghan affairs. Naming Zalmay Khalilzad of the Rana Corporation, who is also associated with the Afghanistan Foundation, as one of the heads of this royalist group, he criticizes the former king for allowing such people to use him. He compares Muhammad Zahir to the late King Amanullah, stating that the latter remained a patriot till his last day, thus guilefully charging Muhammad Zahir with treason and discrediting him and those around him as illegitimate candidates.

The View of the State by Afghans Abroad

While the battlefields of Afghanistan are dominated by uneducated war-hardy warriors, educated Afghans have made print and broadcast media their arena. Publications such as *Omaid Weekly*, *Aaina* (Mirror), Afghan Azadi Radio and Ariana Radio are mostly the unofficial mouthpiece of a particular party or an individual. Some editors make no secret of their sentiments, while others are more discreet about their political/ethnic inclinations. Even some of the most respected scholars and individuals disintegrate into vulgarities and display deep hatred for the opponents of their views, effectively proving that the younger generation, and those who want peace for its own sake, must look elsewhere for inspiration and guidance.

Afghans and Afghan friends abroad have initiated a number of organizations and institutions in support of, or in reaction to, current and/or ongoing events inside Afghanistan. While outwardly these organizations are working for peace and democracy, in actuality they are lobby organizations for a side of the conflict in Afghanistan. Their existence is usually indicative of new alliance struck by a faction and the foreign government(s). The bigger the organization, the better the relation between the two sides. However, members of these support organization by-pass the current dynamics of the Afghan community abroad and play old-school politics. They do not know, nor want to know, that the community is no longer how it was.

Generally speaking, older generations of Afghans abroad have a tendency to express more emotions in their political opinions. With the lack of diplomacy and a misunderstanding of politics, often discussions about their differences end up as personal attacks. In a broader prospective, with their country destroyed and a new brand of people in control of Afghanistan, the older generation finds itself in a precarious position. Added to this is the total loss of control over their lives and their families. In fact, their children have become their means of survival in an environment completely different from where they came from. Clinging on to the old ways and siding with parties that might never call on them, most of the older generation are causing the further fragmentation of their own communities by useless loyalties. Furthermore, by taking sides the older generations still nurse a faint hope that Afghanistan will return to the same state that they left and that they will be able to assume their old positions in society.

Speaking with them, one immediately notices how they boast about their status in Afghanistan and their expectation of being respected in the same way they were used to. I am not a sociologist or a psychologist who is competent to explore this dilemma but it nevertheless is a serious problem facing our ageing community. Sadly, in Afghanistan, where white hair and old age was revered, the older generation is slowly dismantling their own authority by continuously alienating their children.

The late 1990s have seen the slow resurfacing of a group of socio-political activists who had vanished from the Afghan political scene a decade earlier. Convinced of the error of some of their ways and having gone through some self-purification, the former left, as well as a number of right-wing and moderate educated Afghans, are actively, yet cautiously, preaching peace. Most of these people are residing in Europe, both East and West, as well as North America and Australia. They are a small group who have past ties going back to high school and college years. Some have produced publications, others are trying to re-enter the socio-political scene but their public reception has been cold at best. The wounds of the Soviet War, and the subsequent civil war, are still fresh in the minds of most Afghans and they are seen as the cause of the devastation of Afghanistan. This group preaches democracy as they have come to learn it in the West. Some residual former-school ideologies are evident in their analytical disposition, but for the most part they seem reformed. It may be controversial to state, but any future development of Afghanistan will need their expertise if it is serious about rebuilding. To the pre-communist social and political activists, Communism, Maoism, Islamism, Socialism or Democracy was seen as the sole equalizer of all people, in a country of dynastic rule. Most of those who eventually entered political parties were those who were given a chance to go abroad and study. However, on their return, they were provided with few opportunities to express their vision for their country. Much of this is apparent from conversations with such people, who now regret their one-sided approach.

Perhaps the most acceptable segment of the Afghans, capable of effective means of technical support and cosmopolitan attitude, are the young. 'Young' is the key word: this group is well-educated, less antagonistic and full of enthusiasm and energy to set right what has gone wrong, however, at the expense of repatriation. Tired of countless so-called Afghan events, where fights break out repeatedly and vulgarities are a constant companion, the younger generation is disenfranchised and therefore distanced from Afghan activities. It is only in the past few years that young Afghan publications, websites and groups have begun to spring up everywhere. Overwhelmingly, the goal of these publications is more the promotion of culture, and less rhetoric on politics. While ethnic sentiments are still visible, there is still trust and good communication with each other, regardless of ethnicity. Much like the majority of Afghans, politics-related topics have sadly been deemed evil and less explored by the young Afghans. More technical careers have been pursued by the younger generation, and less in social sciences. Therefore, their awareness of statehood, governance, international relations, diplomacy and the like are somewhat limited. One reason is the lack of interest in returning 'home', and another, the absence of inspiring leaders among those who seemingly practise politics. Growing up in their host countries, the young Afghan generation has become accustomed to the local cultures and people; therefore repatriation in a collective sense is not an attractive option needing much exploration. Nevertheless, the young Afghans are a growing segment of the Afghan community that needs to be taken more seriously.

The most common impediment to a viable and continuing peace in Afghan political thought is the leadership paradigm (Moshref 2000). Historically, Afghans often rallied more around a leader than an idea or institution. Thus, stability and strength have always been short-lived. Following the death of a charismatic and strong leader the success and progress that had been initiated have always been replaced by chaos and destruction, taking the nation back to where it started. Two major reasons may account for such tendencies: (1) lack of diplomacy and political consciousness or tolerance, (2) the absence of a culture of peace. A poor country, often regarded as having been carved out of other nations and named by foreigners, Afghanistan was never a solid and united nation, with a national conscience. Loyalties of the individual have been more local than national. Afghans believe in their Afghanistan and not in every Afghan's Afghanistan. Previous governments usually had to survive either by invading other lands for booty or be subsidized – often at an expense to its sovereignty – by foreign sponsors in order to run the state. Although some efforts were made to educate the people, such efforts, for a variety of reasons, were short-lived. In over 250 years of its existence, one can barely name a professional diplomat who ran the state, or part of it. Therefore, Afghanistan has always been in the hands of its more powerful neighbours, diplomatically. Afghans had little self-determination when it came to their political destiny in the regional or international arena. Strategically important, Afghanistan has had unstable borders and therefore was ripe for a for-hire mentality. Foreign powers, in order to stabilize their frontiers, have always paid and armed one Afghan group against another. It was not unusual for Afghanistan to have had a foreign-backed government installed in Kabul. In recent history, however, it has become a norm.

Is there any hope for Afghanistan in the future? With the lack of understanding of the duties and obligations of the state and its citizens towards one another, the first step is the internalization of those two notions. Second is the understanding that Afghans of all ethnic backgrounds have *equal* rights before the state. The legacy of the past can only be an example for all the failed choices and mistakes being made. A state should be run by politically qualified and diplomatically articulate individuals and not by a family, tribe, ethnicity or people in medicine. Meanwhile, a quota system in a joint government is useless if the leadership cannot sacrifice personal issues for the sake of the whole country. Third, unless viable and enduring social and political institutions are created to bridge the gap between the people and the state, as well as alleviating the socio-economic crisis, Afghanistan may pass into history as another failed state.

Bibliography

Akram, E. (n.d.) *Islam Online*, Peace in Afghanistan: What Peace? A Conference Report.

Kakar, M. (n.d.) www.Afghan-Politics.org: Afghan Make or Foreign Make?

Khalilzad, Z. (n.d.) www.AfghanistanFoundation.org: The White Papers.

Kissinger, H. (1994) *Diplomacy*. New York, Simon & Schuster.

Maley, W. ed. (1998) *Fundamentalism Reborn*. Albany, NY, New York University Press.

Mohmand, Q. A. (n.d.) *Sabawoon Journal* (www.theworldpress.com/ru/newspap/afghanistan/sabawoon.htm) Our Solutions.

Moshref, R. J. (1999) Four that Never Return. *Afghan Communicator* (March/April): 2.

Moshref, R. J. (2000) Leadership by Design. *Inter Afghan Youth Summit II*. San Francisco, April.

Rashid, A. (2000) From Deobandism to Batken: Adventures of an Islamic Heritage. A lecture, 13 April.

Saikal, A. (1998) The Rabbani Government 1992–1996. In W. Maley (ed.), *Fundamentalism Reborn?* Albany, NY, New York University Press: 30.

Shahrani, M. N. (1998) The Future of the State and the Structure of Community Governance in Afghanistan. In W. Maley (ed.), *Fundamentalism Reborn?* Albany, NY, New York University Press.

The *Loya Jirga*
– An Effective Political Instrument?
A Historical Overview

Christine Noelle-Karimi

Recent events have caused a flurry of diplomatic activity around Zahir Shah's suggestion that the time-honoured institution of the *loya jirga* might be employed as a means of creating peace in Afghanistan. For many Afghans this term is associated with the good old days before the war, when every segment of the population knew its place in society. Zahir Shah being the last king to rule Afghanistan, his person also symbolizes the last truly functional political system, which combined a certain degree of modernity and social stability. As the *loya jirga* was created in analogy to the tribal council convened among the Pashtuns, this institution furthermore evokes the ideals of democracy and equal rights. In the following, I will explore how this linkage between the tribal *jirga* and its 'grand' version on the state level came about. As will be seen, the *loya jirga* is, historically speaking, a relatively young phenomenon and owes its existence less to inherent Pashtun traditions than to the political needs of the centralized Afghan state emerging in the early twentieth century.

1. The Term *Jirga*

In the early nineteenth century Mountstuart Elphinstone described the *jirga* as the 'internal government' of the Pashtun tribes (1992: i. 215). Interestingly, the terminology employed for the tribal assembly does not suggest that it was a specifically Pashtun institution from the very beginning. The term *jirga* is of Mongolian origin and means 'circle'. In the contexts of hunting and military combat, it designated the circle or semi-circle men formed when closing in on their prey or enemy troops. In the Persian literature of the fifteenth and sixteenth centuries this word was also used in the sense of 'assembly', such as a circle of nobles (Doerfer 1963: i.

292–3). It is thus probable that the term *jirga* was not limited to the Pashtuns during earlier phases of history but may have also been employed for any sort of council in the regions beyond the Pashtun domains, the outlines of which kept shifting due to migrations until the sixteenth and seventeenth centuries. Nor did all Pashtuns call their tribal assemblies *jirga*. According to Glatzer, the western Pashtuns simply used the term *majlis* (from Arabic *jalasa*, 'to sit down') for their meetings in the 1970s (1977: 165). The Pashtun word *loya*, 'big', 'grand', on the other hand, was apparently attached to the *jirga* concept in the early twentieth century, as part of a larger state effort to create a national Afghan identity under the umbrella of Pashtun culture and language.

On the tribal level, the *jirga* forms the only available means of decision making and expresses in many ways the egalitarian ideals of Pashtun society. It is not a permanent institution and is only called to tackle a specific subject which requires the immediate attention of the community. It is open to all men who feel concerned about the issue which has occasioned the meeting and thus may comprise all male members of the tribe. There is no hierarchy of speakers and no one openly exerts authority to direct the flow of discussion, which continues until opposition ceases and a unanimous opinion, rather than a decision by majority vote, is achieved (Glatzer 1977: 165–6; Steul 1981: 120–4). At the same time, local power structures do impinge on tribal politics. The so-called 'white-beards' (*spinzhiri*), men distinguished by their experience, rhetoric abilites and their reputation as good Pashtuns, act as opinion leaders and have great influence on the outcome of the meeting. In order to maintain their prestige, these leaders need to make sure that their ideas find the support of the men present at the *jirga*. Thus it is not unusual for *khans* or men aspiring to this position to do intense 'lobbying' before the assembly takes place, and the *jirga* then merely serves to enact a consensus previously reached in the community.

2. Historical Precedents

Elphinstone assumed that there was a hierarchy of *jirgas* reflecting the various levels of tribal organization:

> The Khaun presides in the principal Jeerga, which is formed by the chiefs of the great branches of Oolooss. Each of these holds his own Jeerga of the heads

The Loya Jirga

of divisions: these again hold their Jeergas; and the members of the lowest Jeerga are either acquainted with the sentiments of the individuals under them, or are able to persuade them to adopt their own. (Elphinstone 1992: i. 215)

Elphinstone was quick to concede that the system he thus described was an ideal one and that he had not witnessed it at work. In fact, modern anthropologists were unable to find a matching arrangement of subordinate and superordinate *jirgas* (Glatzer 1977: 165; Steul 1981: 121). This raises the question of how the 'small' *jirga* on the tribal level developed into the 'grand', national institution. From the perspective of modern Afghan historians, it emerged at a point in time when the various segments of the population gave up their mutual animosities and united to free Afghanistan from the yoke of foreign oppression. This occurred in 1709 when Mir Wais Hotak ousted the Safawid governor of Kandahar with the support of a number of tribal chieftains. A further milestone was the assembly of 1747 which nominated Ahmad Khan Sadozai as paramount leader of the Pashtuns and thus marked the foundation of the Durrani empire after Nadir Shah's demise at Sultan Maidan near Mashhad. Henceforth, it is said, the kings of Afghanistan resorted to this instrument in times of crisis, securing the national consensus with the help of the tribal leadership from all parts of the country. From this point of view, the beginnings of the *jirga* as a supra-tribal institution are indelibly linked to the genesis of the Afghan state.

In this process of projecting the modern Afghan state into the past, some of the historians seem to be tempted to inflate these early constituent meetings to some sort of national level. According to Ghubar, not only Abdali (later Durrani) and Ghiljai chieftains participated in the *jirga* secretly convened by Mir Wais but also Tajik, Hazara, Baluch and Uzbek leaders were present and were forged into a 'united national force'. Yet a closer look at the names he lists suggests that this assembly was more accurately a meeting of Pashtun nobility.[1] Ghubar's description of the meeting in 1747 likewise prefigures the creation of Afghanistan as a territorial entity. In his version of events, this assembly consisted of representatives from all major

---

[1] Ghubar (1981: 319) lists the following names indicative of tribal affiliations: Yahya Khan Hotak (Mir Wais's brother), Muhammad Khan b. Yahya Khan Hotak (also known as Haji Angu), Yunus Khan Kakar, Nur Khan Barech, Gul Khan Babar, 'Aziz Khan Nurzai, Saidal Khan Nasiri. Mihraban (1989: 29–33) adds the name of Nasro Khan Alikozai to the ones enumerated by Ghubar.

ethnic categories that were to become part of Afghanistan at a later date, that is, the Ghiljais, Uzbeks, Abdalis, Hazaras, Baluch and Tajiks. This impression, again, has to be revised on the basis of older historical works. Written in 1781, *Mujmal al-tarikh* describes how Nadir Shah's former Pashtun and Uzbek troops fled towards Kandahar. Three stages from Sultan Maidan, the Pashtun officers (*sarkardigan-i afghan*) nominated Ahmad Khan as their leader (Gulistani 1896: 74). Sultan Muhammad, who compiled the *Tarikh-i sultani* in 1864–5, is of the opinion that this decision was taken by five members of the Abdali confederacy.[2]

The terminology employed in this context is also of interest. While the modern Afghan authors consistently use the word *jirga* for the tribal assembly of 1747, it is called *majlis-i mushawirat*, a consultative meeting, in the *Tarikh-i sultani* (Sultan Muhammad 1881: 122). During his reign, Ahmad Shah formed a council of nine Pashtun leaders (seven Abdalis and two Ghiljais) who had served with him under Nadir Shah. This *majlis* is said to have advised the king in all matters of general policy, both civil and military (Ferrier 1858: 94–5; Singh 1981: 347–8). Another term used for the meeting of 1747 is *diwan-i ahmadshahi* (Mihraban 1989: 38), which would also imply the creation of a consultative assembly. Thus Ahmad Shah's 'old boys' network' represents an interesting transition from the spontaneous tribal assembly to an institutionalized royal council. Although it decided policy at the highest administrative level, it was limited to a few members of the Pashtun aristocracy and closely resembled the traditional tribal *jirga* in terms of size and procedure.

If the Persian chronicles are to be believed, larger meetings extending beyond the royal council did not form a regular feature in Afghan politics. For the period between 1747 and 1900 they mention no more than three occasions on which larger assemblies were convoked. Two of these took place during the reign of Amir Sher 'Ali Khan (r. 1863–5, 1868–78). In 1865 the amir sought the support of the tribal leadership in his ongoing power struggle with his brothers. According to his contemporary Khafi, the king summoned 2,000 tribal representatives (*az har taifa buzurgan-i qaum*)

---

[2] The leaders mentioned by name are Haji Jamal Khan Barakzai, Mahabbat Khan Fofalzai, Musa Khan Ishaqzai, Nur Muhammad Khan 'Alizai, Nasrullah Khan Nurzai (Sultan Muhammad 1881: 122).

to consult with them on the course of action he was to adopt in his confrontation with the rebellious governor of Kandahar, his full brother Muhammad Amin. At the beginning of the meeting, Sher 'Ali Khan encouraged the delegates to state their opinions freely, without fear of royal punishment. Unfortunately, we are left in the dark whether the tribal leadership indeed expressed their sentiments on this issue. Ultimately, they consented to the amir's plan to prepare a military campaign against his brother (Khafi 1957: 95–9). Nur Muhammad Nuri, who chronicled the events at Sher 'Ali Khan's court up to the year 1870, gives a different account of this meeting. In his version of events, it merely consisted of an extended royal council, in which Sher 'Ali Khan informed his loyal followers (*waqifan-i paya-i sarir-i khilafat wa 'ataba busan-i dargah-i imarat*) about the hostilities Muhammad Amin had commenced against the Kabul government (Nuri 1956: 80).

In November 1873 the newly founded newspaper *Shams al-Nahar* reported that Sher 'Ali Khan had invited about 1,000 tribal representatives to Kabul in order to consult them concerning the pending nomination of 13-year-old 'Abdullah Jan as heir apparent (Ahang 1968–70: 75). This meeting apparently took place on 8 November, when, according to the British agent at Kabul, the amir's officials summoned

> all the higher Sirdars, Khans, leading merchants and others of position and influence to the smaller hall of private audience, and explaining to them the views of the Ameer on this subject asked them what advice they had to offer. They all pronounced a blessing on Sirdar Abdoolla Khan as heir apparent. (Kabul Agent, 9 November 1873; For. Sec. March 1874 No. 1, National Archives of India)

Previous to this larger meeting, the most prominent courtiers had deliberated on the question of succession for fifteen days. While the amir declared that he would abide by the decision of this council, all concerned knew that 'Abdullah Jan was his favourite and voted accordingly (Faiz Muhammad 1912: 331; see also Khafi 1957: ii. 110–11). Twenty years later Amir 'Abd al-Rahman Khan (r. 1880–1901) was to hold a *darbar* to inform 400 delegates of his negotiations with Sir Mortimer Durand concerning the eastern and southern frontier of his dominions. This assembly was composed of the tribal leadership and the important army officers from Kabul and its immediate environs. Similar to the meetings called by Amir Sher 'Ali Khan, it merely served to sanction a fait accompli.[3]

The search for the historical roots of the *loya jirga* thus reveals that this term did not exist until the late nineteenth century. Nor was there a state institution suggesting the implementation of the tribal concept of *jirga* on the national level. The two assemblies I have mentioned for the eighteenth century fit into the concept of spontaneous tribal meetings serving to unite local segments in the face of external challenges posed by war or the disintegration of larger power structures. The phenomenon of the *majlis* is not as easily captured for the nineteenth century. While one large meeting of 2,000 delegates did take place in 1865, most of the meetings called by the king merely consisted of a larger version of the court council. A common characteristic of both kinds of meetings is that those invited had no active part in the decisions reached but rather functioned as claqueurs.

Thus, when the Afghan kings set out to 'revive' the *loya jirga* in the early twentieth century, they had no long-standing political tradition to fall back upon. In their endeavour to present modern state organs in the garb of familiar customs they had to reach much further into a mythical past and claimed to tap truly 'Afghan' institutions, which were alive and well in the tribal setting. When Nadir Khan, the founder of the Musahiban dynasty, addressed the newly created Afghan Parliament in July 1931, he admitted that the *jirga* had not been a regular feature of Afghan politics so far and attributed this shortcoming to the neglect of his predecessors:

> In Afghanistan, conferences were held from remote antiquity, since we can consider the Afghan Jirga as the just ruler of the Afghans. If the previous sovereigns did not hold conferences, the nation in their tribes and clans at any rate have not abandoned to this day their Jirga system. (Ali 1933: 195; see also Gregorian 1969: 303)

3. Modern Developments

The first *loya jirga* took place in 1915, when Habibullah Khan invited 540 delegates from all parts of the country to Kabul in order to explain the

---

[3] Faiz Muhammad 1912: 946–8; Sykes 1981: ii. 176. Amir 'Abd al-Rahman Khan also created a permanent royal council consisting of the *sardars*, the local leadership (*khawanin-i mulki*) and the ulama (Kakar 1979: 23–4; Sultan Mohammad 1900: 57, 61).

reasons for Afghanistan's neutrality during the First World War (Mihraban 1989: 51; Sykes 1981: ii. 257). Under Habibullah Khan's successors the *loya jirga* became a regular feature of Afghan politics and grew along with the efforts of the Muhammadzai kings to establish a central state. Even so, it was not convened at regular intervals. In 1931 Nadir Shah stipulated that it was to be called every three years, but this practice ended with his death (Ali 1933: 191; Wilber 1962: 162). In 1923 Amanullah presented the draft for the first Afghan constitution to a *loya jirga* consisting of 939 participants. Despite the fact that the government controlled the selection of delegates (Dupree 1980: 567), this assembly displayed an interesting range of reformist and traditionalist attitudes. Apart from the 'Young Afghan' modernists of Kabul, a number of local leaders and 300 ulama were present. The latter two groups opposed all government endeavours to enhance state control and to interfere with customs considered internal and intrinsic to local culture. Thus many of the reforms Amanullah Khan envisioned, such as a new marriage code, education for girls, as well as the introduction of a new system of conscription and identity certificates, met with harsh criticism (Adamec 1974: 83–5; Kreile 1997: 398–402). The administrative measures, including the establishment of a cabinet (*shura-i waziran*) and a state council (*shura-i daulati*), by contrast, passed without much comment (Mihraban 1989: 58, 65).

Operating on a larger scale than the tribal assembly, the *loya jirga* was designed to reach its decisions on the basis of a majority vote rather than consensus. At the opening ceremony of the *loya jirga* on 29 August 1928, Amanullah Khan encouraged the 1,001 representatives to make their opinions heard but also made it clear that the outcome of the vote at the end of the discussion was binding for all participants: '[O]nce a decision had been reached by majority vote, the delegates would betray their nation, their families, and the Prophet if they resisted the decision'. Accordingly, the amir faced little open opposition as the negotiations went on during the next four days. Only his plan to raise the marriage age for men and women was rejected after a heated discussion. Nonetheless, Amanullah Khan sensed that the delegates did not really approve of his reformist policies. For this reason he gave another sequence of four speeches to a hand-picked audience consisting of the diplomatic corps, Afghan civil and military officials and members of the state council at the beginning of October

(Adamec 1974: 133–6). Resistance to the amir's plans to abolish the veil, to introduce monogamy, and to secularize education had been brewing for a while. After the conclusion of the *loya jirga*, members of the Mujaddidi family collected 400 signatures for a manifesto declaring Amanullah Khan's reforms as contrary to Islam. On 14 November 1928, their agitation led to the outbreak of a rebellion in Khost, which eventually forced him to leave the country (Adamec 1974: 139; also see Ahmad 1930: 27-9).

Less than two years later yet another assembly was convened to pass a constitution. This time around, the circumstances were entirely different. While Amanullah Khan had tried to use the *loya jirga* primarily as a vehicle to publicize his ambitious reformist plans, the new ruler Nadir Khan needed to secure his power by wooing the traditional leadership. In the *loya jirga* of 9 September 1930 he annulled a number of Amanullah Khan's reforms. The ulama regained control of the judiciary (civil and criminal law), the *shari'at* courts were to remain autonomous. The conscription of soldiers passed to the domain of the tribal leadership again; certain frontier tribes became entirely exempt from taxation and conscription. Women were no longer mentioned in the new constitution, and Amanullah Khan's initiatives concerning the marriage code and girls' education were reversed (Olesen 1995: 179–80; Wilber 1962: 159). At the same time, first steps towards institutionalizing the *loya jirga* were undertaken, with the creation of a parliament consisting of a 'house of peers' (*majlis-i a'yan*) and a 'national assembly' (*majlis-i shura-i milli*). While the sixty members of the *majlis-i a'yan* were nominated by the king, the selection of the members of the *shura-i milli* was apparently linked to the *loya jirga*.[4] On paper, the National Assembly enjoyed far-reaching powers, including the right to initiate and pass laws and to examine the national budget (Dupree 1980: 467; Mubariz 1996: 60–1). In reality,

---

[4] Dupree 1980: 463. The information on the number of delegates to the *shura-i milli* and the way they were selected is contradictory. The figures for the deputies are variously listed as 105 (Dupree 1980: 463), 111 (Mihraban 1989: 115), 116 (Gregorian 1969: 303) and 120 (Mohammed Ali 1933: 190–2). While Dupree is of the opinion that members of the *shura-i milli* were selected from within the *loya jirga* with the king's approval, other sources speak more vaguely of nationwide elections by which each constituency of about 100,000 had the right to elect a member to the assembly (Gregorian 1969: 303–4). Also see Ali 1933: 191; Mihraban 1989: 115; Wilber 1962: 161.

The Loya Jirga

however, it wielded little authority and rather reflected Nadir Khan's policy of appeasement than a genuine attempt to include the local leadership in government affairs.

The constitution of 1931 combined various elements from the Turkish, Iranian and French constitutions – as well as some of Amanullah Khan's ideas – with ingredients from the Hanafi school of Islamic law and customary law. While it devised the creation of democratic government institutions, power remained in the hands of the royal family (Dupree 1980: 464). More than thirty years elapsed before Afghanistan received its first democratic constitution. In September 1964 Zahir Shah called a *loya jirga* of 452 participants, six of them women. In an attempt to make this *loya jirga* truly representative, the king stipulated that an equal number of delegates (176 each) was to be furnished by the National Assembly and representatives from the provinces, who were elected by indirect vote. The remaining hundred seats were filled by appointees of the king, as well as members of the senate, cabinet, supreme court, constitutional committee and the constitutional advisory commission. Contrary to the *loya jirga* of 1928, when Amanullah Khan had imposed the look of modernity by insisting that the delegates wear Western clothes, Zahir Shah left it to the participants to express the festiveness of the occasion by their own choice of Western or tribal clothing, or a combination thereof. Decisions were reached by a simple 'yes' or 'no' vote at the end of the discussion but dissenters were allowed to put their opinions in writing. The debates alternatively took place in Persian or Pashtu (Dupree 1980: 567–73).

The new constitution achieved many of the goals Amanullah Khan had vainly striven for. Afghanistan became a constitutional monarchy with a parliament (*shura*) consisting of a 216-member Lower House (*wolesi jirga*) and an eighty-four-member Upper House (*meshrano jirga*).[5] Women and men gained the right to vote and the first parliamentary elections took place a year later. Simultaneously the composition and function of the *loya jirga* changed. Title V of the constitution stipulated that it was to be made up of members of parliament and the chairmen of the twenty-eight provincial

---

[5] Twenty-eight members of the *meshrano jirga* were appointed by the king, another twenty-eight were elected by the provinces and twenty-eight were elected by the provincial councils (Dupree 1980: 587).

councils. The *loya jirga* thus became a state institution (Dupree 1980: 586). No longer subject to appointment by the king and his advisers, it reached a high degree of inclusion and approximated the ideal of representation for all segments of Afghan society. However, its incorporation into the state also deprived the *loya jirga* of its former spontaneity and glamour. The process of institutionalization continued in the 1970s and 1980s, formally elevating the *loya jirga* to previously unknown heights while at the same time cutting it off from its local roots.

The constitutions of 1977, 1985 and 1987 defined the *loya jirga* as the highest state organ but changed its composition to such a degree that it more or less lost its representative character. Both Daud and Najibullah planned to pack the assembly with state cadres.[6] If the constitutions of 1977 and 1987 had ever been implemented they would have turned the *loya jirga* into a state instrument, reducing it to a democratic facade for an authoritarian one-party system (Moltmann 1986: 560). Yet these constitutional changes were never carried out. Daud's constitution became obsolete with the Saur revolution of 1978. During the communist era the idea of instituting a representative *loya jirga* became entirely elusive. In 1980 the communist regime announced that a *loya jirga* could only be established once 'conditions are right for free and secure elections to it'. Until then the Revolutionary Council was to be in charge of government. Shortly afterwards Babrak Karmal's efforts to substitute the *loya jirga* by creating the National Fatherland Front failed miserably (Arnold 1983: 121–3). As the war gained momentum, the government became increasingly alienated from the rural population. The organizers of the constitutional

---

[6] According to the constitution of 1977, the *loya jirga* formally represented 'the paramount power of the will of the people'. It was to consist of the members of parliament (*milli jirga*), the president, his cabinet, the central council of the National Revolutionary Party (*shura-i markazi-i hizb-i inqilab-i milli*), the high military council, the supreme court, and thirty delegates appointed by the president. The provinces were to depute five to eight representatives each. The president of the republic also presided over the *loya jirga* (Dupree 1980: 763–4; also see Moltmann 1986: 552). The constitution of 1987 designated the following composition of the *loya jirga*: members of the National Assembly, the Council of Ministers, the leadership of the National Fatherland Front, governors and mayors of Kabul, the attorney general and his deputies. Furthermore, a number of well-known personalities were appointed by the president on recommendation of the Secretariat of the National Fatherland Front (Olesen 1995: 266).

loya jirgas of 1985 and 1987 thus faced difficulties in mobilizing delegates outside of Kabul.[7] The government's claim that the participants in these assemblies were elected locally seems highly improbable, given the political circumstances of the time (Moltmann 1986: 558–60).

In the early phase of the war, the forces opposed to the communists likewise tried to use the *loya jirga* for their purposes. In mid-May 1980 representatives from all over Afghanistan attended a *momasila loya jirga* – a provisional national council – in Peshawar. This was the first *loya jirga* which was held in opposition to the government and took place outside of Afghanistan. For the next six months, approximately 7,000 participants, representing all administrative districts in Afghanistan as well as the refugee population in Pakistan and Iran, deliberated on a provisional constitution for an Islamic republic and set up a 110-member revolutionary council. Ultimately, however, the efforts of the *momasila loya jirga* were undermined by the Islamist Peshawar parties, which were in turn fostered by the Pakistani secret service (Newell and Newell 1981: 184–5).

4. Conclusion

The *loya jirga* may thus be viewed as a political phenomenon which owed its existence to the rulers' efforts to establish a central state. As the Afghan state institutions grew in the course of the twentieth century, the *loya jirga* became a staple of politics but also lost much of its original meaning. At the core of its genesis lay the basic tension between state and tribe, between centre and periphery. The Afghan kings attempted to bridge this gap by appealing to a well-known tribal institution and tapping its potential for their own purposes. My historical survey shows that the *loya jirga* proved particularly efficient at times of political stability, enabling those in power to give their rule the veneer of broad popular acceptance. This also points to the limitations of the *loya jirga* as an instrument for peace in a setting devoid of functioning state institutions, as is the case in Afghanistan today. For all its positive connotations, it is no panacea for the social and political evils that have befallen the country in recent years. Historically, the *loya*

---

[7] The government managed to hold *jirgas* on a smaller scale among the Hazaras and the border tribes during this period (Schetter 2001: 371 n. 119).

jirga has shown itself to be a useful tool in the hands of well-established rulers, no more, no less. It cannot induce the will for peace on the part of all the political/military players presently involved in Afghanistan.

The same might be said for Zahir Shah. The former king indeed symbolizes an era of stability and a balance of power that cannot seem other than golden in the light of the incessant warfare and massacres the Afghan population is being subjected to. At the same time he and his entourage do not represent a broadly based political movement inside or outside the country. Even if he were to return to Afghanistan, he could not bring the good old days back. The challenge for the future will be to create a representative form of government that includes all segments of society. The first condition for the summoning of a *loya jirga* – or whatever name may be applied to such an assembly – is the establishment of an interim government that has sufficient coercive power to turn the capital into the centre of political gravity again. The next, equally difficult step would be the choice of representatives to attend a national meeting. Who are the local leaders who could rightfully claim to speak on behalf of their fellow Afghans? This most compelling question makes it abundantly clear how uncertain the political future of Afghanistan is.

Bibliography

Adamec, Ludwig (1974) *Afghanistan's Foreign Affairs to the Mid-Twentieth Century*. Tucson, University of Arizona Press.

Ahang, Mohammed Kazem (1968–70) The Background and Beginning of the Afghan Press System. *Afghanistan* 21(1): 70-6; (2): 41-8; (3): 43-7; 21(4): 37-47; 22(1): 28-31; (2): 73-80; 22(3-4): 52-73.

Ahmad, Ali (1930), *The Fall of Amanullah*. L/P&S/10/1285, India Office Library.

Ali, Mohammed (1933) *Progressive Afghanistan*. Lahore, Punjab Educational Electric Press.

Arnold, Anthony (1983) *Afghanistan's Two-Party Communism*. Stanford, CA, Hoover Institution.

Doerfer, Gerhard (1963) *Türkische und mongolische Elemente im Neupersischen*. Vol. I *Mongolische Elemente im Neupersischen*. Wiesbaden, Franz Steiner.

Dupree, Louis (1980) *Afghanistan*. Princeton, Princeton University Press.

Elphinstone, Mountstuart (1992) *An Account of the Kingdom of Caubul*. Karachi, Oxford University Press.

Faiz Muhammad (1912) *Siraj al-tawarikh*. Kabul, Government Press.

Ferrier, J. P. (1858) *History of the Afghans*. London, John Murray.

Ghubar, Mir Ghulam Muhammad (1981) *Afghanistan dar masir-i tarikh*. Qom, Payam-i Muhajir.

Glatzer, Bernt (1977) *Nomaden von Gharjistan*. Wiesbaden, Franz Steiner Verlag.

Gregorian, Vartan (1969) *The Emergence of Modern Afghanistan*. Stanford, CA, Stanford University Press.

Gulistani, Ibn Muhammad Amin Abu al-Hasan (1891, 1896) *Mujmil al-tarikh-i ba'dnadiriya*, 1196/1781. Edition of Vols. I and II by Oskar Mann. Leiden.

Kakar, Hasan Kawun (1979) *Government and Society in Afghanistan*. Austin, University of Texas Press.

Khafi, Ya'qub 'Ali (1957), *Padshahan-i mutaakhir-i Afghanistan*. Kabul, Daulati Matba'a.

Kreile, Renate (1997) Zan, zar, zamin – Frauen, Gold und Land: Geschlechterpolitik und Staatsbildung in Afghanistan. *Leviathan* 3: 396-420.

Mihraban, 'Abdullah (1989) *Tarikh-i shura dar Afghanistan*. Kabul, Majlis-i Sana-i Shura-i Melli Jumhuri-i Afghanistan.

Moltmann, Gerhard (1986) Die Verfassungsentwicklung Afghanistans von 1901 bis 1986, *Jahrbuch des öffentlichen Rechts der Gegenwart*. In: Peter Häberle (ed.). Neue Folge 35. Tübingen, J. C. B. Mohr.

Mubariz, 'Abd al-Hamid (1996) *Tahlil-i waqi'at-i siasi 1919–1996*. No place, no publisher.

Newell, Nancy Peabody, and Newell, Richard S. (1981) *The Struggle for Afghanistan*. Ithaca, NY, Cornell University Press.

Nuri, Nur Muhammad (1956) *Gulshan-i imarat*. Kabul, Government Press.

Olesen, Asta (1995) *Islam and Politics in Afghanistan*. Richmond, VA, Curzon Press.

Schetter, Conrad (2001) Ethnizität und ethnische Konflikte in Afghanistan, PhD dissertation, University of Bonn.

Singh, Ganda (1981) *Ahmad Shah Durrani: Father of Modern Afghanistan*. Lahore, Tariq Publications.

Steul, Willi (1981) *Paschtunwali: Ein Ehrenkodex und seine rechtliche Relevanz*. Wiesbaden, Franz Steiner Verlag.

Sultan Mohammad Khan (1900) *The Constitution and Laws of Afghanistan*. London, John Murray.

Sultan Muhammad Khan b. Musa Durrani (1881) *Tarikh-i sultani*. Bombay, Karkhana-i Muhammadi.

Sykes, Percy (1981) *A History of Afghanistan*. New Delhi, Manoharlal Publishers.

Wilber, Donald Newton (1962) *Afghanistan: Its People, its Society, its Culture*. New Haven, HRAF Press.

Part II

Regional and Cultural Development

A Tense Autonomy
The Present Situation in Nuristan

Max Klimburg

Nuristan presents a special case in virtually all relevant respects, as its ethnic, linguistic and cultural features are highly particular. It is only some 105 years ago that the region was Islamized, and that the feared and ostracized 'Kafirs of the Hindu Kush' were converted by force and then renamed Nuristani, establishing them as members of the Muslim world. Subsequently they enjoyed a special status which was based initially on the reported beauty of their women, and which eventually provided them with official support and exceptional trust. Many Nuristani received generous grants for their education in Kabul, and especially in the military they found good career possibilities. In the world of sports they also held a unique position, as many members of the national Afghan hockey team were Nuristani whose traditional recreational activities included the playing of hockey in both summer and winter (on snow). The Nuristani thus constituted the most favoured among the minorities of Afghanistan, and they accepted wilfully the authority of Kabul in return. Their extraordinary cultural past attained such a reputation internationally that eventually Kafir and also Nuristani objects of even minor value were officially prohibited from being exported (illegal and construed 'legal' export continued notwithstanding). Naturally, the privileged position of the Nuristani made them virtually the first ethnically based victims of the new rulers after the communist coup d'état in April of 1978. Soon one high-ranking man after another disappeared; only a few managed to escape in time to Nuristan. A major exception was General Muhammad Sarwar, as will be shown below. This negative attitude changed, however, to much more favourable dealings after the Soviet invasion and Babrak Karmal's coming to power.

Back in earlier and generally much happier years, the enthusiasm of the newly converted Nuristani for the tenets of Islam was limited. The then still-recent Kafir past with its general life style and comparatively liberal attitudes towards sexuality continued to influence the people's thoughts. On the other hand, growing ties with the outside Islamic world inevitably eroded their former practices and increased tendencies to bedevil the Kafir past. Eventually Nuristan presented a challenge for Islamists in their drive to establish what they deemed as the correct Islam. In the 1960s, groups of mullahs, educated in a *madrasa* in the village of Panjpir close to Mardan in Pakistan's North-West Frontier Province and thus known as Panjpiri, started to preach throughout Nuristan the 'true Islam' according to orthodox tenets, related to those of the Indian Deobandi school which was also to provide the basis of the Taliban movement. Their message was clear and simple: acknowledgment of nothing but what is written in the Quran or established by *hadith*, strict opposition to every kind of deviation in folklore or otherwise, in particular against the cult of saints, dance and music and all non-Islamic feasts, and for an absolute gender-based division of the society. In essence all recreational activities were condemned as distracting from or even obtrusive to the essential duty of worshiping Allah. In this sense the Panjpiri literally thundered with their loudspeakers against typical Nuristani traditions such as feasting for the sake of status, dancing and music, dating (or what was left of it by the 1960s) or simply communicating between the sexes, and locally favoured games and sports, especially hockey. Islamist proselytizing activities must be seen against the background of a culture which once was extremely lively and extroverted, in some respects even 'Dionysiac'.

The impact of this Islamist movement led to tensions particularly in larger villages. Thus, in Waigal, the dominant community in the Waigal Valley, many young men fought against the local mullah's orders to stop playing hockey, their favourite game, and to demolish one of the popular resting platforms, which were located along important pathways in or near the communities. In Kafir times wealthy men had had them built in their names in the context of large feasts of merit. The Panjpiri regarded the platforms as inducive to illicit sexual contacts, be it only by watching women passing on the paths. A few times the platform in Waigal was torn down by one group of men, only to be rebuilt by another. Several years ago the platform disappeared for good.

In one respect, the religious authorities, mainly Panjpiri-inspired, proved successful in a number of villages, especially in Waigal Valley: they managed to reduce the standard Waigali bride price of between 150 and

250 goats to 60 goats. This reduction made it possible for mullahs to enter the competition for 'good' marriageable girls in spite of their generally poor social background. Major social problems remain, of course, if a mullah belongs to the previously ostracized, slave-like class of craftsmen and labourers called *bari*. Today in Waigal Valley, one finds neighbouring villages with vastly differing bride price regulations, greatly complicating inter-village marriage contracts and the settling of the generally very steep fines for illicit sexual relations.

The Islamist battle for the Nuristani soul was in full swing, advancing in particular in the Bashgal and Parun Valleys, when the communist takeover occurred. The new rulers' precipitous reformist regulations and announcements, including those dealing with property rights in forested areas such as, above all, in Nuristan, led to revolts as early as in the summer of 1978, only a few months after the coup d'état. The destruction of the Pashtun inhabited village of Ningalam, located at the confluence of the Waigal and the Pech Rivers, boded more ill to come. Some six months later half of the large Nuristani village of Kamdesh, located in the Bashgal Valley, was burned as a result of the fast-spreading uprising.

During the 1980-92 war, until the fall of the Najibullah regime, Nuristan both suffered and profited. Only the villages in southeastern Nuristan, located close to the border of Pakistan and the hotly contested Kunar Valley with its important supply routes for the Mujahidin, experienced repeated bombardments and were more or less destroyed. Most of the local villagers fled to the Pakistan district of Chitral. In addition, in February of 1987 Kamdesh was again partially destroyed by fire. The main area of Nuristan, however, remained largely unaffected in the physical sense, though it suffered from the heavy loss of men fighting outside of Nuristan against Kabul government forces. For instance, several bombs fell on and near the village of Nisheigram, destroying a few houses which were rebuilt soon afterwards. When I visited the Waigal Valley in autumn of 1987, I observed no ruins and much construction activity.

On the positive side, Nuristan profited from serving the Mujahidin crossing Nuristan on routes leading from Pakistan to Laghman and into the Panjshir Valley. A part of the arms and ammunition supplied to Ahmad Shah Massoud was transported in one direction, and loads of lapis lazuli stones mined in Badakhshan in the other (after the government troops, guarding the mines, had been driven away). Plenty of goats and large quantities of walnuts and clarified butter could be sold to the Mujahidin in transit. A number of 'hotels' were set up in goatherd's lodges or in caves to provide them with food, tea and shelter along the routes, and selling cigarettes, *naswar* (chewing tobacco), chewing gum, biscuits and batteries.

On the other hand, Nuristan not only suffered from loss of life, but also from tensions resulting from the political and religious division which plagued the Afghan resistance from its start. With only one exception, all the well-known 'Peshawar parties' were represented, each competing for more influence and followers with both ideological and financial means, such as access to arms and minimal pay. The carrying of a Kalashnikov quickly became a symbol of martial prowess and virility, and was coveted by most young and middle-aged men.

In Nuristan the most influential of the 'Peshawar parties' were the Jam'iyat-i Islami under Burhan al-Din Rabbani and G. Hikmatyar's Hizb-i Islami, according to some conflicting statements. The essentially royalist and liberal organization Mahaz-i Milli under the leadership of Pir Sayyid Ahmad Gailani seems to have dominated several villages in Waigal Valley. S. Mujaddidi's Jabha-i Milli, Nabi Muhammad's Harakat-i Inqilabi and M. Y. Khalis' Hizb-i Islami played smaller roles.

There was in addition a Nuristani party called Daulat-i Inqilabi-i Islami-i Afghanistan, in short Daulat, based in the northern part of the Bashgal Valley and led by the mullah Maulawi Muhammad Afzal from his home village Nikmuk. By its strictly Wahhabi orientation, it introduced from Pakistan into northeastern Nuristan an Arab Islamist movement, which proved very successful (with the help of generous funding and emissaries from Saudi Arabia), spreading into other Nuristan areas as well. However, the creation of Daulat deepened the traditional antagonism inside the Bashgal Valley between the Kantozi villages to the north and the Kam villages to the south, dominated by the large village of Kamdesh. The south adhered to the dominant 'Peshawar parties', in particular to G. Hikmatyar's Hizb-i Islami.

The fiercely Islamist Daulat was founded in 1982 with organizational advice from the former Brigadier General Muhammad Sarwar, a politically active Nuristani from northwestern Nuristan. Maulawi Afzal became the

'Emir' of a tiny, independent Nuristani 'state of God' with a sort of council of ministers and government offices, with Muhammad Sarwar acting as 'Minister of Defence'. As its main activity, Daulat built mosques and primary schools, the latter called *madrasa*[1], and taxed everybody passing through unless provided with a 'laissez passer' document issued by its foreign relations representative in Chitral.

The tensions between the two halves of the Bashgal Valley were further incited by new fights in continuation of old conflicts between Kamdesh and its much smaller close neighbour, the village of Kushtoz, which formed part of the northern half. The demand of more water for Kamdesh, transported in a channel above Kushtoz, was the main bone of contention. When in 1984/85 Kushtoz closed the channel, the fight led to serious bloodshed, and dozens of men, mainly among the Kamdesh fighters, were killed.

The situation changed in favour of Kamdesh with the seizure of power in Kabul by the Mujahidin (1992). The influence of the Hizb-i Islami grew stronger, and in about 1994 the 'Emir' was forced to pay blood money to Kamdesh for the men killed in 1984/85. Kushtoz had to back down, and the embattled irrigation channel was reopened (de Bures: 2).

In late 1996 or early 1997 Muhammad Sarwar reappeared in Nuristan, and he became interested in mediating between Kamdesh and Kushtoz, seeing a chance to build a new power base for himself after earlier undertakings of his had failed. In around 1983 he had left the Daulat 'Emirate', reportedly irritated by its Islamist zealousness and the constant interference by Arabs. He had moved to Pakistan, had there been jailed for more than a year on grounds of smuggling or the like, had managed to be freed, and had been greatly welcomed in Kabul by Babrak Karmal, who then used Sarwar for

---

[1] The term *madrasa* is generally used to refer to a religious college or even university for males, while 'mosque schools' provide marginal primary schooling for boys and girls. As the Taliban and Wahhabi acknowledge only religious schools, they use the term in a general sense for 'school', thus also for non-mosque-based primary schools or the formerly secular lycées in Kabul. The *madrasa* in the old sense is mostly referred to as *dini madrasa* - 'religious *madrasa*' - a genuinely pleonastic term. Presently there are in all of Nuristan only mosque schools: some six (Arab supported) 'primary *madrasa*', and a few (Western NGO supported) secular primary schools for boys and girls.

undermining the Mujahidin alliances in Nuristan. The bait was the long-coveted creation of a separate province of Nuristan, meant to be carved out of the two provinces of Kunar and Laghman. Accordingly, he started to collaborate with the communist regime, organizing meetings of Nuristani notables with government authorities and calling to arms everybody interested in defending the idea of a new, but neutralized Nuristan province. At that time, this province was limited to northwestern Nuristan, with its centre in Gadmuk, Sarwar's home village. It was a classic 'divide-and-rule' attempt to counterbalance the anti-Kabul Daulat government at the 'other side' of Nuristan. Kabul was quite successful, as the offer of money and Kalashnikovs and also the lure of a relatively liberal and joyful life style in Kabul, if only enjoyed briefly, attracted many young Nuristani. There were cases of runaways such as the one I noticed when I visited, in October of 1987, an old friend in Waigal Village. He was away looking for one of his sons who was thought to have followed the call of recruiters employed by Muhammad Sarwar.

With the fall of the communist regime in Kabul (1992) Sarwar's Nuristan province became obsolete and also the secular lure of Kabul was gone, but the idea of a separate province survived. In spite of all the political tensions and the old and new animosities between neighbouring communities, the Nuristani managed, possibly with the participation of Sarwar, to agree in 1993 on establishing a 'united' Nuristan province. A site near the centrally located village of Pashki in the Parun Valley, in spite of its difficult accessibility, was chosen as the administrative centre. Work on the governor's house had already started when the arrival of the Taliban in 1996 put an end to the work, but not to the idea of a separate province.

As the Taliban refrained from interfering in Nuristan or even trying to disarm the Nuristani, prominent Nuristani like Sarwar and Afzal were free to act. Afzal allied himself with the Taliban, who in return upgraded his stronghold, Bargromatal, to the administrative centre of the Bashgal Valley, thereby angering Kamdesh, the previous centre. Naturally, all this led again to new conflicts in Bashgal, not only between Kamdesh and Afzal's protegé village Kushtoz, but also between him and supporters of the 'Northern Alliance' under Ahmad Shah Massoud, among them Muhammad Sarwar. In 1997 Afzal was attacked and heavily injured, losing one eye (de

Bures, p. 4). Some time afterwards he quit the field and moved to Jalalabad where he presently lives.

Muhammad Sarwar had reentered northeastern Nuristan after the fall of Kabul to the Taliban (September 1996), attempting to regain some influence for the sake of the Northern Alliance. Successful mediation in important cases greatly raises a man's reputation, and thus he occupied himself with the most pressing case, the Kamdesh - Kushtoz conflict. His mediation appeared successful for a while. In late 1997 he joined a large *jirga*[2] in Kamdesh which attempted to find a solution to the conflict. However, he failed and the jirga achieved nothing, with the exception of defaming Sarwar in as much, as it provided a platform for Afzal and other Islamists wanting to attack Sarwar for his earlier collaboration with the communist regime in Kabul. Soon afterwards Sarwar had the courage to meet with the Taliban in the Kunar Valley, undoubtedly lured by promises for his safety, to discuss with them the unresolved issue of Kamdesh versus Kushtoz. He and his numerous body guards were taken prisoner, and he was brought to Kandahar, where he still lingers in jail.

In June of 1998 the conflict between Kamdesh and Kushtoz about the water channel exploded, with Afzal unable to assist Kushtoz. Kamdesh attacked its much smaller neighbouring community, bombarded it with rockets and burned it down, not sparing the large, richly decorated mosque and the magnificent house of Amir Muhammad.[3] There were many casualties, and the inhabitants had no choice but to flee and seek refuge. Most of them ended up in Dungul, Weligal and other communities to the south of Kamdesh. Vengeful Kushtozi continue to bombard Kamdesh from time to time with rockets, thereby keeping alive a war-like situation which can at any time pull in other communities as well.

Tragically, this was the second time that the village was totally destroyed, as the same fate had befallen Kushtoz in 1929, following the uprising against King Amanullah and the collapse of state authority. Then, in around

---

[2] The Pashtu term *jirga* for 'village council meeting' is generally used nowadays in Nuristan whenever one talks of large negotiating meetings involving speakers of different Nuristani language groups.

[3] Both buildings occupy a prominent place in Edelberg 1984: Figs. 101-102 and 164-167.

1930, the newly established government of King Nadir Shah managed to enforce a settlement. This held until around 1982 when the Kamdeshi raised the issue of needing more water.

The Taliban seemed content to leave the Nuristani preoccupied with their fights. Though they uphold the existence of a separate Nuristan province with the location of its capital in Parun, they have not appointed anyone to become what would be a powerless *wali* (governor) heading a remote, predominantly anti-Taliban province. Nevertheless, the Taliban wanted their presence shown, be it only by name, by staffing the nine (formerly six) *uluswali* district centres of the Nuristan province with local Taliban mullahs.

Thus kept more or less alone, the present situation in Nuristan is reminiscent of the one which existed there before Islamization, when the communities, *desh*, were entirely autonomous. Nuristan again can arrange its affairs on the basis of local traditions and decision making bodies, and can also choose between the Islamist tenets preached by Wahhabi or Panjpiri or mainstream Sunni Hanafi mullahs. The Nuristani are free to turn their attention to both developmental issues and internal conflicts, readily seizing their arms whenever the situation gets tense. As many new developmental projects are undertaken, more clashes erupt over conflicting uses of land and water, road construction, power stations, water pipe lines, clinics, schools[4] and the like. The drought in the year 2000/2001 sensitized the population further, leading to serious conflicts, even bloodshed and the burning down of houses, such as in Kusht (Pech Valley) in the summer of 2000. In the summer of 2001 gun fights erupted between Waigal and Zhönchigal (in Waigal Valley) caused by conflicts over a water channel, and six men were killed. In addition, there are the new, very dangerous clashes over the Nuristan forests as, after a long lull in logging activities due to the war, a serious assault on the forests in eastern Nuristan began several years ago. With the precious Himalaya cedars – majestic, straight growing trees – cut in great quantity and then exported to Pakistan and

---

[4] With virtually no other prospects many Nuristani boys are sent each year to attend one of the thousands of dini-madrasa in Pakistan, which provide them for years with free education, board and lodging until graduating as mullahs – adding them to the very many unemployed mullahs already populating Nurtistan.

Arab countries the unique Nuristani environment becomes increasingly threatened.

Caught in between are the western donor organizations such as, in particular, the French organization MADERA[5] and the British NGO Afghanaid. With no powerful government authorities intervening, they depend, like the Nuristani, on the local means of conflict solving, that is with the help of respected local mediators or elders in specially summoned *jirga* meetings. As important *jirga* may last for many days or even several weeks, influential men are often prevented from performing other urgent mediating tasks. Therefore successful mediators are in great demand. Najibullah, the leading Nuristani staff member of MADERA, became one of the most sought-after men.

In spite of the contemporary openness of Nuristan to the outside world, the better knowledge of each other and the greater mobility of its male population, old animosities and prejudices survive. These are partially inspired by the recent Islamist missionary work on the part of different religious schools, which are united only in their efforts to efface all memory of the Kafir past with its liberal and sensuous life style.[6]

The Islamists have succeeded above all in tightening up the separation of the sexes, which could meet quite openly only a few decades ago. Nowadays nearly all Nuristani women veil themselves when encountering unrelated men, and occasionally one even sees the *chador*, the complete veil – a rather shocking image in any rural environment. Newly constructed houses have a new design which helps to keep the women away from the public eye. Music, singing and dancing are strictly forbidden everywhere with the exception of several villages in Waigal, where some 'liberal attitudes' can still be found. At least hockey and other games are still being played.

Everywhere, new hamlets have sprung up consisting partially or mainly of stone-built houses, since many families have opted to move to new locations outside the former clustered village compounds, and to abandon

---

[5] Mission d'Aide au Développment des Economies Rurales en Afghanistan.

[6] As recently as in 1973 Louis Dupree wrote that 'the Nuristani have seen the light of Islam, but any fuzzily practice the true religion, and have incorporated Kafir motifs and mysteries into their brand of Islam' (p. xxvi).

the old wooden house style. The traditional building style of wooden scaffolds filled with stones and earth appeals less and less, in spite of the excellent sturdiness of such structures when earthquakes occur. The new houses are designed with two rooms with small windows and without the open verandah always formerly attached to the house. They are built by masons brought in from outside, who use explosives to break large boulders into small blocks. Likewise, all the new doors and windows are made by carpenters from outside. Thus, in the near future the Nuristani villages will look quite different, and few women will be seen outside on typical sun-lit verandahs.

The wide-spread building activity mirrors the fact that the Nuristani have a relatively good income from the region's highly developed animal husbandry (with transhumant or 'alpine' features), and in many cases even much new income from the sale of timber and precious stones (mainly emeralds) which are mined in many places. There is also the impact of assistance provided by NGOs.

All this, understandably, is bound to create feelings of envy, especially among the much less privileged and relatively resource-poor Safi Pashtuns inhabiting the crowded lowlands of the Pech Valley, through which pass the main transportation and communications routes into the central areas of Nuristan. Many of them have started to express their resentment by causing trouble for NGO employees on their way to Nuristan, by impeding the transport of Nuristani timber, and even by demanding some Waigal land on the basis of vague claims.

All this may change drastically if Nuristan becomes involved in the civil war. Recently, the risks were there, as the crucial question of neutrality was challenged, in the spring of 2001, by the activities of Haji Abdul Qadir, the Pashtun pre-Taliban governor of Nangarhar Province. At the request of the Northern Alliance under Burhan al-Din Rabbani and Ahmad Shah Massoud, he had gone to Wama, the village controlling the Pech Valley in central Nuristan, with the purpose of recruiting men to fight against the Taliban. The Taliban reacted swiftly. In early June they sent a fighting unit into the Pech Valley. Before it reached Wama, Qadir left the field, and the unit retreated, with no shots fired.

A Tense Autonomy

The Nuristani were well advised to hold on to their neutrality and to keep from provoking the Taliban. Any provocation would have endangered their relatively 'good life' with respect to basic conditions, even though this life is negatively affected by internal strife, the lack of proper medical care, and the scarcity of learning, jobs and entertainment possibilities. On the other hand, it must be kept in mind that the Taliban lacked the means for an easy conquest of a well-armed and independent-minded Nuristan. This was very different from the situation in the winter of 1895/95 when the Afghan army invaded an ill-armed Kafiristan which already felt that its time was over.

With the fall of the Taliban regime in November of 2001 some changes will affect Nuristan in the near future. It is likely that a new Nuristani-based administration will be established according to the plans already agreed to in 1993.[7]

Bibliography

Brillet, Marie (1998) Study of the socio-political organisation and identification of village organisations in the Wama-Parun valley (Nuristan, Afghanistan). Unpublished MA thesis. Paris, Université Paris I (Institut d'Etude du Développement) and MADERA.

de Bures, Alain (n.d.) Historique de la succession de conflits qui opposent les communautés de Koustoz et de Kamdesh au Nouristan-est et qui a abouti à la destruction des quatre villages de Koustoz. Unpublished manuscript, MADERA.

Dupree, Louis (1973) Introduction. In: Reprint of Robertson (1896) *The Káfirs of the Hindu-Kush*. Karachi, Oxford University Press.

Edelberg, Lennart (1984) *Nuristani Buildings*. Moesgård, Jysk Arkæologisk Selskab.

Edelberg, Lennart and Schuyler, Jones (1979) *Nuristan*. Graz, Akademische Druck- und Verlagsanstalt.

---

[7] Most of the information on the most recent developments was collected during fieldwork in Nuristan in October 2000. This fieldwork was undertaken in preparation for a book on the Parun Kafirs, to be published as the second part of my study on the Kafirs of the Hindu Kush.

Jones, Schuyler (1974) *Men of Influence in Nuristan*. Seminar Press, London and New York.

Katz, David (1984) Responses to Central Authority in Nuristan: The Case of the Vaygal Valley Kalasha. In: M. N. Shahrani and R. L. Canfield (eds.) *Revolutions & Rebellions in Afghanistan. Anthropological Perspectives*. Berkeley, University of California Press: 94-118.

Klimburg, Max (1990) Kulturformen bei den Kafiren des Hindukusch. *Mitteilungen der Berliner Gesellschaft für Anthropologie und Urgeschichte* 11: 47-60.

Klimburg, Max (1999) *The Kafirs of the Hindu Kush. Art and Society of the Waigal and Ashkun Kafirs*, 2 Vols. Stuttgart, Franz Steiner.

Robertson, Sir George Scott (1896) *The Káfirs of the Hindu-Kush*. London, Lawrence & Bullen.

Finding a Balance
between Religious Orthodoxy and the Maintenance of
Afghanistan's Performative Traditions

Bruce Koepke

This paper provides a perspective on Afghanistan's intangible cultural heritage of embodied artistic practices, the impending loss of which is a result of the ongoing civil war and imposition of ultra-orthodox Islamic injunctions. Special attention is given to some existing non-religious performance traditions in Badakhshan, Afghanistan's most north-eastern province. Before commenting on fieldwork conducted in 1998 and 1999, I will briefly discuss the ethnography of Badakhshan and, in the light of current censorship of non-religious performance traditions, will examine the role of the relationship between performance and Islam.

1. Ethnographic Context

The ethnically heterogeneous province of Badakhshan is the main living area of the predominantly Persian-speaking Tajik people but is also inhabited by other ethnic groups including bilingual Uzbeks, Pashtuns and Kirghiz. Badakhshan, like Afghanistan, is a plural society, both in terms of ethnicity and Islamic sects. The Ismailis of this province, although ethnically related to the dominant Sunni Tajiks of Badakhshan, are a religious minority here.

As a consequence of Badakhshan's mountainous terrain, the province has been historically and geographically isolated. In the north and north-east, Badakhshan adjoins Gorno-Badakhshan in Tajikistan by its natural border of the Amu Darya, or the Oxus River of antiquity. While eastern Badakhshan fringes Pakistan, at its easternmost point, through a short stretch along the Wakhan Corridor, the province is also connected with China. Former rulers strategically took advantage of Badakhshan's alpine landscape with its deep valley encarvements between the Hindu Kush in the south, the Pamirs in the north-east, and the mountains of Darwaz in the north, which acted as political boundaries. Badakhshan was integrated into the nation of Afghanistan only just over one century ago. As I write, it is once again relatively independent, the only province that remains entirely beyond the control of the Taliban, an ultra-conservative Sunni Islamic religious militia that emerged in 1994. The Taliban, whose members are mostly Afghan and Pakistani religious students from Pakistani *madaris* along the Afghanistan–Pakistan border and disillusioned former Mujahidin, Islamic resistance fighters, from predominantly Pashtun-inhabited regions in southern Afghanistan, now control almost 90 per cent of Afghanistan. Other than Badakhshan, regions beyond Taliban control are in Takhar, Kapisa, Parwan, and several pockets in Kunar, Balkh, and Samangan. These non-Taliban territories are, in theory, ruled by the former government of President Burhan al-Din Rabbani and loosely aligned commanders.

Badakhshan's internal infrastructure is extremely poorly developed. This is not surprising given the recent history of over two decades of civil war, as well as long-standing neglect by previous central authorities in Kabul. Currently, no sealed roads exist in the province and the once stone-reinforced roads, constructed forty to fifty years ago, have now turned into rough tracks. Wash-outs are frequent after heavy rain and, depending on the severity, may lead to road closures ranging from one day to several weeks. The main forms of transport in the province remain horse, donkey or foot. Moreover, as a result of Badakhshan's geopolitical position, its ailing infrastructure and recent natural disasters such as earthquakes and droughts, food shortages are not uncommon.

2. Discussion on Intangible Cultural Properties

Before exploring the reasons behind the censorship of performances and commenting on existing performance traditions in Badakhshan, I will briefly look at the concept of intangible cultural heritage and then summarize the recent history of performance traditions in Afghanistan.

Discussion of cultural heritage must inevitably begin with the recognition that all cultures are reflected in their intangible and tangible cultural properties. Culture, when understood as emergent, dynamic, processual, and 'located in the creative act of communicating' (Daniel 1984: 47), is thus manifested when public and private aspects of human experience become 'mutually immanent' or simultaneously present and active in moments of social action (Daniel 1984: 13). As a 'living culture', members of local communities interact with one another and, through their blending, borrowing and reinventing, develop meaningful cultural actions with which they then identify. Culture also includes important physical dimensions through which a person embodies what it means to be a member of a particular society. By their engagement in cultural practices, people continuously recreate, renew and renegotiate their cultural worlds. Culture therefore may be seen to be a dynamic process of performance.

The combination of a culture's tangible or intangible properties, either through chance or purposeful selection, leads to the creation of its 'heritage'. The concept of tangible properties such as material objects, architecture, literature, handicrafts, etc., is generally relatively familiar. In contrast, and although of equal cultural significance, the category of intangible heritage which encompasses events, language and oral history, beliefs, values and knowledge is much less well known. Like places and objects, intangible practices have aesthetic, historic, scientific or social value for past, present or future generations. They hold significant meaning for a community and are integral to its identity. Whilst a landscape may be thought of as a space imbued with human associations, stories, myths, and emotions, it is the intangible cultural contents of this space that often reveal far more about the owners and their society than the place alone.

The genre of performance is wide-ranging, encompassing a diversity of social processes. In differentiating a performative practice from those of ordinary life, the term 'special event' is often utilized. Such events may include music, dance, sport, or rituals and often represent intensifications of some aspect of ordinary practices, but which are marked for reasons such as cultural reflection or entertainment. Ideas of performance are therefore contingent upon how these events are marked in their respective cultures.

3. Afghan Intangible Cultural Heritage

Afghanistan's recent history is characterized by a series of shifts in the nature and type of governance, moving from monarchy, to republic, communism, Islamic governance and, more recently, to ultra-conservative Islamic rule. These different social and political outlooks have led to the existence of divergent views of tradition and culture. From the 1970s onwards, under King Zahir Shah and then the leadership of Sardar Muhammad Daud, and perhaps even later during parts of the communist regime, attempts were made to foster a national cultural identity and heritage. These trends were consistently biased towards the culture of the politically dominant Pashtun ethnic group, with the cultures of non-Pashtun ethnicities as well as those of rural and tribal identities and of the sizeable religious affiliations neglected, if not suppressed.

In almost all Islamic societies, performance traditions represent vital features of their cultural heritage. Likewise, music and dance performances were patronized at an urban and rural level in Afghanistan, especially during the modern period from the 1960s to the 1980s. During that time and in spite of their controversial status in some religious texts, performances occurred freely and without censorship during the life-cycle events of weddings or after the birth of a child, but also at picnics and private functions. Celebrations were generally sought as a positive emotional outlet, for relaxation and the enjoyment of aesthetics at festivities such as *jashn* (Afghanistan's Independence Day), *nauroz* (Persian New Year), *'id-i qurban* (Feast of Sacrifice) and *'id-i ramazan* (End of Ramadan), and in private homes, urban theatres and outdoor public venues. During the communist period, a shift in the interpretation of intangible cultural properties took place. The performing arts began to be utilized as a means of propaganda, with an emphasis on developing a single national identity, and preferably a communist identity, rather than multi-ethnic and religious identities. The stress was on non-religious entertainment and the suppression of Islamic values. Since the collapse of the communist regime in 1992 and with the introduction of Islamic governance, there has been an even larger shift, which this time has led to a dramatic decrease in all non-religious cultural expression.

This lack of patronage of the performing arts has been accelerated by the expansion of ultra-conservative Islamic values. It is most clearly manifested in the cultural policies of the Taliban who within hours of taking the capital Kabul in 1996 introduced the strictest Islamic system of the contemporary world, banning all forms of non-religious and most forms of religious performances.

Given that this marked change in attitude towards the performing arts is a relatively recent phenomenon, it comes as little surprise that some confusion about cultural identity and heritage currently exists at a local level in Afghanistan. Uncertainties about the appropriateness of the expression of local cultural practices within an Islamic society have thus arisen. Many locals interviewed during my fieldwork in Badakhshan professed that their culture now consisted only of strict Islamic cultural practices such as regular prayers. But when questioned further, the Badakhshi informants acknowledged the value of and their love for other cultural practices, such as performing music and dancing at weddings, picnics and social gatherings, as experienced pre-extremist Islam and pre-communism. It is critical therefore to explore why injunctions against such valued performance traditions have been imposed by most Islamic groups currently in power in Afghanistan.

4. Injunctions Against Performance Traditions

Since the mid-nineteenth century, religious establishments in Afghanistan have been among the most powerful groups in the country and until 1925 *shari'at* law shaped all legal processes in Afghanistan (Rashid 2000: 83). Modernization in Afghanistan has always had to contend with the influence of Islamic institutions which exercised authority both in the political sphere and in the regulation of social norms and values. Certainly, attempts by the Musahiban rulers in the 1970s and the communist regime in the 1980s to develop a national cultural heritage that placed emphasis on performance traditions tended to undermine the social control exercised by these religious establishments.

In tracing the history of Afghanistan's religious groups and their ideological influences, we are taken to the Subcontinent and to the system of *madaris* and especially to the Islamic reformist ideology of the Deobandi- but also Wahhabi-style *madaris*. Whilst Afghanistan has never been colonized, if one considers that its religious institutions were influenced by these centres in British India and later, Pakistan, especially in the sense of developments in education, curricula and print technology (Zaman 1999b: 304), then one may construe the Islamic ideology originating from the *madaris* as a form of cultural imperialism. In fact, many current leaders in Afghanistan have either formally trained at, or at least been influenced by, Deobandi- and Wahhabi-style *madaris* in Pakistan.

The Islamic reformist ideologies taught at Deobandi- and Wahhabi-style *madaris* in the Subcontinent promoted a theory of 'liberation ... through a return by the whole society to its former faith' (Roy 1986: 56) and introduced a renewed emphasis on the study of *hadith*. Many students and their teachers from these *madaris* fought for the establishment of a truly Islamic society based on their understanding of the conditions of the Prophet Muhammad during the seventh century. In the process, they became strongly opposed to non-Sunni minorities, Islamic modernists (Rashid 2000: 23; Zaman 1999a: 81) and any expression of embodied artistic performances.

One can easily recognize the influence of Deobandi ideologies on the Taliban's condemnation of customary beliefs and practices. Furthermore, Taliban supporters are mostly ethnic Pashtuns and the Taliban's interpretation of *shari'at* law displays a syncretic amalgam of orthodox Islam, Deobandi and Wahhabi ideologies but also draws on the influences of local traditions such as *pashtunwali*, the tribal code of the Pashtuns (Rashid 2000: 112). Nevertheless, even the *atan-i milli*, the well-known ethnic Pashtun dance that until the rise of fundamentalist Islam was valued as Afghanistan's national dance, has been banned. Afghanistan's cultural heritage is to be expressed now only in terms of Islamic intellectual scriptural heritage, ideally through 'purely sacred, formal and serious activities' (Werbner 1996: 93) which are primarily based on the Taliban's ultra-conservative interpretations of *hadith*.

When the Taliban took over Kabul at the end of September 1996, they immediately made public their views on performance traditions and entertainment. Among other things, music, dancing, television and cinemas were banned, as were all social institutions including libraries and entertainment venues (Paik 1997). This censorship is now enforced by special Taliban units under the Religious Police and within the Department of Promotion of Virtue and Prevention of Vice. In an interview, the Taliban's Education Minister, Mullah 'Abd al-Hanifi, claimed that music must be opposed 'as it creates a strain in the mind and hampers study of

Islam' (Associated Press 1996; Rashid 2000: 115). Some recent comments made by one of the Taliban's senior officials further substantiate their radical Islamic views. In an interview in *Time* magazine, the Justice Minister, Mullah Nuruddin Torabi, stated:

> We are Muslims and we are required to follow the Holy Koran and implement ... Shariat. If we don't follow it we are committing a sin ... We are following the instructions of God. It is not me saying what should be done. We are told by God what to do ... Our legal code is not something the Taliban has created ... every vice has to be stopped and every virtue promulgated. (Fathers 2000a)

When asked why it had been necessary to ban non-religious music and dance, the Minister replied that these performance activities 'can lead you astray. It is wrong to think the people want them' (Fathers 2000a). The Taliban's Foreign Minister, Mullah Wakil Mutawakkil, was also interviewed for the same *Time* magazine edition. When asked about the Taliban's concerns for human rights, Mutawakkil responded: 'We do not believe we have denied anyone their rights. If there are some restrictions it is because of our culture. People accept this. It is not a Taliban issue, but something which people have always followed' (Fathers 2000b). This statement further indicates that Islamic extremists within Afghanistan, and especially in Taliban-controlled areas, believe that there is only one culture, namely an Islamic culture that is based on the early Islamic cultural heritage as it was known during the Prophet Muhammad's life 1400 years ago. Moreover, the Taliban assert that Afghanistan has always been an austere society based on these principles.

Yet Muslims worldwide are interpreting the same Quran and *hadith*, and some conservative Islamic nations such as Saudi Arabia are based on elements of *shari'at* law, but continue to integrate and safeguard their intangible cultural heritage. How then can the Taliban defend its extremist policies on religious grounds alone? If one refers to Islam's primary authoritative religious text – the Quran – one does not find any explicit mention of the illegality of performance traditions. Among the *hadith*, there is no clear indication that performance traditions should be censored. However, the references to immoral behaviour in these texts have often been interpreted by ultra-conservative forces as applying to embodied artistic performances. The Taliban's statements must be seen as a misappropriation of the primary authoritative Islamic texts.

Unlike the Taliban's public declarations on performance traditions, in Afghanistan's non-Taliban northern regions an official decree has not been issued. My field research experiences in Badakhshan, however, have confirmed that some commanders of the anti-Taliban alliance have been exposed to the same ideological influences as the Taliban and consequently hold similar views. A general trend towards extreme, ultra-conservative Islam is thus also noticeable in Tajik-dominated Badakhshan, among the local population and commanders alike.

It would seem that the framework of interpretation of Islam by Taliban leaders and ultra-conservative commanders elsewhere in Afghanistan is being appropriated for the purpose of political domination and is based on 'primitive Islamic injunctions which have no basis in Islamic law' (Rashid 2000: 33).

5. Modern Patronage of Intangible Cultural Properties in Badakhshan

In Badakhshan, in direct response to the increasing influence of religious orthodoxy and strict interpretation of *shari'at*, non-religious performances are now rarely practised. Currently, entertainment, either private or public, occurs only if the local commander or community leader condones such performances. During fieldwork in 1998 and 1999, however, I was fortunate to experience some rare and spontaneous activities. These events included artistic performances and tended to be mostly of a covert nature, occurring amidst much secrecy. On a few occasions, however, I also witnessed some public events performed outdoors.

In 1998, at an event celebrating *jashn* in a small town in north-eastern Badakhshan, a public *buzkashi* tournament was organized as part of the festivity. Interestingly, this public event was accompanied by one of the district's main performers, a singer, musician and master of several instruments such as the *dambura*[1], *ghichak*[2], and the harmonium,[3] who had

---

[1] The *dambura* is a long-necked, two nylon-stringed and finger-plucked, fretless, pear-shaped lute.

[2] The *ghichak* is a two metal-stringed, bowed, spiked fiddle with a tin resonator as the instrument's body. A single piece of wood is affixed to the tin resonator. The bow is made from horse hair.

been invited by local authorities to perform. Paradoxically, the festival of *jashn* commemorates the defeat of the communist regime and the beginning of Islamic governance on 28 April. Once, *jashn* was marked by days of public music and dance performances and also included *buzkashi*, the traditional Afghan horse tournament. In this game, groups of riders, often numbering thirty to a hundred, from various district teams aim to score points by grabbing a decapitated calf, riding around a flag pole and then placing the calf in a specially designated circle before it is again snatched by another competitor. *Buzkashi* is now only permitted in the anti-Taliban territories of northern Afghanistan.

According to local informants, the sanctioning of a public music performance during a *buzkashi* tournament had not occurred since 1992. I must stress therefore that this event must be seen as an exceptional incident in contemporary Afghanistan. Prior to the Islamic revolution, this musician was accorded an extremely prestigious status with the filming of his songs by Kabul Television. Such an appearance on national television was then the pinnacle of success for any performer in Afghanistan. He was a celebrated musician, especially in the Persian-speaking regions, earning regular money for his performances and travelling frequently to provincial capitals. Since Islamic governance, however, like all musicians across Afghanistan, his performing career has become virtually non-existent and he now ekes out an existence as a subsistence farmer.

The genre of the music performed on this occasion was mostly local folk songs – *falak*s – with sad, comical, romantic and at times even sensual content. *Ghazal*s and *rubai*s from both the local Badakhshi area and other Afghan provinces were also performed. As performances have been rare since the onset of civil war, the renditions were greatly appreciated by the local male spectators who encircled the performer and listened attentively.

One of the songs performed by the musician was a *ghazal* written most possibly by a local poet with the pen-name 'Omed', which translates as 'Hope'. The lyrics of this *ghazal* may be translated and summarized as follows:

---

[3] The harmonium is a free-reed aerophone with a keyboard.

[*fard*]
The freshness of the garden and flowers and the rosy cheeks have gone.
Loyalty, love and kindness have disappeared from the friends.

[*matla'*]
Think about your weaknesses but don't ask about the weaknesses of others.

Don't despise your friends in front of those you don't know.
You must not blame others, it is better to blame yourself for your mistakes.

One day your enemy may be your guest.
Everything that you have – give to him, and don't tell him any lies.

Sometimes you will be in a garden of flowers.
Don't flood your friend's wall with your tears.

Respect your real friends and don't accompany bad friends.
Don't break off the relationships with your loyal friends.

It will bring happiness if you bow in front of friends and Omed.
Don't bow in front of a person with weaknesses.

6. Implications of Subversive Performance Events in Badakhshan

This public outdoor performance is embedded in relations of power. It seems that the music performance accompanying the *buzkashi* at the *jashn* festival was tolerated by the district's commanders and community leaders as a means of demonstrating their authority to override increasingly prevalent orthodox Islamic injunctions. This sanctioning of a public artistic performance stands in stark contrast to the bans on all forms of entertainment and non-religious artistic performances imposed by the Taliban and like-minded ultra-conservative authorities. According to my informants, it was the first time since Islamic governance that music had been condoned at an outdoor festival in that region of Badakhshan. It is also conceivable that the performance was organized in honour of my visit, indicating that performance traditions continue to hold considerable value for individuals and communities as local cultural property. Local music was thus appropriated as a sign of identity and as a means of demonstrating Badakhshi cultural heritage in contradistinction to other Afghan provinces and domains of governance. Such a performance thus serves to reveal the artist's intention and reflects upon Badakhshan's socio-political situation.

7. Recommendations and Conclusion

The safeguarding of Afghanistan's cultural heritage is a crucial factor in ameliorating its current crisis. Importantly, intangible cultural properties have the potential to bring together different ethnic and sectarian groups by peaceful, non-violent means. Although Badakhshan has historically been isolated in every sense of the word, the variety of songs performed at the outdoor festival exemplifies Afghanistan's multi-ethnic cultural heritage and identity. During the *jashn* festival, 60 per cent of the songs were local and of the remaining songs, 40 per cent were from other ethnic regions, mainly in northern Afghanistan but also from Logar and Kabul.

It seems unlikely that the war in Afghanistan will cease in the near future and I can only emphasize that the safeguarding of Afghanistan's cultural heritage cannot be left until the return of more peaceful times. By then, a large portion of Afghanistan's intangible heritage may have been irreversibly altered, or irretrievably lost. International law has had limited impact to date on the protection of Afghanistan's cultural heritage. Undoubtedly, the safeguarding of cultural properties can only be assured through effective laws and enforcement at a local level (Dupree 1998: 5, 10). Ordinary Afghans must also be encouraged to take pride in their cultural heritage. In particular, the interest in and appreciation of Afghan intangible culture outside of Afghanistan must be fed back to communities within Afghanistan. Public awareness may be initiated through meetings between local residents, authorities, NGOs, donors and experts (Dupree 1998: 10–11), with the intention of also encouraging communities to collect and record intangible materials. International heritage agencies have so far been willing to support the safeguarding of tangible cultural properties and may be able to fund and assist also with intangible projects. Positive relationships of collaboration between NGOs active in Afghanistan, various international heritage organizations such as UNESCO, ICOMOS (the International Council of Monuments and Sites), ICOM (the International Council of Museums), ICCROM (the International Centre for the Preservation of Cultural Property) and also SPACH (the Society for the Preservation of Afghanistan's Cultural Heritage), ruling authorities and Afghan communities may lead to the creation of a balance between religious orthodoxy and performance traditions and may thus secure Afghanistan's intangible cultural heritage for future generations.

Bibliography

Associated Press (1996) Taliban Restrict Music (18 Dec.).

Daniel, Valentine E. (1984) *Fluid Signs: Being a Person the Tamil Way*. Berkeley, University of California Press.

Dupree, Nancy Hatch (1998) *Status of Afghanistan's Cultural Heritage*. Peshawar, Society for the Preservation of Afghanistan's Cultural Heritage.

Fathers, Michael (2000a) An Eye for an Eye. *Time* 155: online.

Fathers, Michael (2000b) Washington Needs an Enemy. *Time* 155: online.

Paik, Choong-Hyun (1997) *Final Report on the Situation of Human Rights in Afghanistan, in Accordance with Commission on Human Rights Resolution 1996/75*. New York, United Nations, Economic and Social Council.

Rashid, Ahmed (2000) *Taliban: Islam, Oil and the New Great Game in Central Asia*. London, I. B. Tauris.

Roy, Olivier (1986) *Islam and Resistance in Afghanistan*. Cambridge, Cambridge University Press.

Werbner, Pnina (1996) 'Our Blood is Green': Cricket, Identity and Social Empowerment among British Pakistanis. In: Jeremy MacClancy (ed.) *Sport, Identity, and Ethnicity*. Oxford, Berg Publishers: 87–111.

Zaman, Muhammad Qasim (1999a) Commentaries, Print and Patronage: Hadith and the Madrasas in Modern South Asia. *Bulletin of the School of Oriental and African Studies* 62(1): 60-81.

Zaman, Muhammad Qasim (1999b) Religious Education and the Rhetoric of Reform: The Madrasa in British India and Pakistan. *Comparative Studies in Society and History* 41(2): 294-323.

Hazara Research and Hazara Nationalism 1978-89

Rolf Bindemann

1. The Beginnings

Towards the end of the first period of government under Muhammad Daud (1962/63), shortly before the start of the 'Constitutional Period' of Afghanistan, there were the first signs in Afghan publications that the country was being recognised as a multi-ethnic state. Even authors who in the 1940s had vehemently argued – some with falsified, pseudo-academic findings – that the original inhabitants of Afghanistan were Pashtuns (e.g. 'Abd al-Hayy Habibi), started to take note of the country's other cultures. Now they even discussed the possibility that all these different peoples, including the Hazaras, had an equal claim deriving from common pre-Islamic roots in Afghanistan (Habibi 1962).

The moderate opposition journal *Payam-i wijdan* (Message of Conscience), founded by the Hazara intellectual 'Abd al-Rauf Turkmani (1966), published articles calling for equality for all the peoples of Afghanistan, short stories critical of the deplorable position of women, and articles on the culture and history of the Hazaras. This period can be regarded as the start of Hazara research in Afghanistan. Further scope for liberal, academic discussion was offered by the publications of the University of Kabul, in such journals as *Adab* (Literature) and *Kitab* (The Book).

2. Exile

Following the putsch of Muhammad Daud Khan in 1973, Hazara refugees fleeing this new phase of oppression came up against the descendants of their fellow countrymen who had fled to Baluchistan after the wars of 'Abd al-Rahman Khan at the end of the 19th century. In Quetta they founded an association, the Tanzim-i Nau-i Hazara-i Moghul (Organisation of the new generation of Hazaras), which published the magazine *Zo al-faqar*[1]. It contained articles in Urdu, Farsi and English on religious and political themes, and on the history and culture of the Hazaras. Tanzim also published the Persian translation of the monograph on the history of the Hazaras, called the 'New History of the Hazaras' by the Soviet academic Litfin Temirkhanov.

The April coup d'etat by the Khalq/Parcham party (1978) put an end to the Daud regime, but the attempts of the government of Taraki and Amin to introduce revolutionary change to Afghan society very soon prompted a majority of the population, particularly in the countryside, to react with armed resistance. Following the success of the general uprising of the Hazaras in their heartland in central Afghanistan a range of journals appeared, from safe exile in Iran and Pakistan – published by the various, mostly Khomeinist-oriented Islamist resistance organisations. The articles in these journals showed that a study of the history of the Hazaras, its great historical figures, its oppressed and underdeveloped situation in Afghanistan and the events and consequences of the war with the Kabul rulers in the 19th century, also offered important lessons for strategy and tactics in the current struggle. Indeed a number of the religious party leaders strongly dependent on the Iranian revolutionary guard made great efforts to win over the Hazara Mujahidin to Iranian-style pan-Islamism. Individual figures, even entire groups of people, were denounced as 'moghulists' and Hazara nationalists, pursued and even killed. Yet the founding of Hizb-i Wahdat-i Islami (Party of Islamic Unity, 1989), an alliance of eight ethnically-based Shi'ite parties, showed that in the end it was the nationalist tendencies among the Hazaras that predominated.

One of the most productive of these writers in exile was Muhammad 'Isa Gharjistani who published many books and pamphlets in Quetta about ancient and modern Hazara history and on Hazara ethnography. Although his nationalist orientation brought him initial opposition from the Iran-oriented Hazara mullahs, his main work (entitled 'Skull pyramids in Afghanistan') was later reprinted in Qom, a centre of learning for Iranian clerics. This showed that Iran, too, was finally having to recognise Hazara

---

[1] The name of the sword of 'Ali, the son-in-law of Prophet Muhammad and the founder of the Shi'ite branch of Islam.

nationalism, and, I am told, this book has recently started to be used to train Hazara theology students. Sadly, the trail of M.I. Gharjistani goes cold at the beginning of 1993, following his return to Kabul; it is feared that he was killed in the murderous struggles of the ongoing conflict.

Another important author in exile writing about the Hazaras was Husain 'Ali Yazdani, a Mujahidin commander and a mullah, who went to Iran following a serious injury and there started to research into the Hazaras. He published first a few articles in the journal of the 'Nasr' party, *Payam-i mustas'afin* (Message of the Suppressed) and then in 1989 his main work, 'Research on the history of the Hazaras'.

3. Afghanistan under the PDPA Government

Following the putsch of April 1978 – in Taraki's words the second true socialist revolution after the October Revolution – set pieces from the Soviet nationalities policy were immediately adopted. Afghanistan was declared a multinational state, one recognition of this fact being the foundation of the journal *Payam-i khalq*[2]. Here Pashtuns, Uzbeks, Turkmens and also the Hazaras published articles on literature, politics and culture. In 1980, under Babrak Karmal, four more languages – in addition to Pashtu and Dari – were given official recognition (Baluchi, Turkmani, Pashai, Nuristani – in reality Kati), and in 1981 Radio Kabul started broadcasting in these languages.

In 1986 Babrak's successor, Najibullah, launched a 'National Reconciliation' plan aimed at persuading as many Mujahidin groups as possible to lay down their weapons or come over to the generously equipped *qaumi* (tribal) militia. This it attempted with the aid of government officials and neighbouring and associated groups from the Mujahidin areas and through organisations created as part of the 'nationalities policy' of the communist government.

As an expression of this, a new constitution was adopted in December 1987, article 13 of which states explicitly that Afghanistan is a multinational state the job of which is to secure the equality, welfare and

---

[2] The title means 'Message of the People'. After the downfall of the Khalq faction, the publication was re-named *Payam-i mardom* which is synonymous in meaning.

development of all nationalities and regions. The article even stated – very much in tune with the long-standing demands of the Hazaras – that 'The state shall gradually prepare the grounds for the creations of administrative units based on national characteristics'. Then, in article 14, it said: 'The state shall adopt necessary measures for the growth of culture, language and literature of the people of Afghanistan as well as preserve and develop the worthy cultural, traditional, linguistic, literary and folklore legacy of all nationalities, clans and tribes'.

Two months before, in August/September 1987 the Central Committee of the PDPA called a general assembly (*jirga*) of the Hazara nationality in the Polytechnic of Kabul. The assembly was chaired by Dr 'Abd al-Wahid Sarabi, a Hazara *khan*, who was a member of the Academy and a representative in almost all governments since the days of the king. The importance of the assembly was underlined by the presence of high-ranking speakers – head of state Najibullah, the Minister of Tribal Issues, Sulaiman Layiq, and Minister-President Sultan 'Ali Kishtmand, the first Hazara in the history of Afghanistan to hold this post. Previously there had been a National Central Council of the Hazaras (over 350 members with a 34-strong executive committee), which at this *jirga* elected six members of the board, including Sayyid Mansur Nadiri, the head of the Isma'ilis of Afghanistan. The text of the speeches and the list of participants in the *jirga* were collated in a brochure, thousands of which were printed[3].

4. The Journal *Gharjistan* and Its Authors

On 20 November 1987 the Central Committee of the PDPA decided to found the bi-monthly journal *Gharjistan*, as the central organ of the National Central Council of the Hazaras. In the first issue – Jan./Feb. – Feb./Mar. 1988 – the editorial and several introductory articles set out the journal's goals: to further the cultural development of the Hazaras, to inform the other peoples of Afghanistan and the world 'about the economic, historic and cultural life of the noble brother people of the Hazaras' (p. 9), and to provide information on the contribution of the Hazaras to the defence and reconstruction of the country. The programme was enormous:

---

[3] *Jirga-i sarasari-i milliyat-i hazara.* Kabul, August/Sep. 1987.

themes to be covered included 'history, regional geography, culture (dialect, folklore, music, customs, education etc.), the economy, political events, ecology of the Hazara region, the wishes and demands of the population, important scientific research, information on important people (men and women) and on historic geography, crafts and the arts, on peace, and national reconciliation, religious guidance on peace and prosperity, dissemination of the goals of the constitution and the *loya jirga*, appropriate and well-founded criticism, opinions and proposals for the Central Council' (p. 12 ff).

I have two incomplete year's issues of this journal which, along with other original material on the Kabul Hazaras, were kindly placed at my disposal after the fall of the Berlin Wall, by Afghanistan scholars at the Humboldt University of Berlin.

The most productive contributor to *Gharjistan* was the professor and candidate of the Academy of Science, Sayyid Shah 'Ali Shahristani, editor of the journal and deputy chairman of the Central Council of the Hazaras. He had accompanied the Royal Danish Expedition to the Hazarajat in the 1950s and was a 'linguistic consultant' to Klaus Ferdinand (Poladi, 1989). Between 1956-58 he had translated from Arabic two volumes on the Islamic faith for the Ministry of Finance; in 1975/76 he wrote a book on the customs of the Hazaras which was not published until 1984/85, by the University of Kabul. Before (1982/83) his book 'Dictionary of the Dari Dialect Hazaragi' was published (also in the Kabul University Series). On the same theme, a preparatory study on grammar, called 'Farhang-i khalq', appeared in *Gharjistan*.

Shahristani's second specialist area is the early Islamic history and geography of the old province of Gharjistan. Through an analysis of the old Arabic and Persian geographers and historians, published in several long articles in the journal, he reaches the conclusion that the present-day Hazarajat equates with the territory of Gharjistan, the inhabitants of which are reputed to be the ancestors of today's Hazaras. This theory had occupied him for some time, as shown by his articles in *Jughrafia* (Geography) and *'Irfan* (Knowledge), *Kitab* (Book) and *Adab* (Education), which were also mostly known by the Hazara authors in exile mentioned above. Hence the name of the journal, and hence also the *nom de plume* of the author, M.I. Gharjistani (and of another employee of the said journal whom I do not know). Shahristani also has profound knowledge of the work *Siraj al-tawarikh* (Light of History) by Mullah Faiz Muhammad Katib. Based mainly on this important history book, Shahristani also wrote another series of articles on special questions of Hazara history in the last two centuries.

Siraj al-tawarikh and the life and other works of its author, Faiz Muhammad, are also a specialism of one other author and editor of the journal, Husain Nail from Bihsud[4]. Before *Gharjistan* was founded, he wrote an article called 'The Work and Struggle of the Hazaras, in Solidarity with the Other Nationalities', which aligned with the policy of 'National Reconciliation'. This appeared in 1983/84 in the first issue of *Milliyatha-i baradar* (Brother Nationalities) published by the Ministry for Tribes and Clans. Another article in the second issue of the same journal takes the argument about the origin of the Hazaras one step further – an argument which I believe is impossible to settle: Are they the original inhabitants of Afghanistan or are they Mongolian immigrants from the time of Chingiz Khan?

The only work by Husain Nail that I found in *Gharjistan* is a historical-biographical article and a geographical description of the Bihsud region, but Husain Farmand, the literature critic of *Gharjistan*, regularly presented the more important books published by this author in his own articles. The subject of Nail's article on cooperation with the other brother nations of Afghanistan also dominates his book entitled *Shade and Light in the Situation of the Hazara Society* (published 1985/86 by the Nationalities Ministry press) – at least this is what reviewers report, as I have not seen it. In addition to its obligatory political and ideological content, this monograph is also a mine of previously unknown information on ethnography, geography, language, archaeology and history, and on the possibilities of future economic development of the Hazaras.

In April 1983, again organised by the Ministry for Tribes and Clans (which was renamed the Directorate of Nationalities in 1989) a seminar was held on Mullah Faiz Muhammad Katib, in conjunction with the Academy of Sciences and the Faculty of History at the University of Kabul. Husain Nail

---

[4] Author of the 'Directory of books printed in Dari in Afghanistan', published in 1977/78 as publication no. 120 of the Anjuman-i Tarikh (Historical Society of Afghanistan).

edited the *festschrift* (*Memories of Katib*, 1986/87). At the beginning of 1988, to mark the 130th birthday of Katib, another seminar was held, at which Husain Nail presented a two-volume register of persons, place-names, tribes and related groups that appear in *Siraj al-tawarikh*. The first part refers to Afghanistan in general, the second lists all the places related to the Hazaras. Any historical researcher who has battled through the over 1000 large-format pages of *Siraj al-tawarikh* will know the real value of such a register. Key information concerning volumes 4 and 5 of this work, which were supposedly lost (or suppressed by the Afghan rulers in the first quarter of the 20th century), is provided in issues 6 and 7 of *Gharjistan*: In 1979/80 the son of Mullah Faiz Muhammad sold a private manuscript of his father's to the National Archive. Entitled *Tazakkur-i inqilab* (Memories of the Uprising), it was not written upon the orders of the emir, and thus is uncensored. It describes mainly the events during the period of the uprising of Bachcha-i Saqqa against King Amanullah at the end of the 1920s. Fewer than a handful of Afghan authors have so far dared to write about this period, and so the records of the eye-witness and participant Faiz Muhammad could give researchers into this difficult period a whole new basis for understanding what happened and why. Unfortunately *Tazakkur-i inqilab* has not yet been published in Persian, but it has been translated into Russian, by a Soviet researcher, A.I. Schkirando, and published in spring 1988 at the Institute of Oriental Studies at the Russian Academy of Sciences.[5]

Another member of the editorial team was Muhammad 'Iwaz Nabizada from Bihsud, who was also a member of the Central Committee of the PDPA and, since the end of August 1988, Head of the Directorate of Nationalities, which emerged from the old Ministry of Tribal Affairs. No articles by him appeared in *Gharjistan*, but he did write about the Hazaras in a second ministry publication, *Milliyatha-i baradar* (Brother nationalities). I also have two brochures by him, entitled *Ethnography of the Hazaras and the April Revolution*, and *Common Dialectical Expressions of the Hazara People*, which appeared in 1986/87 as special supplements to this journal.

---

[5] The book was translated into English and annotated by McChesney in 1999.

The editor-in-chief, Riza Miskub, contributed a new short story to each issue. But some other contributions seem to be rather out of place in the journal. For example, Karim Mishaq, finance minister in the days of Taraki (1978/79), and a revolutionary writer, wrote a short story that was published in *Gharjistan*. His amazing discovery that the Khazars that featured in Pushkin's lyric poem 'Ruslan and Liudmilla' were in reality Hazaras is either an attempt to curry favour against the background of the new nationalist spirit among the Hazaras or, alternatively, a gross satire of the sometimes over-extravagant Hazara research of the authors of the journal (no. 8: 56).

I will not here detail the inestimable wealth of content in the sources quoted – which shines through the ideological stance obligatory under the state system at the time – nor will I attempt a deeper scientific analysis of the material, but, to conclude, I would like to present a brief comparison of the Hazara-related literature produced in Kabul and in exile.

The Shi'ite or Hazara literature in exile is strongly influenced by the theme of the 'Islamic Revolution', by the battles and successes of the Mujahidin against the government in Kabul. On the other side, there was the Hazara militia put together to fight the Mujahidin since 1987 by the chief of the Isma'ilis in Afghanistan, Sayyid Mansur Nadiri, and his brother. Reports on this militia and its successes are contained in the news section of *Gharjistan*. Religion is only mentioned in *Gharjistan* in connection with Isma'ili celebrations to mark the birthdays and anniversaries of the Aga Khan, whereas in exile literature questions of religion dominate.

However, the principal concerns of the Hazaras in Afghanistan and in exile are remarkably similar. All Hazara writers, whether in exile or in Kabul, tackle in detail the following issues, in each case with great personal involvement:

- all the inhabitants of Afghanistan, above all the Hazaras, have equal claim to being the original inhabitants of the territory;
- the historic region of Gharjistan is the present-day Hazarajat;
- the Hazaras of today and in the last few centuries have fought for the territorial integrity of Afghanistan, side by side with other peoples ('brother nationalities' in the jargon of the Kabul government at the time);

- the desperate situation and oppression of the Hazaras after the wars of Abd al-Rahman Khan at the end of the 19th century;
- the Hazaragi dialect as the ancient form of Persian, Mongolian and Turkish components being played down;
- the discrimination against the Hazaras by the regimes of past decades.

In the historical perspective, however, the authors do differ: For the Mujahidin the uprising against the Khalq/Parcham regime and the struggle against the Russians also represented a liberation from historic oppression and underdevelopment, and the chance to establish some kind of Islamic system of order. On the other hand, in their introductory paragraphs of all their articles in *Gharjistan*, the pro-government Hazaras in Kabul praised the April Revolution, the PDPA and the people's democracy as the progenitor of a new freedom and self-confidence of the Hazaras.

Through all of this, the one issue about which all very firmly agree is the urgent need for proper study of the history of their own people, in order to strengthen the new self-confidence of the Hazaras and thus secure their equal place among the other peoples of Afghanistan. The common ground in the publications presented above already points to the ethnic/nationalistically defined recruitment criteria of the now very powerful political and military organisation of the Hazaras, the Hizb-i Wahdat-i Islami, to which large numbers of former pro-government Hazara nationalists in Kabul were also admitted after the Mujahidin took Kabul. Incidentally, since then this party has played a hardly less inglorious role in the present civil war than the other parties involved (and, indeed, given the circumstances, how could we expect anything else).

Bibliography

Faiz Muhammad (1912) *Siraj al-tawarikh*. 3 vols. Kabul, Government Press.

Faiz Muhammad (n.d.) *Tazakkur-i inqilab*. n.pl. (translated, abridged, re-worked, and annoted by R.D. McChesney (1999) *Kabul under Siege: Fayz Muhammad's Account of the 1929 Uprising*. Princeton, Markus Wiener Publishers).

Gharjistani, Muhammad 'Isa (1980) *Shikast-i rus-ha dar hazarajat*. n. pl.

Gharjistani, Muhammad 'Isa (n.d.) *Kalla monar-ha-i afghanistan*. Quetta.

Habibi 'Abd al-Hayy (1962) Is Hazara an old word? *Ariana* 5 (20) (in Persian).

Nail, Husain (ed.) *Memories of Katib*, 1986/87 Kabul, Kabul University Press (in Persian).

Nail, Husain (1985/86) *Shade and Light in the Situation of the Hazara Society*. Kabul, Nationalities Ministry Press.

Poladi, Hassan (1989) *The Hazaras*. Stockton/California, Mughal Publishing.

Temirkhanov, Litfin (1972) *Khazaretsui ocherki novoi istorii*. Moscow (Persian edition: 1980. Translator: 'Aziz Toghiyan. Quetta)

Yazdani, Husain 'Ali (Hajj Kazim) (1989) *Pazhuhishi dar tarikh-i hazara*. Qom

Part III

The Role of NGOs

About the School System under the Taliban Government

Peter Schwittek

Since the beginning of 1998 I have headed COFAA (Caritas Organization for Aid to Afghanistan), an office financed by several national Caritas organizations in Kabul. When we started determining COFAA's tasks a little bit by chance we happened to get involved in the field of elementary education. The Taliban's attitude towards schools, especially towards girls' schools, has essentially contributed to their international reputation. Girls' schools are an important challenge for the ideology of the Taliban. The policy of a government has to be implemented by its administration – by 'the state' or any kind of substitute for it. So if you are dealing with schools you will be confronted with something like an Afghan state whose very existence is called in question by the main topic of this book. I will tell you the history of COFAA's mosque-school programme and its coexistence with the Taliban administration. Perhaps the materials I submit will make it easier for you to decide whether you want to attach to the 'country Afghanistan' a 'state Afghanistan' or not. It is a question which seems to me to be semantic – I beg your pardon for this unscholarly attitude of a pragmatist.

In 1998 all girls' schools were closed. When foreigners were pestering the Taliban government about girls' schools they were told to be patient. After the war the government would deal with this problem. The Afghan citizens got to hear quite different slogans. The loudspeakers of the mosques instructed the population that girls' schools were infernal stuff and had to remain closed. In the big cities, especially in Kabul, they had indeed been closed. In the countryside there are girls' schools, sometimes till class nine. Some even had the written approvals of provincial or district authorities. In Kabul the only school classes being offered to girls were 'home schooling'. In their apartments teachers – mostly women – give lectures to children of their neighbourhood. These are private initiatives often stimulated by relief agencies with money and materials. The Taliban did not allow such activities officially, yet during longer periods they seemed to tolerate them. But then they suddenly forcibly stopped such lessons. Some teachers even disappeared and have never been seen again. Home schooling is a delicate matter. Sponsors supporting such activities have problems in verifying whether such classes take place at all. Visits from outsiders, especially foreigners, easily raise suspicion and endanger all participants.

The conditions in the governmental boys' schools are deplorable. The equipment has been looted. The classrooms mostly have no doors or windows. A senior teacher earns an equivalent of $6 per month. Even in Kabul nobody can live on this salary. The teachers must try to get by with other jobs. Only one or two times a week they can afford to give school lessons. Under these circumstances the pupils hardly learn anything. Put briefly, in Kabul the girls' schools are closed and the boys' schools are not much better.

These conditions should be a matter of concern. After the long war the youngest Afghans who enjoyed a sound education are at least 45 years old. Illiterates can hardly be trained to take over duties in the administration and in the economy. The reconstruction of Afghanistan will only be possible if there are enough Afghans who have had a certain level of school education. Without reconstruction no political stability will return. At the moment there is no economic revival in the city of Kabul. Even this is essentially due to the conditions of the school system. Afghans having a certain level of education and a spirit of enterprise – i.e. persons able to organize a company or a factory – have left Kabul, mostly because of the education of their children.

Soon after it was opened the COFAA office was visited by mullahs. All of them explained that every priest has the duty to care for the knowledge of all human beings – men and women, girls and boys. They asked for support for school lessons for boys and girls. This I did not expect, but it was foreseeable. The 'Afghan mullahs' are not the 'Taliban movement'. Usually mullahs enjoy a sound preparation for their profession. In former times nobody became a mullah after studying nothing but a crash course by a Pakistani fanatic. What an ordinary mullah knows about his religion differs remarkably from what the leaders of the Taliban claim.

About the School System under the Taliban Government

School lessons – even for girls – in mosques – and priests taking responsibility – this was a brilliant concept. How could the Taliban refuse it? What could they do against it? Nevertheless, it was still delicate. We asked the mullahs whether the government would allow such activities. And then the next surprise happened. They showed us written approvals from the Ministry of Education – and even approvals signed personally by the minister of Amr bi al-Ma'ruf wa Nahi al-Munkar, the religious police. This ministry gets young guys from the southern deserts to beat women for not being totally veiled. It arrests men because their beard is too short. But its head personally issues approvals allowing school classes for girls. It was rather confusing.

We made use of two of such approvals and supported schools for boys and girls till class twelve, one of them in Mikro Royan 4, a Soviet-style district of tenement blocks built of ready-made concrete slabs. Within one week 1,500 children attended this school, 1,000 of them girls. This was too much. The security authorities pressed for the closure of the school. Cautiously the mullah did not resist these demands. He asked the crying women teachers to interrupt their classes for some days. He was arrested – but was released after one week. Mind you, he had done nothing but what was approved in writing by high authorities.

Then a decree came from Kandahar, making the assistance to women and girls especially difficult and explicitly prohibiting home schooling. The ministry for Amr bi al-Ma'ruf called the relief agencies in and announced the edict. Additionally all approvals of activities now forbidden by the new decree were pronounced inoperative. The minister declared his own signatures given only three weeks before null and void. Under such legal security it is not easy to implement programmes. You plan, you get a written approval, you make investments and then suddenly you are told: stop it!

Rather depressed we returned from this meeting to our office. The mullahs were waiting for us. Recently they had asked us to support their school activities. Now they asked whether we had decided about their request. Didn't they know what had happened? Yes, they knew. And they even had understood: girls' schools till class twelve were too dangerous now. But schools for boys and girls till class four would still be possible. They had to be called *madrasa* now. It should be easy for COFAA and the mosques to find an agreement about the content of the lessons. Again they had written approvals for their purposes – again signed by the minister of Amr bi al-Ma'ruf. We could continue.

But then a delegation of the Ministry of Hajj and Islamic Affairs came and asked about our activities. We explained them to the gentlemen and were told that the approvals of any other authorities were inoperative. In the mosques only their ministry has a say. But they did not want to put us off. Their ministry only wanted to ask us to run our programme in co-operation with it. I paid a visit to the deputy minister. The minister himself usually lingers at court in Kandahar. His deputy was a very open-minded personality and we were ready to sign a protocol.

This furious beginning of our school activities took place in the first half of 1998. In July suddenly all relief agencies were ordered to shift their offices to the war-damaged dormitory of the Polytechnic Faculty. We refused to go there and had to leave the country. At the beginning of 1999 we returned. In June we signed our contract with the Ministry of Hajj and Islamic Affairs.

We started the adventure at first in six, later in ten mosques: teaching boys and girls, up till class four. Two lecture units take place after the morning prayer, i.e. from 5.30 to 7.00 a.m., and two in the afternoon. So our pupils can also attend the classes of the government schools from 8 to 12 a.m. Even the teachers and the other government employees giving lessons in our schools can perform their official duties. Public services are only active in the morning. Six of the weekly twenty-four lecture units have a religious content. This was like the situation in the government schools before the Taliban came into power. We pay a monthly salary of Rs 1,200, about $22.

The say of the Ministry of Hajj and Islamic Affairs is restricted to the compounds of the mosques. There we can work. For every kind of teaching beyond the mosques the Ministry of Education is responsible, but is not entitled to allow classes for girls. The space in the mosques is restricted. A lot of classes sit in the gardens of the mosques. This becomes a problem in October at the latest. There are school buildings in the neighbourhood of some of the mosques. School buildings are not needed by the Ministry of Education in the early morning and in the afternoon. We could shift some

About the School System under the Taliban Government

of the boys' classes to these school buildings. The girls have to stay in the mosques.

The co-operation with the mostly spiritual gentlemen of the ministry went smoothly and was friendly. But then the minister of Hajj and Islamic Affairs came himself from Kandahar. When he realized what had happened in the mosques of Kabul he simply ignored the fact that the teaching was based on a contract. He instructed us that we must not supply the girls with writing materials. They only should learn to read. Writing is for boys. Furthermore he issued new timetables. From the twenty-four lecture units now not eighteen but only eight should be other than religious instruction – this for boys. For girls there should only be six hours. Our colleagues in the ministry appeased me: 'We simply will ignore this. When he asks we will tell him that such changes only can be introduced in the beginning of the next school year. Until then nothing will be changed.' The mullahs of the concerned mosques were more radical: 'Let him say whatever he wants! We simply continue the programme we had up till now.' In the following weeks we indeed continued to run the initial programme. We had several tough negotiations with the minister. He was concerned that we had made schools from his mosques. We had good reasons – which I need not explain here – for insisting on our initial programme. We rejected support for the programme the minister wanted to introduce. By the way, during these controversial negotiations good personal relations with this man were established.

The matter remained pending till October. I had to apply for money for the activities for the year 2000. Who wanted to finance the programme under these circumstances? I needed a decision. The allies in the ministry advised us to contact the second deputy minister. He has a good personal relationship with his boss, and he is a fan of our programme. He was imam of one of the mosques belonging to our programme. Every early morning he scrutinized whether the lessons in his mosque were taking place properly. He wanted to have the best mosque school in Kabul. We approached this man. He had an idea. He wanted to invite his boss to his mosque and then ask a girl to write a religious statement on the blackboard. Then he wanted to ask the minister what was so wrong in doing this that he wanted to forbid it.

Soon after this a delegation of my staff paid a visit to the minister and unofficially sounded him out about what could be done in future. Hear what happened! The minister allowed us to continue our initial programme. How did this change of mind happen? I cannot prove it, but I believe that the girl writing on the blackboard brought the decision. Indeed the whole environment was favourable. A lot of dignitaries from mosque and state had urged the minister again and again to allow the continuation of our programme.

A week later another event took place. I believe that it indeed happened as it was told to me and as I will tell it to you now. The second deputy – the same man who had called the girl to the blackboard – spread the rumour that older girls were sitting in our lessons. The cabinet was concerned. It appointed a commission of several ministers to investigate what was happening in the mosques. The commission did not find older girls. Instead the second deputy used the chance he had prepared to show the other ministers the good religious knowledge of the children. The commission was enthusiastic and proposed in the report about its investigation to introduce this mosque-school system throughout Afghanistan. The deputy prime minister issued a decree that this should be done.

From then on we continued this programme fruitfully. By the end of 1999 more than 13,500 children attended our mosques, with around 400 teachers. Since then we even have fifth classes. Nearly half of the children are girls. As the girls could not go to school for several years the boys are the majority in the higher classes while the girls dominate the first and now even the second class. Furthermore we established an accompanying teacher training programme. The teacher training was inaugurated by a ceremony in the Intercontinental Hotel. Several ministers made speeches emphasizing the importance of school education. And I even had the opportunity to explain our programme. All this was transmitted by the radio.

COFAA as well as the Ministry of Hajj and Islamic Affairs had seen our programme merely as a crutch for the languishing governmental school system. Because of the decree of the deputy prime minister it became the official government school system. That is why leading people in UNICEF blamed COFAA for supporting 'the mullahs' in destroying the governmental school system. The Ministry of Education is now deprived of the whole school system as it has shifted to 'the mosques'. Now everything will perish.

This is a very Western kind of thinking, using the categories of institutions and competencies. No, here there was no ingenious plan for the destruction of the school system. Here the second deputy minister managed to get high-calibre approvals for our programme by applying two shrewd tricks. He made it much safer for small girls and boys to have reasonable classes. We would be glad if we had enough funding to enable us to offer the programme to the whole city of Kabul. An extension to other provinces will not be possible. Beyond the city of Kabul there is virtually no competency of the Ministry of Education for the school system that could be transferred to the mosques. There, provincial or district authorities make the decisions, or the people themselves.

There is no danger of those who want to destroy the school system of their country making subtle preparations and changing the competencies of ministries. People who believe that schools are superfluous don't cook up ingenious plans. They don't reflect for a long time. Nevertheless there are Afghans brooding and ruminating about the future of the schools. These are the people who are concerned about the conditions of the education system. These are the ones who want girls to go to school again. I got to know a lot of such Afghans, even in the Taliban movement.

But the leading Taliban had drummed for too long into the heads of their supporters that Islam prohibits girls' schools. They can't simply reopen the girls' schools without upsetting their own rank and file. The way through the mosques seems to be a secret path by which the reopening of the girls' schools can be achieved. Even this should not be understood as a secret plan of the government or of an internal opposition. Such a development is hoped for even by priests and by influential personalities of the Taliban movement. Once it is initiated it should get strong support. Someone had to dare to try the secret path. The Ministry of Hajj and Islamic Affairs and COFAA are now en route.

Country Without a State –
Does it Really Make a Difference for the Women?

Heike Bill

Afghan women appear not to have been involved at all in the topics considered by the title of this book 'Afghanistan: Country without State'. Yet, it is their situation which is being used so effectively to manipulate public opinion in Europe and America. Much attention was attracted by Emma Bonino's campaign, 'Flowers for the women of Kabul', at the International Women's Day of 1998 and by the 'Feminist Majority'.

We do know that with the emergence of the radical Islamist Taliban in 1994, and certainly after the capture of Kabul and Jalalabad in 1996, the situation in Afghanistan, particularly that of Afghan women and children, has changed for the worse. On the basis of a very arbitrary interpretation of Islam, the Taliban introduced laws which profoundly affected the lives of women, especially pertaining to freedom of movement and action. One example is the insistence that women may only leave the house when accompanied by a male, husband or relative (*mahram*), and must wear a veil which covers the entire body. Another example is the general ban on education for girls and women and on employment for women (except in the field of health).

Is this really new? Were these restrictions such decisive changes in the countryside where, after all, about 80 per cent of Afghan women live? And if not, why are we instrumentalizing, for our own interests, an indeed outrageous yet insignificantly altered existence, to such an extent that we use it to justify the current orientation of foreign policy? At the same time we are unfamiliar with the actual situation of women in Afghanistan. This ignorance is further compounded by the fact that, aside from family members, only women have access to houses where other Afghan women live. The conditions of Afghan women today are similar to those prior to 1978, but under another disguise, bad conditions under different cloaks. The history of Afghan women has been used as a means to an end and, simultaneously, what we see are primarily symbols and external criteria.

Do we not miss the core of the matter when we focus on what is branded as 'progressive' and 'retrogressive'?

Although the laws of the Taliban are particularly rigid ones, they merely continue long-established cultural and religious traditions rather than breaking from them or establishing a new canon. In this respect, Taliban policy is nothing less than the continuation of institutionalized structural and personal violence against women in Afghanistan. Through the Taliban, existing social systems and gender relations receive further strengthening and justification, and therefore, legitimacy.

To what extent do political attempts made by an Afghan state or, rather, as is the case with Afghanistan today, a political superstructure which could be interpreted as a state, affect traditions? How do they affect memory, which becomes increasingly transfigured, as does the present? How did, and does, war, a very violent and tragic event, affect these traditional conditions? Did, and does, war create niches; did it set up new forms of living together, particularly between women and men?

Thirty years ago, traditional conditions were reasons for providing aid. Today, on the basis of the violation of human and women's rights, these same traditional conditions are reasons for removing or minimizing aid. This way, the focus is not on the impact of aid but, rather, on the justification behind it.

Certainly the Taliban interfere with the work of aid organizations in Afghanistan. They can restrict, if not prohibit, access to women. In any case, the Taliban want control. Decisive influence on the range of aid for women and men does not, however, come from the state, the Taliban, but from the communal and family structures. In other words, circumstances, ways of acting and mentalities are not to be changed by the state alone, but rather, particularly in the case of Afghanistan, these changes must be made from within traditional structures. Other influential aspects are the physical infrastructure, land property, jurisdiction and authorization, and monetary possession.

For whom in Afghanistan have the conditions changed for the worse and on what basis is this being bewailed in the West? Why are there so few changes for some and none at all for others? On the other hand, why were there so many changes for still others, particularly for members of former elites and, even more specifically, for women of those elites? It seems necessary to break through the moralism that taints our knowledge and judgements.[1]

A common, if not the most common, characteristic of the regionally and also ethnically different Afghan cultures is gender segregation. This gender segregation is a prominent feature of Afghan identity and defines a system of standards and values which, beside others, is a basis of the various traditional codes of law. The *pashtunwali* is probably the most noted of these codes of law. The principle of gender segregation demands that all living areas be split into a 'male' (*mardana*) and a 'female' (*zanana*) domain. These categories thereby constitute a system of order and value and correspond to the exterior domain defined as public, the *bakhsh-i khariji* or *bakhsh-i umumi*, and the interior domain, defined as private, the *bakhsh-i shakhsi*. The public domain is off limits for women and girls. Access to the private domain is permitted only to related family members and other women. The mobility of women is restricted and this is justified with the argument that this confinement to houses protects the women from the outside and its hostile and perhaps immoral influences. The protection of female family members is also important because virginity is of highest moral value. This could mean physical virginity of unmarried females or figurative virginity of married females, being kept safe from external influences such as contact with non-relatives. The protection of this virginal honour (which is also a guarantee of honour for the future husband and his family) is the job and duty of men. The virginity of the women and girls of a family serves as an indicator for honour, both their own and that of the male family members, and is often found to be a weak point. The sexual harassment and rape of a woman are common ways for a man to deprive another of his honour.

The Afghan veil, the *chadari* or *burqa'*, is an excellent symbol of the moral integrity of a woman or, more precisely, a symbol of male honour. The less a woman has a face, the more righteous is a man. The woman does not attract attention and is therefore protected from any unwanted outside

---

[1] I would like to thank Deutsche Welthungerhilfe for their support and for making it possible for me to participate in the conference at which this paper was originally given. I would also like to thank Nellika Little for her patience and help in editing this lecture.

influence (Duby 1995: 11). The *burqa'* reinforces the preservation of gender segregation when a woman leaves her house. As a traditional Afghan form of *hijab*, the *burqa'* is an expression of Muslim and Afghan identity, even if it does not play a role in the specific ethnic culture. At the same time it symbolizes conservative values and, therefore, is not compatible with modern ideas.

To many Afghan men, the *burqa'*, although strictly a female garment, is conducive to their identity, for if a woman wears a *burqa'* her husband or father is an honourable man and therefore a good Afghan, a believing Muslim and advocate for the continuation of tradition. He is adhering to gender segregation and contributing to the social order by shielding his personal life and taking responsibility for the internal organization of his household.

The organization of the *bakhsh-i shakhsi* is a private matter and in a patriarchal society, such as the Afghan society, a man's business. This includes the determination of the rights and duties of individual family members and the character of relationships among them. It is the privilege of a man to determine the participation of women in decision-making processes, their access to education and training, and to health services. A man has the right to interfere with, from the Westerner's point of view, very personal matters and even take possession of them. Thus, for instance, the choice of future husband or future wife, use of contraceptives, number of children and how a woman shall dress, the form of *hijab*, and so on, are all under a man's control. In this context it should be pointed out that the Afghan understanding of an 'individual' and his or her personal matters greatly differs from that of the West. Here the focus is on the family and on men.

This private domain is *haram*, or prohibited, for the public, as it is defined and protected by religion and tradition. It is beyond the influence or control of the outside world. Even state institutions with their respective executive organs, if they exist, are not responsible for this domain and cannot seize this internal decision-making power for themselves.

King Amanullah violated these distinctions between public and private matters with his reforms. He attempted to abolish the veil, thereby giving the symbolic power of the veil revived importance as a decisive characteristic of ethnic, national as well as religious identity. Because he advocated the abolition of the veil in his political programme, all other issues, such as the advocation of equal rights for both sexes, free choice in marriage matters (already known from the reign of Amir 'Abd al-Rahman, monogamy, setting up of (primary) education for girls and boys and literacy campaigns,[2] were instrumentalized and repudiated by the opposition as anti-Islamic.

Queen Soraya, the wife of Amanullah (indecent private photos of whom, as legend has it, considerably contributed to the fall of her husband), lived in Kabul, one of the few cities in Afghanistan. With her background and connections as a member of a social elite, it is very likely that she was unfamiliar with the life of lower class urban women, not to mention with the circumstances of women in the countryside, whose lives were hardly influenced by the politics of the urban world. Even today, the lives of these women are defined by the concessions of the family and thus practically unaffected by state decisions or public policy.

However, in the cities, particularly in Kabul, state endeavours had a strong effect on patterns of behaviour. Considering later developments, it remains questionable to what extent the 'new' forms of behaviour influenced mentalities or to what extent they were internalized by the people, particularly by men. For the important decisions, those concerning schooling, education, profession, spouse and so on, were still for the most part not made by women, but rather by respective male family members.

By the end of the 1970s, Afghan women had received a number of rights: the right to education, to work and to vote. They had fought for none of these rights themselves nor had they founded an independent women's liberation movement. Women came out unveiled from their houses because their husbands, either out of free choice or pressure to conform, had decided that their daughters and wives were allowed to do so. A male-dominated society had granted women their rights and a male society was going to deprive them of these same rights (Dupree 1996).

With the coup d'état in April 1978, the speed and the direction of the social transformations changed. The invasion of the Soviet army in December of

---

[2] Further information on Amanullah's reforms can be found in Emadi (1993: 36ff.).

1979 was to alter the quality of these transformations again. Millions of refugees left the country. The majority of these sought refuge in Pakistan and Iran, while a significant number left for Western countries. At the same time, many fled to the capital from the fighting in rural areas. Kabul burst at its seams. Various groups of the Mujahidin took advantage of the conditions in the refugee camps in Pakistan, particularly those in Peshawar, and organized resistance groups against communist Afghanistan. The Mujahidin shared the different refugee camps among themselves and attempted to conform the refugees to conservative values. They demanded *hijab*, the retreat of women from the public domain, and wrote threatening letters to those who did not comply.

Meanwhile, the 'new socialistic society' developed in Kabul and other major cities of Afghanistan. It was regarded as progress and ideal that women should work as judges, drivers of trolley buses and tractors, in the few factories and, naturally, as teachers, nurses and so on. Women went to universities, wore what they liked and still married, willingly, the man the family had chosen for them. Meanwhile the countryside raged with war.

The Soviets left and the Mujahidin took over, levelling to the ground major parts of Kabul in the winter of 1993–4. They took not only what they needed but also what they wanted. By this time boundary incursions were part of everyday life. Social control had collapsed, traditions had lost their impact and private domains were violated and destroyed. Mujahidin, originally fighting 'The Holy War' in the name of God, were overwhelmed by their own power hunger. Kabul's skeletal remains of destroyed houses give evidence of this hunger. The stories about deportations, rapes, forced marriages, suicides of violated women, and of murdered children who originated from these sad liaisons, give further witness to the scope of encroachment on the security of society. The increasing untrustworthiness of the Mujahidin, their hunger for power and their mutual rivalry are root causes for the recent political movement. The start of the movement is surrounded by the myth that religious students, *taliban*, were united for the first time in Kandahar in July 1994, spurred by the public rage concerning the abduction, rape and murder of three women by a Mujahidin commander. A mullah and former mujahid, Muhammad 'Omar, mobilized a group of students of a *madrasa*, a religious school. These students became known as the Taliban and, under the bidding of Mullah 'Omar, pursued this commander and killed him. This action created for Mullah 'Omar a profound following and much public support (Christensen 1995: 40).

In 1997, I organized questionnaires in the refugee camp Hisar-i Shahi, situated between Torkham and Jalalabad. I spoke with 120 women and each one attested that she felt more secure under the Taliban than previous regimes. The *burqa'* was no reason for defiance. The Afghan women who worked at this time for the Deutsche Welthungerhilfe in Jalalabad wore the *burqa'* with an admirable nonchalance It is too ingrained a custom to create much inner anxiety, at least on most days.

On trips with my Afghan colleagues who work as health educators I have been permitted to enter numerous private houses. An entirely different world is found behind each door. I take advantage of this access to the so-called 'interior domain', where my male colleagues are not permitted, and seldom experience restrictions. Often the women are quick to speak frankly. They mourn and cry but will also laugh and enjoy themselves. One of their most prominent worries is the health of their children, but under the current circumstances, little consideration can be given to this, for there is a hard workload to be reckoned with. The women of the house must collect firewood, fetch water, prepare dough for bread, light the furnace, bake bread, care for children, sweep, collect food for the animals and milk them, prepare food, wash dishes and clothing, by hand of course, and so on. As soon as a child is able to walk, she or he will be integrated in these duties. More often than not the girl will have the larger portion to perform. Some girls are married before they even have their first period. The bride must leave her parents and move in with her husband's family and from this point on her toil increases. She was paid for and, as a daughter-in-law, must take on practically every household job. Her work is so indispensable that a woman in the countryside must often relinquish childbed. In this case it matters little that the Quran clearly states a childbed period of forty days. This was and is nothing new; nothing has changed. As it would be said: *Khoda mehraban ast* – God is merciful.

The situation was different for the women of the urban areas in Afghanistan. Some of them enjoyed the advantages of a completed education or training, work and salary at their disposal. A few of their children went to kindergarten or school and, somehow, these women had to endure a double burden of household and job. For them, the take-over of the Taliban has had drastic consequences. Now, with the exception of the few who worked in the health sector, women are banned from their jobs, schools and universities are closed to girls and women, and no woman is allowed to be in the streets without being accompanied by a male relative. Hardship is plentiful. Many children have to support their families by working as daily labourers. For some women, there is no other way to get by than to work as a prostitute.

For the time being, Afghanistan will have to continue to be one of the countries where Deutsche Welthungerhilfe provides emergency and development aid. The question arises, however, whether the continuation of aid activities and expenditure of donations can be justified under the current political circumstances. Many outsiders think that, as long as oppression of the women of Afghanistan continues, no assistance should be rendered. As an employee of Deutsche Welthungerhilfe, I think that one of our duties is to familiarize ourselves with the conditions at hand and that we should continue to work in Afghanistan and implement projects which take the interests and needs of women and men into consideration. Yet, so long as Afghan women are subject to their own ignorance and to the control and violence of others, they cannot be expected to act on their own behalf, nor to make decisions that impact on their lives. In spite of emergency and development aid, so long as women are excluded from decision-making processes and are not empowered by the state or other influential power, their situation will continue to get worse. We can, however, make offers and try to show or provide choices. Actual changes and effort would need to come from the women of Afghanistan, despite all obstacles. Their efforts should be encouraged and supported since they receive neither assistance nor support from the Taliban, nor, for that matter, from the majority of Afghan men. We should keep in our minds that the outcome is uncertain. It will need time and patience.

Bibliography

Christensen, Asger (1995) *Aiding Afghanistan: The Background and Prospects for Reconstruction in a Fragmental Society*. Copenhagen, SIDA Publication.

Duby, Georges (1995) *Die Frau ohne Stimme: Liebe und Ehe im Mittelalter*, 2nd edition. Frankfurt a.M., Fischer Verlag.

Dupree, Nancy Hatch (1996) *The Women of Afghanistan*. Stockholm, Swedish Committee for Afghanistan, with the support of the UN coordinator for Afghanistan.

Emadi, Hafizullah (1993) *Politics of Development and Women in Afghanistan*. New York.

Part IV

Aspects of a War Economy

The 'Bazaar Economy' of Afghanistan
A Comprehensive Approach

Conrad Schetter

1. Introduction

Following the guiding question of this book and analysing the current economic situation of Afghanistan, this article will come to the conclusion that *Afghanistan is a country without a state*. The essential argument is that the mere existence of a 'war economy' can be considered as a salient indication of the erosion of state structures and the disappearance of state order. Thus, there is a close coherence between the decline of state structures and the emergence of a 'war economy'.[1] Or, in terms of a market economy: in a world which is entirely made up of states and which, in the political sense, is only conceivable in terms of states, the disappearance of state structures and the absence of an internationally recognized government in a particular country result in some respect in an economic advantage for this country. It offers opportunities for economic practices which are not available or authorized in any internationally recognized and responsibly acting state of the world.

It is true that the war which has been going on for more than twenty years has left Afghanistan as one of the most destroyed countries in the world. But the other side of the coin has to be borne in mind as well: some branches of the Afghan economy are alive and have been booming for several years. Most of these branches may be labelled as belonging to the 'war economy'.[2] However, in the following approach the term 'war

---

[1] It has to be taken into consideration that there are also a few exemptions such as Sierra Leone, in which a war economy has emerged, but government structures have remained more or less intact (Reno 1997).

[2] The general criticism of the term 'war economy' must be taken into account (e.g. Duffield 2000). The distinction between 'war economy' and 'peace economy' is tied to the Hobbesian credo, that a strong nation-state guarantees peace and that the absence of state authority mean a state of disorder, chaos and war. However, due to

economy' will embrace not only illegal or illicit economic actions, such as drug traffic or smuggling (Rubin 1999).[3] Rather, the term 'war economy' will refer to the economic actions of an entire society under the conditions of war. I pursue a comprehensive approach. With respect to the endemic Afghan terminology I define the economic practices in Afghanistan as a 'bazaar economy'. The general framework of the Afghan 'bazaar economy' is that the capitalistic free-market economy regulates all economic activities in the absence of any state regulation. Private trade constitutes the most important economic activity, while the production of real goods and the influence of a public sphere almost completely disappear. Furthermore the 'bazaar economy' on the Afghan territory is not contained by its national borders, but interwoven with the world market through an informal transnational network (Duffield 2000).

I will first demonstrate how the erosion of the state enabled the emergence of bazaar economy activities. Subsequently I will deal with the main branches of the Afghan 'bazaar economy'. In addition to kinds of illicit economic activities like drug traffic and smuggling, I will draw the attention to the 'market of violence', as elaborated on a theoretical level by Elwert (1999), and I will emphasize that a symbiosis of interests between the war parties and traders characterizes the 'bazaar economy' of Afghanistan. On the one hand the traders show interest in particular military and political decisions, on the other hand the combat units behave like economic actors. In the last part of this article I will scrutinize how the 'bazaar economy' has changed Afghan society and indicate how the 'bazaar economy' is leading to a disintegration of Afghanistan.

2. The Vanishing of State Structure

Almost all published development reports rate Afghanistan as one of the poorest countries in the world. Prior to the coup d'etat of the communist People's Democratic Party of Afghanistan (PDPA) in 1978, the Afghan

---

the lack of an adequate term, I will denote the economic situation in Afghanistan as a 'war economy'.

[3] The equating of 'war economy' with illegal economy seems to be problematic. Economic activities are seldom isolated phenomena, due to the fact that illegal and legal economic activities are generally interwoven (Keen 2000).

economy was characterized by rural subsistence agriculture and pastoral nomadism. According to Grötzbach (1990), approximately 60 per cent of the national GDP came from agriculture and pastoralism, with 80 to 85 per cent of the Afghan population directly depending on the rural economy (Rubin 1995). In the non-agricultural sector most jobs were concentrated in the state-run administration and in the military. The Afghan state received the bulk of its budget (40 per cent) from development aid, supported by opponents on both sides of the Cold War (e.g. USA, Germany, Soviet Union). Thence Afghanistan was characterized as a 'rentier state' (see Rubin 1992).

The absence of modern industries and the economic weakness of the state were reflected in the Afghan politics. The history of modern Afghanistan can be characterized as a power struggle between decentralized tribes and the central state. This struggle involved persistent arguments between proponents of tradition and modernity, and it determined the Afghan political setting throughout the twentieth century (Grevemeyer 1987). However, in the 1970s Afghanistan was ruled by a more or less functioning government. Even when the physical presence of state officers in the countryside was rare, the central government maintained supremacy over Afghan territory. At that time only the Pashtun tribes of the border area with Pakistan opposed violently the exertion of any state influence. Hence this area was the only region where illicit economic activities were recorded on a large scale. The smuggling of timber across the border into Pakistan turned out to be a profitable business. Although the planting of opium and other drugs occurred in climatically advantageous regions of Afghanistan (e.g. Hilmand), it took place only on a small scale. Drugs were primarily produced for domestic consumption, and rarely for export.

State control, which was arduously and slowly installed during the twentieth century against the will of the ordinary people, eroded with the outbreak of the Afghan War in 1979. The war, which has been going on for more than twenty years, completely changed the society. Approximately two million fatalities and the exodus of more than six million Afghans to neighbouring Pakistan and Iran – the largest forced migration in numbers on a global scale during the last 50 years – were obvious results of the ongoing war. I would like to draw attention to other consequences of the war which are worth specifying:

- The ongoing war led to a devastation of large regions. Especially in the vicinity of the cities and of the grand Afghan circular road, large parts of settlements as well as agricultural and pastoral land were razed to the ground in the aftermath of fighting. In several provinces, such as Paktia, Herat or Kandahar, almost each village was affected by war destruction. Furthermore large areas of cultivated land were contaminated with land mines. It is estimated that more than ten million mines were scattered in Afghanistan.

- The destruction of the agricultural and pastoral basis of the ordinary Afghan who remained in Afghanistan led to an economic dependence on staple food supply by the Afghan government. Due to the lack of any revenues, this situation fostered the Afghan government's dependence on foreign aid. Thus, in the 1980s the Afghan government was completely dependent on the supply of military equipment and of food from the Soviet Union.

- The continuance of the military activities resulted in the transfer of power from state institutions to war factions. This development started in the early 1980s. Against the background of the regular Afghan army being increasingly ineffective and deeply affected by mass desertion, the Afghan government supported the establishment of ethnically or tribal based militia organizations (Giustozzi 2000). The most notorious and powerful militias were the Jauzjan militia in northern Afghanistan and the Ismailia militia in Baghlan. In the late 1980s several regions were completely controlled by these militias. Most of the other regions of the country were under the control of a multitude of locally or tribal based combat groups, who were related to the resistance parties based in Peshawar or Mashhad. Owing to the lack of a 'counter-government' which directly controlled the 'liberated areas', these regions were, like the regions controlled by the pro-governmental militias, affected by the arbitrariness of the combat groups and resistance parties. The state authority was only maintained on a small scale and was concentrated in main urban areas such as Kabul, Mazar-i Sharif and Kandahar.

To bring these strands together, during the Afghan War the state lost its economic as well as political power and thus, what was perhaps much more important, its legitimacy to rule the country. The consequence of this development was the shift of power to 'military entrepreneurs', most of them organized on a local basis and using communal networks (*qaum*). The wide destruction of the rural economy was compensated by foreign aid either from the Soviet Union or the Western allies of the resistance parties.

The collapse of the Najibullah regime and the seizure of power by the Mujahidin parties in 1992 highlighted the end of all state structures. On the one hand the new government had to deal with a state apparatus which lacked legitimacy as well as economic resources. On the other hand, the resistance parties were not able to establish a functioning government. They expelled the bureaucrats of the PDPA regime, but they could not replace them with qualified civil servants from their own ranks. In addition, the continuing state of war between the remaining war factions led to a situation in which the hands of the government were tied. Between 1992 and 1994, myriads of belligerent groups related to one or other party controlled parts of the country, yet often not beyond the territory of a village or a valley. Only warlords such as Rashid Dostum in north Afghanistan or Isma'il Khan in west Afghanistan were able to establish fragile administrative structures on a regional level between 1992 and 1996.

The appearance of the Taliban in 1994, their successful expansion and their control of nearly 90 per cent of the country from 1998 did not lead to re-establishment of a strong state. The governmental activities of the Taliban were limited to the provision of security by incorporating local combatants into their own military structure and to the introduction of a bizarre and harsh version of Islamic law. The political decision-making of the Taliban revealed their lack of state legitimacy: all decisions are made by the closed and opaque leadership of the movement in Kandahar, and not by their government in Kabul. The Taliban use positions in the government (such as the rank of minister) as rewards for martial bravery. They do not link them to governmental duties. With regard to the economic situation, it is safe to say that the Taliban allow all kinds of activity, provided that these do not affect either their supremacy or their interpretation of Islamic law.

To summarize: the ongoing protracted Afghan War entailed the vanishing of state structures. The state lost its legitimacy to rule the country and its responsibility for the Afghan people and country. Power shifted to 'military entrepreneurs' who only have responsibility for their own clientele. To maintain their own clientelistic networks these 'military entrepreneurs' need inescapably economic means and thus became the main players in the Afghan 'bazaar economy'. This will be elaborated in the next section.

3. Important Sectors of the Afghan 'Bazaar Economy'

Since Berthold Brecht's novel *Mutter Courage,* we are familiar with the economic side of war. In Afghanistan the conditions of war also resulted directly in the emergence of economic services that supplied the war factions. In once remote areas, such as Nuristan or the southern rim of the Hazarajat, a new infrastructure including roads, hotels and bazaars developed, due to the need for secure supply routes for the resistance. Moreover, private truck and bus drivers profited from transporting *mujahidin* to the frontlines.

The fighting parties, each of them more or less headed by a powerful 'military entrepreneur', were the major economic winners throughout the time when the Afghan War was defined in the terms of the Cold War (1979–89). At the height of the war, the Afghan government as well as the resistance parties received armaments for their combat units and food for the people to an annual value of approximately US$3 billion (Rubin 1995). The main sponsors were on the one hand the USSR and on the other hand the USA and Saudi Arabia. It is an open secret that, after supplying certain combat units, the parties sold the bulk of foreign aid and armaments in the bazaars to obtain liquid funds. Particularly the Jabha-i Milli of Sibghatullah Mujaddidi and the Harakat-i Inqilab of Muhammad Muhammadi were notorious for selling weapons instead of directing them against the communist enemy (Roy 1986). The end of the Cold War brought an abrupt end to the channelling of aid to the resistance parties as well as to the Najibullah regime in Kabul. The lack of external patronage caused a slow disbandment of the relations between the combat units on the one side and the resistance parties as well as the Afghan government on the other side, because the latter were not able to open up new resources. Only those political parties which developed and controlled new means to gain economic profit (e.g. opium trade, exploitation of natural resources) were able to survive. The fact that the Najibullah regime was no longer able to pay for the militias was the main reason for the breakdown of the government in 1992.

The above-mentioned economic activities and actors were directly linked to the acts of war. In the following sections I will focus on some important features of economic activities in Afghanistan:

- economy of violence
- training of militant Islamists
- exploitation of natural and cultural resources
- cultivation of opium poppies
- trans-border trade

These fields of the Afghan 'bazaar economy' resulted from the combination of a collapse of state structures and destruction of traditional economic resources.

Economy of Violence

The term 'economy of violence' focuses on a self-perpetuating system, in which violence itself emerges as a marketable good. From an economic point of view the immense number of combat groups which existed at least until the appearance of the Taliban in 1994 can be regarded as 'war enterprises' adapted to a 'market of violence'. Their main capital was their armaments and their main business was the maintenance of security for a certain territory and its inhabitants.

It has to be stressed that, through the emergence of these combat groups, the vocational training of an entire society changed drastically. Due to the devastation of agricultural resources, the inclination to be trained in agricultural or pastoral techniques declined. The ordinary Afghan adapted his labour to the shifting economic situation in Afghanistan. Membership in a combat unit was much more profitable and even more secure than a civil occupation, such as being a farmer, with the daily risk of stepping on a land mine and without adequate arms for self-defence. Membership in a combat unit was not as precarious as it seems at first glance. The main tasks of these units were to collect taxes from the inhabitants in return for ensuring security and to take tolls from foreigners crossing their checkpoints. The militias were the largest and best-paying employers. The guarantee of security was the fundamental reason for the existence of these combat units. Thus, generation or maintenance of a feeling of general insecurity was the driving force which made the combat units indispensable. Lootings, raids and plundering of rival villages, as well as the occupation of third-party property, not only promised a material profit, but were also the main strategies in upholding a general feeling of insecurity. Impending danger underlined the necessity for the existence of combat units. As long as the inhabitants of an area were in fear of raids by neighbouring enemies, they would support the militia.

Only the Taliban, which emerged in 1994, managed to monopolize the 'economy of security'. In other words, one of the essential reasons for the emergence and the success of the Taliban was the initial lack of security, which particularly affected the traders. Rashid (2000) highlighted the alliance between the Taliban and the Pashtun trade networks. The traders expected high profits from the re-establishing of secure trade routes through Afghanistan. Previously the traders had to pay various combat units at dozens of checkpoints. Through the emergence of a transit trade, the Taliban received a profitable source of revenue. The Taliban required these revenues to bribe and employ the previously independent combat units. Thus, the strategy of the Taliban was to absorb the combat units, who directly profited from the security business in the past, into their own ranks. The maintenance of the state of belligerency as well as the omnipresence of the Taliban guaranteed the sustained employment of these warriors. Nevertheless, due to several defeats of the Taliban with high casualties (e.g. in Mazar-i Sharif, 1997, and in Shomali, 1999), being a soldier lost its attractiveness for many combatants, who increasingly preferred to accept a more secure occupation (e.g. in trade or opium cultivation) than to risk their lives on the frontline. The Taliban met the resulting shortage of warriors by recruiting enflamed and indoctrinated students of the Pakistani *madaris*.[4] At the time of writing from one quarter to one third of all Taliban are Pakistanis or Arabs.

---

[4] For the problem of the 'mushrooming' of *madaris* in Pakistan refer to Malik (1989)

The 'Bazaar Economy' of Afghanistan

Training of Militant Islamists

The 'market of violence' in Afghanistan includes an international dimension. In the eyes of Western observers Afghanistan appears to be a stronghold of an international Islamic militancy (Borke 1999). Indeed, there are indications that the Taliban and, prior to the emergence of the Taliban, Islamic parties such as the Ittihad-i Islami of Sayyaf or the Hizb-i Islami of Hikmatyar incorporated or tolerated groups of militant Muslims from the entire Islamic world. Osama Bin Ladin is the most notorious of these militant Muslims, suspected of being the mastermind behind the bombing of the American embassies in Nairobi and Dar es Salaam in 1998. Nevertheless, many other radical Islamic groups, among them Harakat al-Ansar, Harakat-i Islami-i Uzbekistan and Abu Sayyaf, have training camps in Afghanistan preparing men to fight in Kashmir, Chechnya, Central Asia, West China or the Philippines (Rashid 1999). The lack of state structures is an essential advantage for the establishment of training camps for militant Islamists. Afghanistan offers excellent training conditions: a strictly religious daily life, possibilities of practising war techniques by participating in the Afghan civil war, and security against persecution by enemies from outside the country. In return, the hosting Afghan war parties receive financial supplies from the Islamic militants. For example, it is well known that Osama Bin Ladin not only supported the Mujahidin resistance parties with military equipment and money, but also built a hospital and imported bulldozers to help in reconstructing the infrastructure (Davis 1994).

Exploitation of Natural and Cultural Resources

The exploitation and sale of resources which once were state property or under state protection is an obvious strategy for gaining profit. The smuggling of timber, which already occurred before the Afghan War, increased again from the end of the 1980s, when the Soviet troops withdrew from Afghanistan and when transport into Pakistan became easier. In particular, Nuristan, a once thickly forested region, is affected by heavy deforestation and denudation. The combat units involved in the smuggling of timber became prosperous. As a result they are now well supplied with military equipment. Neither the Taliban nor the Northern

Alliance have attempted to extend their authority into Nuristan. Thus, this region is still under control of independent combat units (see the contribution by Klimburg).

The main revenue of Massoud, the strong military leader of the Northern Alliance, derived from the exploitation of emerald and lapis-lazuli mines in Badakhshan. Massoud started this business in the 1980s. When his party, the Jam'iyat-i Islami, came to power in 1992, he made sure that the mines were nationalized and came under his control. Since then he had exploited the mines with the assistance of a Polish company. It is estimate that Massoud collected up to US$200 million per year from the trade in gemstones.

Ruins and remains of the former Afghan infrastructure were also exploited. For example, all products made out of steel (e.g. rusting factories, destroyed tanks, electricity and telephone poles) were shipped to Pakistan and were recycled in the steel mills of Lahore, as is discussed by Rashid (2000). The sale of Afghan culture is another economic strategy. Since 1992, when state structures broke down in Kabul, the national Afghan museum has been robbed several times. Its antiquities have been sold to traders in Pakistan and elsewhere.

Cultivation of Opium Poppies

Probably the most prominent branch of the Afghan war economy is the cultivation of opium. Already in the 1980s some combat units started to plant opium on a large scale in the Hilmand valley. Combat units allied with the resistance parties (e.g. Harakat-i Inqilab) as well as with the Afghan government were involved in this business. The cultivation of opium increased and spread steadily. In many places the agricultural land which was cleared of mines was immediately cultivated to grow opium. Although the profit of the opium business lies almost exclusively in its trade, as expounded in the contribution by Schulenburg, farmers gain a much more regular and higher profit from opium than from cultivating other crops. The war parties also gained from the opium cultivation by collecting a tax of 20 per cent on harvested opium from the dealers (Rashid 1999). In 1999, the peak of the Afghan opium production was reached: in that year 75 per cent of all global seizures of opiates were produced in Afghanistan.

Pressure from the UN resulted in a ban on the cultivation of opium which was imposed by the Taliban in 2000. According to a recent UNDCP report (http://www.undcp.org), the planting of opium almost came to a complete stop in 2001. It is difficult to comprehend why the Taliban decided to abolish the cultivation and production of opium. It is probably too early to give a satisfying answer. The decision can be interpreted as an attempt to obtain international recognition for the Taliban's government. Other arguments are that the Taliban found a way to substitute their profits from the drug fees, or that the decline in production is simply a market strategy. However, the producers and traders of the drug should be taken into consideration too. What would be the incentive for the farmers to abolish opium cultivation, and where will the traders find ways of gaining sufficient profits with the trade of other goods? It seems as if the Taliban must have entered into economic arrangements with opium producers and traders. Otherwise they will face fundamental problems in the future. Reported riots against the Taliban in poppy cultivation areas of southern Afghanistan in June 2001 may be connected to the prohibition of cultivation and trade of drugs.

Trans-Border Trade

The collapse of the Soviet Union led to a new geopolitical interest of several countries in the Central Asian states, known as the New Great Game. In this context Afghanistan, situated on the southern rim of the Central Asian states, gained an enormous geo-economic importance. Under the rule of the Taliban south and west Afghanistan became the turnstile of smuggling between Pakistan, Dubai, Iran and Turkmenistan.

Based on the Afghan Transit Trade Agreement (ATTA) dating back to the 1950s, goods were permitted to be imported tax-free via Pakistan (Karachi) into landlocked Afghanistan. Already in the 1970s the ATTA was misused for smuggling: goods arriving in Afghanistan via Pakistan were smuggled back to the Federally Administered Tribal Area (FATA) of Pakistan, where they were sold in open bazaars. While this smuggling decreased in the period of the Soviet occupation, it emerged again with the advent of the Taliban, but this time on a larger scale and via several trade routes.

Afghanistan has taken advantage of enormous disparities in trade policies between the countries in its vicinity. From Dubai, the largest free port in the world, consumer goods (e.g. video recorders, television sets) were imported by air to Kandahar and Jalalabad. Fuel from Iran, where oil products are heavily subsidized and where fuel costs less than US$0.04 per litre, enters Afghanistan via Herat. From Turkmenistan a range of goods, such as automobile spare parts, are imported into Afghanistan. Most of these goods are destined to be smuggled into Pakistan. Goods from Pakistan are also imported into Afghanistan. Rashid (2000) stressed the steady increase in car-theft in Pakistan, where 63,000 cars were stolen in Karachi alone in 1992-8. Most stolen vehicles are transferred to Afghanistan. The required transportation network, which integrates Afghanistan into the regional economic structure, is used for drug traffic, too. To sum up, all goods traded in Afghanistan are either produced or consumed in the region. Drugs and emeralds are exported from the region to developed countries. To a large extent war materials, fuel and manufactured consumer goods are imported into Afghanistan from global markets. Today's Afghanistan is at the crossroads of an international trade with an immense variety of products: 'The consignments range from Japanese camcorders to English underwear and Earl Grey tea, Chinese silk to American computer parts, Afghan heroin to Pakistani wheat and sugar, East European kalashnikovs to Iranian petroleum' (Rashid 2000: 189).

At the same time as this transnational trade increased, state borders became permeable. According to Rashid (2000) the Taliban are interwoven in a trading network of smugglers, transporters, drug barons, bureaucrats, politicians, police and army officers, not only in Pakistan, but also in Iran, Turkmenistan and Dubai. This trading network was conducive to the breakdown of state authority on the borders and to the abrogation of toll duties and taxes. As pointed out above, this trading network affected political decisions: it not only gave financial support to the Taliban from the beginning, but it also triggered the Taliban's offensive against Herat in 1995 – against the vote of the Taliban's Pakistani military advisers. The basis for this trading network are Pashtun tribal connections. The border between Pakistan and Afghanistan criss-crosses the Pashtun tribal area;

large Pashtun communities are economic pillars in Dubai and Karachi. Kandahar and Quetta, cities which are situated in the heartland of the Pashtun tribal belt, are the hometowns of most of the traders and not by accident the strongholds of the Taliban. Like traders and bribed officials, the Taliban directly profit from the trade. They make an effective charge of 6 per cent on each item imported into Afghanistan (Naqvi 1999). The Taliban earned US$2.1 billion from trade in 1997. Many Taliban, also, personally profit from the trans-border trade. They put up service stations, restaurants and garages along the highways between the border-crossing checkpoints of Spin Buldak, Islam Qal'a and Torgundi.

4. Social Consequences of the 'Bazaar Economy'

The collapse of the state and the emergence of the 'bazaar economy', controlled only by the rules of the market, caused profound changes in Afghan society. The most salient problem of the 'bazaar economy' is that it is based solely on trade and the production of 'violence'. Besides agricultural production, which was highly linked to the 'bazaar economy' due to the opium production until recently, no other real goods are produced in the country. Furthermore a state apparatus is absent, which might give economic impetus, establish producing industries, regulate market mechanisms or transfer a surplus to Afghans who are not gaining from the 'bazaar economy'. Therefore, only the Afghans who are engaged in trade and are integrated in the above-mentioned trading networks profit from the 'bazaar economy'. In contrast, the majority of the Afghan people suffers enormously from the 'bazaar economy'. The gap between the handful of people who make an enormous profit by trading and the ordinary Afghans who depend on the low and uncertain crops of the subsistence economy and on the help of the NGOs is immense. The Taliban as well as the Northern Alliance have transferred responsibility concerning, for example, education, training, occupation, agriculture, irrigation systems, to various NGOs. By outsourcing these tiresome and expensive tasks, which are usually undertaken or stimulated by the state, in the eyes of the ordinary Afghan inhabitants the war parties lost their justification for ruling in a civil government. The war parties concentrate solely on the fixing of conditions under which the NGOs are allowed to operate in Afghanistan (e.g. the employment of women, the location of NGO offices).

The continuing Afghan War has fostered the emergence of a Kalashnikov culture not only in Afghanistan, but also in the bordering areas of the neighbouring countries. The serious effect of this culture is the collapse of traditional social structures (see the contribution by Goodhand). In the past each Afghan community was characterized by a highly fragile balance of power between various representatives (e.g. *malik*, *mirab*) and groups of interest. Old men (*rish safid*) had an enormous social status owing to their generally presumed experience and wisdom. Usually conflicts were mediated in a peaceful way by codes of conduct (e.g. the *hamsaya* system) and informal gatherings (e.g. *jirga*, *majlis*). With the war, the balance of power between various actors and groups has been replaced by warlordism. Nowadays young men with arms are the 'big men' in their communities. They make most decisions. In solving conflicts the persuasion of arms has replaced traditional peaceful means. The Kalashnikov culture may be considered as a strong indicator of the brutalization of the Afghan society – a phenomenon which is usually observed in countries under the conditions of a protracted war. More seriously, arbitrary decisions by the warlords, based on the power of arms, enlarge the gap between today's Afghan society and the ideal of a state which regulates conflicts by law and in a civil way. Another social consequence which has to be mentioned is that the number of people addicted to drugs has increased due to the cultivation of poppies.

A problem directly deriving from the conditions of war is the insecurity of property rights. The shift of political power and the arbitrariness of the warlords were accompanied by a redistribution of real estate, such as agricultural land and houses. Until 1978, the Afghan economy was characterized by a subsistence economy. Insecurity regarding real estate as well as the destruction of subsistence economy and the rapid increase in export-oriented poppy cultivation has resulted in a monetization of the Afghan economy (Rubin 1999). This monetization of the Afghan economy is a strong incentive for the involvement of the Afghan economy in the global economy.

5. International Dimension of the Afghan War Economy

The ruin of the Afghan currency (Rubin 1999) and the dissolution of a national market reflect the regional disintegration of Afghanistan. Since 1992 the national integration of Afghanistan has been replaced by the inclusion of the main Afghan regions in the economic circles of its neighbours: for example, the Herat region under the rule of Isma'il Khan was interlinked with Iran. Trans-border trade has increased, regular flights between Herat and Mashhad have been installed, and agreements for a close cooperation between the Iranian province of Khurasan and the Herat region were concluded. The dependence of north Afghanistan on the Central Asian States, particularly on Uzbekistan, also increased. Since the early 1980s Uzbekistan had supplied north Afghanistan with electricity and received natural gas in return. From 1992, when Dostum controlled north Afghanistan, the trade and transport system of this region was fully integrated into the economic circle of Uzbekistan. The economy of north-east Afghanistan (e.g. Badakhshan), which was mainly under the rule of Massoud, was oriented to Tajikistan. Massoud received military supplies via Tajikistan and the trade of drugs, gemstones, etc. from Badakhshan went via Tajikistan. The trade and transportation system of south and south-east Afghanistan was strongly related to Pakistan. Especially since the rise of the Taliban, the state boundary between Pakistan and Afghanistan has been blurred. The connection of the western region to Iran, and of the south and south-eastern regions to Pakistan, was strengthened by the fact that some millions of Afghan refugees have been living in both neighbouring countries for many years, and a frequent cross-border trade has been established.

Obviously, the ongoing war and the 'bazaar economy' in Afghanistan affect the economic and state structures of the entire region. Political and economic destabilization in Pakistan is unquestionable. Not only have state revenues suffered from the ATTA, but Pakistani society faces a sneaking talibanization. It has to be taken into account that the Pakistanis are the most important 'foreign workers' in the Afghan 'market of violence', and the *madaris*, scattered all over Pakistan, are the most important education and recruitment fields for the Taliban.

The war in Afghanistan also has had a strong impact on the economic prosperity of the Central Asian States. While at the beginning of the 1990s some observers declared Central Asia would be a booming zone in the future, the war situation in Afghanistan is still a major obstacle to foreign investment in this region. Thus the war in Afghanistan is perceived as an outstanding threat to the political order of Central Asia. Central Asian governments are particularly worried that the war activities in Afghanistan will extend into the region north of the Oxus, and militant Islamists, trained in Afghanistan, will gain influence in Central Asia.

Besides the regional impact of the Afghan 'bazaar economy', the global dimension has to be taken into consideration. Western observers assess the Afghan 'bazaar economy' as a salient threat to the world order and to international security. The cultivation of poppies and the training of militant Islamists are usually considered to be the most dangerous threats of all.

6. Conclusion

In this article I elaborated different schemes of the 'bazaar economy' in Afghanistan. It can be concluded that the destruction of the traditional economy (agrarian land, pastures) and the collapse of the state structures are the main reasons for the emergence of the 'bazaar economy'. The destruction of the traditional economic basis of the ordinary Afghan people led to a drastic change in the labour market. In order to survive in a devastated country the people have been forced to accept work related to the business of war (e.g. militias) or to illegal economic actions (e.g. smuggling, drug production and traffic). The collapse of the state is the clear reason for the emergence of the 'bazaar economy' in Afghanistan. On the one hand, economic activities which are ostracized by international agreements are mushrooming in the absence of a state authority which recognizes the international standards of law. Since the outbreak of the Afghan War, economic fields (e.g. monopoly of security, trade, drug production and traffic), controlled or prohibited by the state in the past, were established as branches regulated only by the terms of a free market. On the other hand, the lack of state structures meant that impulses to establish productive industries or a social infrastructure are disappearing. Moreover, the non-existence of state structures means that not even a social and economic minimum standard for the majority of the indigent Afghan people is guaranteed. This article has clarified and underlined that the re-establishment of state structures has to be considered as the first and major step towards overcoming the 'bazaar economy' and thus the global menaces proceeding from Afghanistan.

Even though I have drawn a picture of an unbridled and in some respects alarming 'Wild East' economy in this article, it can be assumed that the (first) peak of the 'bazaar economy' has been reached and that there is now a slight decline. This development is less an indication of the re-establishment of state structures than of international pressure and changing economic conditions in the neighbouring countries and the world market. The endeavours by the Taliban to receive international recognition led to a decrease in poppy cultivation. The reform of Pakistani import law as well as international sanctions against Afghanistan's international flights resulted in a dampening down of the ATTA. The Taliban's profit from the ATTA decreased from US$3 billion in 1999 to US$900 million in 2000 (Naqvi 1999).

But even if some branches of the Afghan 'bazaar economy' disappeared, the state vacuum in Afghanistan will still offer unprecedented opportunities for economic activities. Possibly the economy of smuggling people will turn out to be the most profitable business in the future. Natural catastrophes, such as several heavy earthquakes in north-west Afghanistan in recent years or the countrywide droughts in 2000 and 2001, further weakened the poor living conditions in Afghanistan. Under these circumstances the situation of the ordinary Afghans, excluded from the benefits of the 'bazaar economy', in Afghanistan itself, but also in Pakistan and Iran, which are still harbouring several million Afghan refugees, deteriorated. The inhuman situation in the Maslakh camp near Herat and in the Jalozai camp near Peshawar was recognized worldwide. Under the compulsion of dire living conditions, many Afghans consider the request for asylum or the illegal migration into Europe as the very last resort to survive. From all the approximately 300,000 to 500,000 illegal immigrants smuggled annually into Europe, it is estimated that Afghans and Kurds compose the largest nationalities numerically (http://www.demographie.de). The hijacking of an Afghan aircraft and its forced landing in London to apply for asylum in February 2000 and the Australian rejection of Afghan refugees, rescued on a Norwegian tanker, in September 2001 clearly illustrate the new dimension of the migration problem. By smuggling Afghans, unscrupulous hauliers earn a lot of money (see Maley 2001). However, the business of smuggling people has just commenced. What dimension this 'new economy' will reach in the future is still uncertain.

Bibliography

Borke, Astrid von (1999) Die Bewegung der Afghanistan-Veteranen im militanten Islamismus und das Phänomen Osama Ben Laden. In: Conrad Schetter and Almut Wieland-Karimi (eds.) *Afghanistan in Geschichte und Gegenwart* (Schriftenreihe der Mediothek für Afghanistan 1). Frankfurt a.M., IKO-Verlag: 129-52.

Davis, Anthony (1994) The Battleground in Northern Afghanistan. *Jane's Intelligence Review* (July): 323-7.

Duffield, Mark (2000) Globalization, Transborder Trade, and War Economies. In: Mats Berdal and David M. Malone (eds.) *Greed and Grievance: Economic Agendas in Civil Wars*. Boulder, CO, Lynne Rienner: 69-89.

Elwert, Georg (1999) Markets of Violence. In: Georg Elwert et al. (eds.) *Dynamics of Violence: Processes of Escalation and De-Escalation in Violent Group Conflicts* (Supplement to Sociologus 1). Berlin, Dunker & Humblot: 86-101.

Giustozzi, Antonio (2000) *War, Politics and Society in Afghanistan 1978–1992*. London, Hurst.

Grevemeyer, Jan-Heeren (1987) *Afghanistan: Sozialer Wandel und Staat im 20. Jahrhundert*. Berlin, Express Edition.

Grötzbach, Erwin (1990) *Afghanistan* (Wissenschaftliche Länderkunde 37). Darmstadt, Wissenschaftliche Buchgesellschaft.

Keen, David (2000) Incentives and Disincentives for Violence. In: Mats Berdal and David M. Malone (eds.) *Greed and Grievance: Economic Agendas in Civil Wars*. Boulder, CO: Lynne Rienner: 19-41.

Maley, William (2001) *Security, People-Smuggling and Australia's New Afghan Refugees*. Australian Defence Studies Centre, Working Paper 63.

Malik, Jamal S. (1989) *Islamisierung in Pakistan 1977–84: Untersuchungen zur Auflösung autochthoner Strukturen* (Beiträge zur Südasienforschung 128). Stuttgart, Franz Steiner Verlag.

Naqvi, Zareen (1999) *Afghanistan–Pakistan Trade Relations*. Islamabad, World Bank.

Rashid, Ahmed (1999) The Taliban: Exporting Extremism. *Foreign Affairs* 78(6): 22-35.

Rashid, Ahmed (2000) *Taliban: Militant Islam, Oil and Fundamentalism in Central Asia*. New Haven, Yale University Press.

Reno, William (1997) Welthandel, Warlords und die Wiedererfindung des afrikanischen Staates. *Welt Trends: Internationale Politik und vergleichende Studien* 14: 8-29.

Roy, Olivier (1986) *Islam and Resistance in Afghanistan*. Cambridge, Cambridge University Press.

Rubin, Barnett R. (1992) Political Elites in Afghanistan: Rentier State Building, Rentier State Wrecking. *International Journal of Middle Eastern Studies* 24: 77-99.

Rubin, Barnett R. (1995) *The Fragmentation of Afghanistan*. Chelsea, Michigan, Yale University Press.

Rubin, Barnett R. (1999) The Political Economy of War and Peace in Afghanistan (Paper Presented at the Meeting of the Afghan Support Group, Stockholm, Sweden, 21 June 1999).

Illicit Opium Production in Afghanistan

Michael von der Schulenburg

1. Illicit Drug Production Trends in Afghanistan

In the history of the opium trade, one can observe a geographical shifting in illicit opium production and the illegal trafficking of opium (and its derivatives such as morphine and heroin) in response to the changing political fortunes of countries. Whereas in the 1980s illicit opium was produced and illegally exported from more than nine countries, its cultivation is now concentrated in two; indeed, about 95 per cent of all illicit opium now originates in Afghanistan and Myanmar – two countries with substantial internal political and socio-economic problems.

Prior to the 1980s, Afghanistan was not a major exporter of illicit opium. Afghanistan's opium was produced primarily for domestic, traditional consumption and, to a far lesser extent, for a limited number of thrill-seeking 'hippy' tourists en route to India. The subsequent prolonged war turned Afghanistan into a 'failed state', thus preparing the fertile environment for an explosion in illicit poppy cultivation and opium production. It is no coincidence that Afghanistan is today not only one of the poorest countries in the world but by far the most important producer of illicit opium. In 1999 Afghanistan became the source of over 75 per cent of global illicit opium production.

The most recent Poppy Survey of Afghanistan by the United Nations International Drug Control Programme (UNDCP) reveals that during the 1998/9 planting season, an estimated 91,000 ha were under illicit opium poppy cultivation. This represents a 43 per cent increase in area under opium cultivation from the previous growing season (1997/8). The provinces of Hilmand and Nangarhar remained the two dominant areas for opium poppy cultivation, representing 49 per cent and 26 per cent, respectively, of the total area under cultivation. But in 1998/9, opium cultivation spread to new areas, especially in northern and north-eastern Afghanistan.

The increase in the volume of illicit opium produced was even more dramatic than the geographic expansion of poppy cultivation. The output of raw opium is estimated to have jumped from 2,700 metric tonnes in 1997/8 to 4,600 metric tonnes in 1998/9 – a staggering increase of 70 per cent. Favourable weather conditions explain why the increase in the volume of opium production so exceeded the increase in area under cultivation.

Final results for the 1999/2000 harvest were not available at the time of writing but initial reports from the poppy cultivating areas of Hilmand and Nangarhar suggested that both the area under cultivation and the yield have declined. It is believed that the area under cultivation is now between 70,000 and 75,000 ha (a decline of about 16 per cent) and the total production of raw opium between 3,000 and 3,300 metric tonnes (a decline of about 30 per cent). It is difficult to ascertain whether the reduction in area was prompted by the decline in the price of opium or by the decree issued by Mullah 'Omar in August 1999 to reduce poppy cultivation by one-third. The decline in production, in contrast, is closely linked to adverse weather conditions – i.e. the heat wave in April 2000 and the subsequent drought in many parts of the country.

Yields from poppy cultivation in Afghanistan have always been substantially higher than those in other opium-producing areas of the world. The average yield in Afghanistan is estimated by UNDCP to be 50 kg/ha, with the highest yields, in irrigated areas, reaching 90 kg/ha. Compared to this, the estimated average yield in Myanmar are relatively modest at 10 kg/ha; the figure is even lower in countries such as Laos (5.5 kg/ha).

Although Afghanistan has substantially higher yields than Myanmar, farm income from the opium poppy is lower on a per-hectare basis, since farm-gate prices are much lower. UNDCP estimates that, in 1998, the weighted average farm-gate price of one kilogram of opium was about US$60 in Afghanistan and US$340 in Myanmar. For the year 2000, the price discrepancy between the two countries may have widened even further. At present, about 96 per cent of the areas under opium cultivation are under Taliban control, with the remaining 4 per cent under the control of the Northern Alliance.

2. Trade-Offs

To focus solely on the aggregate volume of illicit opium production in Afghanistan risks overshadowing the importance of micro-level decisions taken by farmers throughout the country. Indeed, what distinguishes Afghanistan from other countries is the extent to which entire farming communities now view the poppy as the foundation of the local economy. It is in this context that twenty years of conflict and Afghanistan's drug problem are inextricably linked.

In Afghanistan, the farmer's decision to illicitly cultivate the poppy is, as elsewhere, based on a careful weighing of risks and financial benefits. The conflict in Afghanistan has not only tipped the scale so that perceived risks are minimized and benefits more pronounced, but it has at the same time eliminated virtually all other viable options for the farmer. The opium poppy is widely perceived by Afghan subsistence farmers to be the one crop that allows them to meet their basic needs.

Under conditions of political and economic instability, the cultivation of the opium poppy provides Afghan farmers with a relatively secure source of cash income. Opium has a number of advantages: the relatively short time of six months between seeding and harvesting, its resistance to major natural diseases and the high cash value of its harvest. Opium also has a long 'shelf life' and is thus easily traded throughout the year; in this regard, it is an ideal investment for farmers. That the opium poppy is one of the few crops for which farmers can receive advance credits is testimony to its dependability from a business perspective.

In Afghanistan, poppy cultivation has had an impact on food production that is not self-evident. On the one hand, according to one estimate, the poppy 'crowded out' approximately 360,000 metric tonnes of potential wheat yield in 1999, thus exacerbating the country's chronic food deficit (FAO–WFP). At the same time, the cultivation of poppy has allowed families in many communities to purchase more food than they would be able to grow on their own, thus reinforcing, rather than eroding, food security in some parts of the country. In this respect, local economies dependent on poppy appear to demonstrate a process of product-specialization, with food and opium forming the core of mutually reinforcing bartering networks. Indeed, it is noteworthy that poppy is grown mainly in communities that have enough resources to allocate to both food production and poppy cultivation – rarely is it grown in the poorest communities, which must devote limited agricultural inputs exclusively to food production.

In view of widespread unemployment and underemployment, the impact of poppy cultivation on the labour market is more straightforward. Poppy cultivation and harvesting are labour-intensive activities that provide sharecroppers and migrant labourers with additional income. Itinerant harvesters come from all over Afghanistan, even from as far as refugee camps in Pakistan. They often start in the lowlands in May and move to fields in the mountains where the higher altitude can postpone the harvest until as late as August. The itinerant workers are typically paid a share of the final yield. They also represent the most likely reason for the wide diffusion of poppy-cultivating know-how throughout the country.

Although it is believed that only about 2.6 per cent of agricultural land is used for the cultivation of opium poppy, the proportion of Afghan families who derive at least part of their annual income from opium is much higher. It is believed that about three to four million Afghans – or about 20 per cent of the population – are dependent on the poppy for their livelihood.

3. Opium as a Source of Income

Though opium constitutes the most significant source of cash income for the civilian population in Afghanistan, total income from the 1997/8 poppy harvest is likely to have been less than US$200 million – a small fraction of the hundreds of billions of dollars that the global drug trade generates each year. The earnings in Afghanistan include farm income as well as the mark-up for traders, storage, internal land transport and local 'taxes'. Of this amount, US$130 million, or about 65 per cent, goes to farmers and itinerant harvesters, with the rest going to traders, transporters and 'taxes'.

Speculation abounds as to whether the two main factions, the Taliban and the Northern Alliance, are systematically involved in the drug trade. For either side, income from opium would be gathered through the collection of two types of taxes: *'ushr*, a flat 10 per cent tax on farm products, and *zakat*, a 20 per cent tax generally levied on traders. These taxes are not evenly collected throughout Afghanistan and, in any case, not all tax revenues are intended for the use of de facto rulers. *'Ushr* for example, is in many parts of the country used to support the local mosque and religious services by the local mullah. Estimates of the income the Taliban receive through taxing the cultivation, production and trade of opium vary between US$10 and US$30 million per year. No corresponding estimates exist for the Northern Alliance. It should be emphasized that, compared to the taxes levied on opium, a greater amount of tax revenue is collected from Afghanistan's thriving illegal economy in smuggled goods.

The cash proceeds from the opium trade fuel a much larger illegal economy. The local profits derived from opium provide the needed 'start-up' capital for an economy that is increasingly dominated by illegal entrepreneurs. Afghanistan is a major importer of goods from Dubai, covering merchandise from refrigerators to vehicles, from spare parts to luxury items. Goods are transported duty-free into Afghanistan, only to reappear in neighbouring countries, where they are sold in illegal markets; prohibitive local import duties are, in this manner, easily circumvented. A recent World Bank study valued the illegal border trade between Afghanistan and Pakistan at US$2.5 billion annually. To a lesser degree, such illegal cross-border smuggling also exists between Afghanistan and its other neighbours. A plausible estimate of the volume of illegal trade through Afghanistan is US$3.0–4.0 billion per year.

4. The Structure of the Opium Trade in Afghanistan

Opium is freely traded in Afghanistan. The main opium markets, Ghani Khel Bazaar in the east and Sangin and Musa Qal'a Bazaars in the south, are regularly replenished from smaller markets throughout the country. Due to high levels of opium production in 1999, opium prices collapsed in early 2000: at the time of writing the average price for one kilogram of opium gum was about US$20, down from over US$60 less than a year before.

The structure of the opium trade differs markedly between the southern (mostly Hilmand) and eastern (mostly Nangarhar) regions. The southern region is characterized by a relatively free market structure. In the eastern region, in contrast, the trade is more organized by larger traders. Quality also varies, with distinctly better quality products found in the eastern regions; predictably, this has led to a visible price difference between producing regions.

Because of considerable price fluctuations over the years and the ease of storage, it is believed that large quantities of opium and its derivatives are stockpiled in Afghanistan. Following the abundant opium harvest of 1998/9, these stocks might now further swell, creating additional pressures to find new markets for these products. Given that the Western European markets are believed to be saturated, excess supply could be absorbed in Central Asia, Russia and even Africa.

Typically, Afghanistan's illicit opium is exported as morphine base, which is more attractive to traders and traffickers because it is less bulky and has a less noticeable odour. At present, there is little information on the network of laboratories in the country. However, given that most of Afghanistan's opium is converted into morphine base prior to being exported, it is highly likely that Afghanistan has considerable refining capability. There are reasons to believe that many of the laboratories are located along Afghanistan's southern and northern borders. In the past, local laboratories produced heroin base solely for consumption within the region; though unconfirmed, recent reports suggest that the quality of heroin has improved and that some Afghan laboratories are now capable of producing white, high-grade heroin – a product tailor-made for Western markets.

5. Diversification of Trafficking Routes

According to information collected by UNDCP, in 1998 total global seizures of opiates amounted to 740 metric tonnes in opium equivalent, of which the largest portion is believed to have originated from Afghanistan. Of these worldwide seizures, 510 metric tonnes, or about 69 per cent were captured in the region. Iran had total seizures of 400 metric tonnes measured in opium equivalents, representing 55 per cent of the worldwide total. This was followed by 54 metric tonnes, or 7 per cent, in Turkey and 39 metric tonnes, or 5 per cent in Pakistan. Western countries, despite the much higher allocation in financial and technical resources, seized 68 metric tonnes, or 9 per cent, during the same time interval. Western Europe is by far the most lucrative destination for illicit drugs from Afghanistan. A recent forensic study in the United Kingdom shows that over 85 per cent of all seized heroin in the UK was produced from Afghan opium; it is likely that similar proportions exist for other Western European countries.

Traditionally, opium and morphine base from Afghanistan have been trafficked through Pakistan and Iran to heroin laboratories in Eastern Turkey. There, the raw materials are processed into white high-grade heroin (heroin hydrochloride), which is then transported over the so-called Balkan route en route to consumer markets in Western Europe. The risk of trafficking drugs along the Balkan route has recently increased due to a strengthening of enforcement efforts in Iran, as reflected in the significant seizure totals mentioned above. This development, as well as similar trends in Pakistan, has elevated the importance of other trafficking channels. The northern routes through the Central Asian countries, for example, appear to have grown in significance. Part of the northern traffic finds its way through the Caucasus back into Turkey's heroin laboratories. There are increasing indications that heroin produced in northern Afghanistan is reaching Western Europe via Russia without going through Turkey. The illicit drug traffic through the Persian Gulf states seems to be on the increase as well, although to a somewhat lesser degree; shipments are intended for markets in the Arabian peninsula, Middle East, the United Kingdom and even the United States.

6. Central Asia's Increase in Drug Abuse

Only twenty years ago, heroin consumption was unknown in the Central Asian region. Opium consumption was carefully regulated according to social custom. Today, in contrast, countries such as Pakistan and Iran have some of the highest heroin addiction rates in the world. Central Asian countries, generally, show signs of rapidly increasing heroin abuse.

These developments can be attributed to the illicit drug trade that originates in nearby Afghanistan. Of course, the tremendous supply source gives rise to the spillover phenomenon. Furthermore, traffickers often pay for services in kind, thus fuelling a vicious cycle of abuse, dependence and drug peddling. A UNDCP study conducted in 1998 found that about 50 per cent of Afghanistan's opium production was consumed within the region.

According to one survey carried out by the authorities of Pakistan, 1.5 million people in the country are believed to consume heroin. Iran reports approximately 1.2 million drug addicts, of which about 450,000 are said to abuse heroin. No precise figures exist for Central Asia but there are indications that the number of heroin addicts in the region now exceeds the corresponding figure for Western Europe as a whole.

7. Considerations for the Future

In recent years, the main emphasis of strategies aimed at checking the flow of illicit drugs from Afghanistan has been on border control assistance to countries in the region; the international community has thus far been reluctant to support any programmes that tackle head on the cultivation of opium poppy *within* Afghanistan. For various reasons, the time may have arrived to reconsider this approach.

Border controls, in and of themselves, have rarely succeeded in substantially reducing the flow of illicit drugs over extended periods of time. Focusing on border controls, in isolation from other drug control measures, is akin to treating the symptoms of a chronic illness without addressing the underlying causes. An emerging consensus supports adjusting the focus of drug control efforts in Afghanistan so that the illicit cultivation of poppy, and the socio-economic needs that have given rise to it, can be addressed directly.

There are a number of reasons why 'internal' strategies might prove more effective in Afghanistan. First and foremost, the socio-economic forces that have spurred opium production in Afghanistan will not be sufficiently mitigated by interventions that seek to sever the multitude of trading channels between Afghanistan and the rest of the world. At the same time, as mentioned above, the income for farmers involved in illicit poppy cultivation in Afghanistan is low – profits generated at country level are minimal compared to earnings at global level. Combined with the fact that most farmers have only in the past two decades turned to poppy cultivation, this suggests that the involvement of small-scale farmers in Afghanistan's drug trade, while widespread, may not be deeply rooted. The entrenchment of viable alternatives, in this regard, could meet with results that would not be attainable in countries with longer traditions of, and deeper financial immersion in, poppy cultivation.

It is self-evident that permanent reductions in illicit poppy cultivation in Afghanistan will come about only insofar as today's growing areas are given the foundations of sustainable development. Indeed, 'alternative development' programmes should not be seen as distinct from conventional development programmes, but rather as extensions of them. It should be recognized that compared to law enforcement-oriented strategies that are funded in expectation of quick results, alternative development strategies must be designed and funded with a medium- to long-term planning horizon. In Pakistan, it took nearly fifteen years of development work to rid the Dir district of illicit poppy. The experience of Dir reinforced the view that, in order for illicit crop elimination programmes to be credible, there must be a long-term commitment by the international community to support drug control as part and parcel of development. Such long-term commitment is rarely in evidence today.

In Afghanistan, the main problem is the prospect of the Taliban becoming the de facto rulers of the country. Even in this age of global markets, international development programmes require a functioning state in order to be effective; this is true particularly for development efforts that are aimed at eradicating illicit poppy cultivation. Therefore, the question is: could the Taliban become acceptable partners in drug control matters? This is a political question that needs to be answered by the international community.

Editors' note

Michael von der Schulenburg wrote this text in the first half of 2000 before he left the United Nation Drug Control Program (UNDCP) for another assignment. In the meantime, during July 2001, the Taliban government stopped the poppy production in Afghanistan. UN secretary general Kofi Annan confirmed the '... almost total disappearance of opium poppy in areas controlled by the Taliban'.

From Holy War to Opium War?
A Case Study of the Opium Economy in North-Eastern Afghanistan[1]

Jonathan Goodhand

This paper examines the recent growth of the opium economy in north-eastern Afghanistan. A detailed analysis of one village in Badakhshan province reveals profound changes in the local economy and social institutions. The paper describes two major shifts in the local economy: (1) the switch from wheat to poppy cultivation and (2) the shift from the livestock trade to the opium trade. It then examines the underlying causes and impacts of the opium economy on social relations in the village. Although this is a case study of a community living on the margins of the global economy, it is argued that these changes have important implications for international policy-makers. The emergence of the opium economy in north-eastern Afghanistan is symptomatic of new and expanding forms of cross-border trade, associated with the restructuring of the global political economy.[2]

1. Introduction – Globalization and Conflict

Traditional neoclassical analysis of conflicts viewed them as irrational. Since aggregate consumption and production declines, comparative

---

[1] This article was previously published in *Central Asian Survey* 19(2), pp.265-280 and is reprinted here with the gracious permission of Taylor & Francis Company. For further information please contact http://www.tandf.co.uk.

[2] The research in Afghanistan was part of a wider DFID-funded research project conducted by University of Manchester/INTRAC on the role of NGOs in complex political emergencies. The findings in this paper are based on a field trip to the village of Deh Dehi in north-eastern Afghanistan. A team of international and Afghan researchers spent five days in the area interviewing villagers, before having to evacuate because of nearby fighting.

advantages are lost and capital destroyed, why do people behave so inexplicably (Goodhand and Hulme 1999)? However recent writings on conflict have developed new insights through the analysis of global processes that contribute to systemic conflict. Duffield (1988) argues that protracted conflict is symptomatic of new and expanding forms of political economy. Today's conflicts are characterized by long-term innovative adaptations to globalization, linked to expanding networks of parallel (illegal) and grey (semi-legal) economic activity.

As Keen notes, conflict is not the irrational breaking down of societies and economies: rather 'it is the re-ordering of society in particular ways. In wars we see the creation of a new type of political economy, not simply a destruction of the old one' (1997: 7). Elite strategies in war economies may, for example, involve the control and export of high-value commodities such as narcotics and precious stones (Duffield 1999b); the opium and lapis lazuli economies in northern Afghanistan are just two examples. Afghanistan may be on the periphery of the global economy, but elites within the country profit from state breakdown and the deregulated environment at a local and global level. It has created the space and linkages for local assets like opium and lapis to be realized on global markets.

Clausewitz characterized traditional nation-state-based war as the continuation of politics by other means. However, in many conflicts today, it may not be so much about winning the war as maintaining one's sphere of influence. As Keen concludes, internal forms of war may now be better understood as the continuation of economics by other means (Keen 1998). This analysis has important implications in terms of our understanding of contemporary conflicts and policy aimed at preventing or resolving endemic insecurity.

> ... in conflicts where violence is decentralised and economically motivated, war cannot simply be 'declared' or 'declared over'. A lasting end to violence is likely to depend on meeting many of the needs of those carrying out acts of violence as well as the needs and interests of some of the more highly developed actors, orchestrating and perhaps funding violence. (Berdal and Keen 1997)

I will return to the policy implications of this analysis at the end of the paper. The next section examines a case study of the opium economy in north-eastern Afghanistan. It is an attempt to present the 'view from the village' in terms of changes brought about by the opium economy and its impact on social relations. An analysis of these changes then follows, in the light of the recent writing and analysis on complex political emergencies (CPEs) as outlined above. Although there is an emerging body of writing on conflict and insecurity, which helps map out the broad terrain of the new world disorder, there is a lack of fine-grained[3] case studies which examine how global processes impact on local actors and communities. A key conclusion of our work in north-eastern Afghanistan is that action has got ahead of understanding and more detailed contextual analysis is important for both improved understanding and policy.

2. Background

2.1. The Afghan Conflict

The Afghan conflict is a potent example of contemporary conflict resulting from a complex mix of factors, caused by years of bad development, Cold War politics, militarization and tribal and ethnic schisms. The conflict has been going on for twenty years. In the 1980s one-third of the population was displaced and rural subsistence economies were deliberately destroyed. The withdrawal of Soviet troops in 1988 did not signal the end of the conflict. A process of 'Lebanonisation' followed in which the contradictions within the resistance movement surfaced (Roy 1989). The conflict thus mutated from a counter-insurgency war with an ostensibly ideological basis into one characterized by warlordism and banditry. Since 1995 the war entered a new phase with the emergence of the Taliban who now control around 80 per cent of Afghanistan, while the remaining area is controlled by an alliance of opposition leaders from the previous government.

It is beyond the scope of the paper to examine in detail the history and dynamics of the Afghan conflict. However, the following points will be relevant to the analysis.

---

[3] A term coined by Paul Richards (1996).

Conflict as Process

Conflict is a social process in which the original structural tensions are themselves profoundly reshaped by the massive disruptions of CPEs. As Tilly argues, 'war is a form of contention which creates new forms of contention' (Keen 1998: p14). The Afghan conflict needs to be seen as less the outcome of a predictable pattern of causes and effects and more as a result of combinations of contingent factors. During the course of the conflict there have been periods and regions of stability mixed with instability, and the boundaries of the conflict are constantly changing.

Systemic Nature of the Conflict

Received wisdom has it that Afghanistan has moved from a holy war into a civil war. The reality is far more complex; Afghanistan is part of a multi-layered and interdependent conflict system, in much the same way as the Great Lakes region is part of a wider zone of instability (Jones 1999). This conflict system is characterized by great volatility and constantly shifting alliances which have a ripple effect on the whole system. This applies externally in terms of the competing interests of the surrounding countries and internally in terms of the fluid and shifting alliances between the warring groups.

Far from being anarchic and irrational the conflict system is being directed and influenced by actors with clear strategic objectives. This applies at all levels, whether we are talking about the interests of Pakistan and Iran, warlords like Dostum and Massoud or local-level commanders. All have a stake in the current system.

The War Economy

A war economy has developed in Afghanistan, which means there are strong vested interests in the continuation of the current situation. As noted above, to a great extent non-state entities are competing with one another for the control of spheres of influence and resources, leading to the fragmentation of Afghanistan. Hard facts about how this economy functions are difficult to ascertain, although one can outline a number of broad defining features.

Kabul has become an economic and political backwater; Kandahar is now the Taliban's centre of power and most of the important transport and trading links of the provincial cities now radiate outwards to the neighbouring countries rather than inwards to Kabul. Cross-border trade has been a strong centrifugal influence leading to the peripheralization of the Afghan economy. The largest source of official revenue for the warring groups is customs duties from the smuggling trade between Pakistan, Iran and Central Asia, which uses Afghanistan as a land bridge. The war is now affecting the economies of all Afghanistan's neighbours.

Another important factor in the equation has been the competition between two oil companies, Bridas of Argentina and the US company UNOCAL, to build a gas pipeline across Afghanistan from Turkmenistan to Pakistan. UNOCAL has now pulled out of the initiative in response to US pressure.

A main source of unofficial revenue in Afghanistan is the drugs trade. Afghanistan has become the biggest producer of opium in the world. In 1998 opium production in Afghanistan rose by 9 per cent. The area under poppy cultivation was approximately 63,674 hectares, while it is estimated that dry opium produce was 3,269 tonnes. Many of the Afghan warlords have used drugs money to fund their military campaigns, while approximately 90 per cent of drugs production is currently taking place in Taliban-held areas.

Finally, it has been estimated that upwards of half a million people are directly dependent on war-related activities for their livelihood (Ostrom 1997). This includes men enlisted as soldiers in the main regional factions, as well as those operating at the district level under local commanders.

2.2 Badakhshan Province

At the time of writing, Badakhshan province is one of the few areas left under the control of the opposition forces of the Northern Alliance. It is a mountainous region bordering Tajikistan and has traditionally been peripheral, geographically, politically and economically, to Kabul. Badakhshan has always been one of the poorest areas in Afghanistan, relying on subsistence agriculture and trading. The main crops are wheat and barley. In most areas only one crop a year is possible, inputs are rarely used and yields are very low. Historically Badakhshan has been a food deficit area and vulnerable to food insecurity. Before the war local food production met only 50 per cent of the province's needs and at present it only meets one-third. The conflict has disrupted agricultural production and markets and destroyed basic infrastructure. During the Soviet period this area benefited from subsidized cereal imports but these were withdrawn in the early 1990s.

Tajiks are the majority ethnic group, but there are also a significant number of Uzbeks (who came from Central Asia in successive migrations in the last two centuries) and Pashtuns[4] (who were resettled in northern Afghanistan in the 1930s). At the time of writing, the province comes under the remit of Ahmad Shah Massoud's administration, the Shura-i Nizar, which has military and civil functions. The political context in Afghanistan has however always been characterized by shifting alliances and extreme fluidity (Kapila, Templer and Winter 1995). This means that the situation on the ground varies from district to district and from village to village. The level of security depends to a great extent on the status and power of the local commander and his relationships with the Shura-i Nizar and other commanders in the area.

2.3 Deh Dehi Village

Deh Dehi is a village of 138 households situated 20 km from the district centre of Faizabad. The road to the village was washed away by flash floods in 1997 and villagers travel to Faizabad by donkey or on foot. Deh Dehi originated 300 years ago when Uzbeks from Bukhara (now Uzbekistan) settled in the area.

It is still an Uzbek village – 'We belong to the same fathers, the same relatives and the same religion' (old man from Deh Dehi) – although the area is ethnically mixed with Uzbek and Tajik villages scattered around the district. Traditionally the economy of Deh Dehi has centred around agriculture – mainly wheat and barley – and livestock. However the local

---

[4] Pashtuns are the largest ethnic group in Afghanistan, constituting 40 per cent of the population. The Tajiks and Uzbeks are 20 and 6 per cent respectively of the total population of 20.1 million.

economy and the social structures of the village have been transformed by twenty years of conflict.

Violent conflict began in the area when the communists came into power in Kabul in 1978. Events in Badakhshan mirrored the growing divisions between the Islamists and communists at the national level. An uprising amongst the intellectuals in Faizabad was put down ruthlessly by the government and fighting spread when the Russian forces came into the area in the early 1980s. A Russian camp was located on the hill behind Deh Dehi and there was often shelling and firing into the village as the Mujahidin fought with the communist forces. Many of the people in the village were conscripted to fight with the Mujahidin.

The villagers were caught between the two warring parties; during the daytime the army demanded water and food from the village while at night the Mujahidin would come and ask for fighting men and for food. The communist forces eventually retreated from the area and then followed a period of infighting between the two political parties of the Hizb-i Islami and Jam'iat-i Islami. The last five years, however, have been relatively peaceful, with the area being under the control of the local Hizbi commander: 'Now that the Russians have left, we have a good life. We can walk around outside at midnight and move from village to village without any problems' (mullah in Deh Dehi).

3. Poppy Cultivation and the Opium Trade

Although wheat farming and livestock trading are still important sources of livelihood, over the last seven years, poppy cultivation and the opium trade have become the key economic activities in the village. Now virtually all the irrigated land is given over to poppy cultivation, and most of the men who would previously have been involved in the livestock trade are either involved in the opium trade or working overseas.

One farmer estimated that he could get 1,000 to 2,000 lakhs annual profit from poppy cultivation, compared to 20 lakhs if he cultivated wheat. Women from Deh Dehi commented: 'Just recently, people's lives have improved because of the cultivation of opium. Now people have two to three sets of clothes and many household goods.'

Shopkeepers from Deh Dehi or traders from outside buy resin from farmers and then transport it to the border of Tajikistan. Here the resin is sold to dealers linked into the Central Asian mafia networks. The journey to the Tajik border is very arduous and dangerous and it is a trade monopolized by young men. Although the dangers are real (one man from the village recently had $1500 stolen) the profits are great; it is estimated that opium which is sold at the farm-gate for $25 per kg has already reached $3000 by the time it reaches the border with Central Asia (Johnson 1998). With the capital gained from the trade many of these men have invested in small shops and businesses in Deh Dehi. Ten years before, there were only four shops in Deh Dehi and now there are over twenty and many of them are seasonal, based upon the currency of opium resin.

The opium economy is controlled and taxed by local commanders. Villagers have traditionally paid two forms of Islamic tax: *zakat* which is a tax of 2.5 per cent on capital and given to the poor and *'ushr* which is a tithe, or tax on income, that went to the state. Both of these taxes now go to the local militia or *jabha*: 'Before the war everyone gave *'ushr* and *zakat* directly to poor people. During the war we cooked food and sent it to the Mujahidin and now our *'ushr* and *zakat* go directly to the *jabha* (villager from Deh Dehi).

The following article from the Itar Tass news agency gives an indication of the scale and quasi-feudal nature of the opium economy in Badakhshan:

> A stable rise in illegal drug trafficking across the Tajik–Afghan border to smuggle narcotics to other CIS countries and Western Europe is a serious threat to the common interests of the Russian Federation and Tajikistan, Lieutenant-General Nikolai Reznichenko, commander of Russian border troops in Tajikistan, told a news conference here on Sunday.
>
> To substantiate his words, the Russian general noted that 135 attempts at crossing the border, mostly by smugglers, were thwarted by border guards. The number of armed clashes increased as compared with the last year. In 1998, 35 transgressors were killed and seven wounded as a result of 40 armed clashes with smugglers.
>
> According to Reznicheko, the Moskovsky and Pyandzh sections of the Tajik–Afghan border remain the main areas for smuggling narcotics. According to border guards, several dozen tonnes of drugs, including about two tonnes of pure heroin, are hoarded at these sections on the Afghan territory. The general stressed that border guards detain smugglers at these sections almost every day.

Afghan drug barons now send threats to commanders of border posts, promising to murder them if border guards continue sealing off smuggling paths. (Dushanbe, 24 January 1998)

4. Factors Behind the Emergence of the Opium Economy

Badakhshan has a long tradition of poppy cultivation having come from China and Bukhara via the silk route. Parts of Badakhshan have a high rate of drug dependency, although this does not appear to be the case in Deh Dehi. Why then has opium only in recent years become a central part of the local economy? The answer to this question lies in processes at the international, national and local levels.

4.1 International Level

The end of the Cold War and the final collapse of the communist government in Kabul marked an important shift in the Afghan conflict. Declining levels of external patronage (in comparison to the mid-1980s) forced the warring parties increasingly to develop their own means of economic sustainability. This meant moving beyond the Afghan state in pursuit of wider alternative networks in the regional or global market. Similar strategies have been employed by non-state warring groups elsewhere, from UNITA in Angola to Charles Taylor in Liberia:

While globalisation and liberalisation have not caused these new forms of instability, market deregulation has made it easier for warring parties to develop the parallel or grey international linkages necessary for survival. (Duffield 1999a)

The drugs trade, which now accounts for an estimated 8 per cent of world trade, can to an extent be linked to the breakdown of superpower patronage and control. In spite of a Northern consensus for elimination, the trade is growing and benefits from a deregulated global environment (Duffield 1999a).

At a regional level, the opium trade in north-eastern Afghanistan has profited from the erosion of strong central authority in neighbouring Tajikistan. The increased porosity of the border with Central Asia and the growth of mafia networks have created the space and linkages necessary for the trade to flourish. In recent years, border controls with Pakistan and Iran have been tightened up, so much of the trade now uses routes through Central Asia.

4.2 National Level

A number of factors which encouraged the growth of the opium economy are a direct consequence of the conflict, while others are rooted in long-term processes that preceded the war.

The Collapsed State

Although one should not exaggerate the power and reach of the pre-war Afghan state, it did play an important law and order function. – 'Life was peaceful in Zahir Shah's and Daoud's time. In that time the doors of our houses were never closed, even at night' (women from Deh Dehi). – Villagers talked about the periods of King Zahir Shah and Daoud in the 1960s and 1970s as a time when the state was more powerful. They claimed to remember government soldiers burning poppy crops. Some described strategies they employed to avoid detection, for example planting wheat around the outside of fields and poppy in the middle. In general, therefore, the state appears to have played an important law enforcement role in relation to poppy cultivation.

A second important factor was the removal of state subsidies for wheat in Badakhshan with the collapse of the Najibullah government in 1992. This, combined with the disruption of the wheat supply from neighbouring Kunduz province, led to sharp rises in wheat prices and probably precipitated the switch by poor farmers from wheat to high-value poppy production.[5]

---

[5] Interview with Paul Clarke, World Food Programme, 15 Nov. 1998.

From Holy War to Opium War?

Filling the Power Vacuum: The Role of Commanders

The collapse of the state has created a power vacuum that has been filled at the provincial and local level by alternative military and political structures. Political parties and commanders have emerged as the new leadership during the course of the war.[6] The military structure created by the commanders is known locally as the *jabha* and it depends on recruitment of local men (about 30 per cent of the young men from Deh Dehi are involved with the *jabha*) and taxation of the population. Leadership has come with the gun (as opposed to consent) and commanders have a vested interest in the continuation of weak central authority in which there are few restraining influences on their local 'fiefdoms'.

Although in Badakhshan there is a provincial administration of sorts – the Shura-i Nizar – in practice it lacks the legitimacy or finance to perform public functions. In reality, spheres of influence are franchised out to local-level commanders who are responsible for generating much of their own income locally. The opium economy is an important source of revenue. The Hizbi commander, for instance, who controls Deh Dehi and the surrounding district benefits directly from the opium trade, through taxation of the farmers and traders. Far from being actively discouraged, as in the past, farmers are now encouraged to grow poppy with the provision of softer loans from money lenders.

4.3 Village Level

Economic and Environmental Pressures

At the village level, important factors behind the development of poppy cultivation are economic and environmental pressures, which predate, but have been aggravated by, the conflict. The population of Deh Dehi has increased steadily from around forty households at the beginning of the

---

[6] At the time of writing, Badakhshan was still under the control of the forces of the Northern Alliance. In other parts of the country where the Taliban are in control, the power of local-level commanders has been circumscribed.

twentieth century to its present population of 138: 'When our children become bigger, the land will not be enough for us all. There are no other jobs for our sons, what will they do?' (women from Deh Dehi).

Land scarcity (about one-third of the population is landless) is a growing problem and a source of conflict. For example, recently there was armed conflict with a neighbouring village over the use of pasture land. Common property resources have been eroded due to intense competition for scarce resources and the breakdown of traditional rules and regulations for managing these resources. Destructive floods in the spring have contributed to severe soil erosion and the decreased productivity of the land. All these factors have contributed to growing poverty in the village. The conflict has further increased people's vulnerability because they can no longer take their livestock to Kabul – the animal trade was a major source of income before the war.

> Livestock used to be a good source of income but now the pastures and markets have been destroyed (farmer from Deh Dehi).

Villagers have few economic options beyond labour migration (about 25 per cent of the young men are involved in labouring work outside the village), joining the *jabha* or cultivating poppies. Money lenders are prepared to provide loans on relatively good terms for opium production. Moreover poppies require less irrigation than wheat, the residue provides fuel for the winter,[7] it has medicinal value, the oil is used for cooking and oil cake for winter fodder and finally the opium resin is high-value and easily transportable – an important factor considering the bottle-neck of the road from Deh Dehi.

The poppy has evidently been an important factor in mitigating the impacts of conflict, poverty and environmental degradation, at least in the short term. It is doubtful, given the advantage of the poppy compared to other crops, whether farmers could be persuaded to switch back to, say, improved varieties of wheat. Farm-gate prices for the poppy have a great deal of elasticity; if an NGO tried for example to introduce improved

---

[7] One farmer interviewed said that the dried poppy stalks from his fields provided fuel for up to six months of the year, an important consideration since fuel takes up a quarter of the family income.

varieties of wheat, the traders would simply increase the buying price for poppy because their profit margins are so great already.

Increased Contact with the Outside World

Another factor behind the growth of the opium trade in Deh Dehi is the widespread displacement and migration caused by the war and economic stress. Many of the villagers of Deh Dehi were refugees and economic migrants in Pakistan and Iran. In Pakistan, in particular, through contact with other refugees and Pakistani businessmen, they saw the potential and profitability of poppy cultivation. Many of the younger men came back to the village and started poppy cultivation. Though it is still in many ways an isolated, inward-looking village, the conflict has increasingly opened its doors to the outside world.

> We have more contacts with outsiders now. We feel like a silk worm coming out of its pupa. (White beard – village elder)
>
> When I came back I compared my village to Pakistan, where I saw good conditions and development like roads and big buildings. I looked at my village and it was like a graveyard. (Young religious leader)

5. Impacts on the Village

The transition to the opium economy has played an important role in transforming social relations in the village.

> Before the population was much smaller and people relied on agriculture. There was less money and there was no trade or business. Now the population is large, agriculture is not sufficient and trade has developed (young man).

5.1 Wealth Distribution

The opium economy has created new tensions within the village in terms of how wealth is produced and distributed. It has created a 'new rich': the young men involved in the opium trade and the commanders who tax and control it.

> Some of our relatives have become rich through trade and smuggling and their lives have changed. My husband is old and he can't do these things. Some of them were our shepherds but now they won't even invite us to social occasions because we are so poor (Woman in Deh Dehi).

The conflict and the opium economy have therefore restructured economic and social relationships.

5.2 Village Leadership and Institutions

In many respects villages institutions and leadership have proved to be remarkably resilient and adaptable to the changing context. It has been argued that civil society in Afghanistan has reasserted itself during the course of the conflict:

> As a result of the decade and a half of successful local community-based resistance struggles, civil society, especially in non-Pashtun territories of northern, central and western Afghanistan has been re-established and is today much stronger than ever before. (Sharani 1998: 232)

Afghan civil society is not made up of formal, rule-based organizations à la Putnam (Putnam, Leonard and Nanett 1993), but consists of a complex web of informal, norm-based networks: 'Power in Afghan peasant society resides neither in a specific locality nor in a person, but in an elusive network which needs constant maintenance and reconstruction' (Roy 1986: 22).

In Deh Dehi traditional leadership and networks still function effectively. The white beards and the *nimayanda* (village representative) are still the gate-keepers between the village and the outside world. They are responsible for collecting taxes and organizing recruitment for the *jabha*. They also resolve disputes and organize the community for public works like road construction. On the face of it, the survival of these institutions indicate that social fabric has not been a casualty of the conflict; relationships of trust and reciprocity and local associational life have been sufficiently resilient to adapt to the new environment.

However, as already mentioned, it is mainly the young men who control the opium trade and who own the shops in the village. Although this, as yet, has not led to conflict with the traditional leaders in the village, it is evident that tensions are likely to increase. Not surprisingly, the young and the old have very different perceptions of recent changes in the village. The following comments were made by old men:

> Life was simple then. The only food was bread, qurot and tea. Everyone worked on their own land.

efore if the elders said something everyone would listen but now the young men don't respect them. If they want something they do it even if that means killing someone. It's everyone for themselves now.

And these by young men:

People have been to other places and they are more broad-minded and educated now.

Life is better now than in the past. People are working and trading. Before people just grew wheat and led simple lives.

Money was scarce before, but now people have money because of poppy cultivation.

The opium economy has also consolidated the position of the local commanders. It has enabled them to pay for the *jabha* and to maintain and extend their patronage networks. There is, however, little respect for this local leadership since it lacks accountability and reciprocity:

Sometimes the people are asked to work to build a school or bridge or something and then the money goes to the pocket of the commanders or one or two of the elders who are close to the commanders. (Young man)

Although at the time of the research, leaders from the Northern Alliance were in the area trying to mobilize anti-Taliban support, the response from villagers was very sceptical: 'People feel that when we start fighting, all the leaders will run away to Tajikistan.'

5.3 Social Capital[8]

Redistributive mechanisms have been and still are very important in mitigating the effects of the conflict. Interviews with villagers, particularly with women, presented a consistent picture of sharing within the extended family. Redistribution within the extended family is a risk-spreading strategy that has been adapted to the conflict. Many families, during the jihad years for example, might have one family member with the Mujahidin, another with the communists, while others stayed in Deh Dehi

---

[8] We use Putnam's definition of social capital as 'features of social organisation, such as networks, norms and trust, that facilitate co-ordination and co-operation for mutual benefit' (Putnam, Leonard and Nanett 1993). Such norms and networks constitute endowments of capital for societies. Conversely, where norms and networks of civic engagement are lacking, as is often the case in internal wars, the potential for collective action would appear to be limited.

or went to Pakistan as refugees or migrant labour (see Glatzer 1998). This helped spread risk in both economic and political terms. Interviews with villagers indicate the persistence of family- and kin-based loyalties and the strength of Afghan systems of mutual support and informal social security.

The resilience of village institutions and networks also indicates that levels of co-operation, trust and reciprocity may not have been adversely affected by the war. The communal irrigation system, for example, organized by the *mirab* (controller of the water system) still functions effectively. This demonstrates that there are still sufficient endowments of social capital for community action when it is clearly in everyone's economic interests to co-operate. Also the mosque is still very much the heart of the village; it constitutes a place for religious worship, a meeting place to swap news, a space where elders come to discuss problems and resolve conflicts, and finally somewhere to accommodate strangers.

Although there is this evidence of resilient coping mechanisms and continuity with the past, there are also signs that these institutions and relationships are beginning to show the strain:

Before the war there was respect and we helped our neighbours. But now if your neighbours die no one will even acknowledge it. Everybody is out for themselves these days. The war has also had a bad effect on relations between fathers and sons.

A number of respondents mentioned changes in the relationship between fathers and sons; sons who had been to Pakistan or Iran or fought in the *jabha* were less inclined to listen to their fathers. Now it was becoming more common practice for sons, once they were married, to move into a separate house with their own family. Villagers also talked about the decline of *hashar* – voluntary communal activity such as helping with a farmer's harvest, or building a house. Now people are either too poor or those who have worked outside the village are used to being paid for their labour.

Other indicators of a move from co-operative to more self-interested, if not predatory forms of behaviour include the payment of *'ushr* and *zakat* directly to the commander rather than redistributing it to the poor. The erosion of common property resources like grazing lands indicates the breakdown of traditional rules and rights of usage.

Finally, as mentioned earlier, contact with the outside world has had an impact on people's attitudes and behaviour. Young boys who were trained in the *madares* (religious schools) in Pakistan brought back ideas about Islam that are often at odds with the 'folk Islam' of traditional Afghan villages. The present mullah was one such boy. This again has increased intergenerational tensions: 'I went to the mosque to pray this morning and I could see that the children didn't feel comfortable with the way I was praying' (old man from Deh Dehi).

5.4 Gender Relations

Existing gender roles appear to be very resistant to change. However, there are contradictory forces at play in terms of gender relations; on the one hand, there appears to be a 'Taliban effect', even in areas which are not under the control of the Taliban. This is manifest in more conservative attitudes towards religion and freedom for women. On the other hand, as already mentioned, the conflict has opened the doors of the village to the outside world. Women have moved with their families to Pakistan and taken on new economic roles. Poppy cultivation, for example, is very labour-intensive and women now play an important role in this.

6. Implications for Policy and Practice

This paper has attempted to explore the development of the opium economy in north-eastern Afghanistan from the perspective of Afghan villagers living in Deh Dehi. This, we hope, responds to the need for more fine-grained case studies, which link the emerging thinking on the political economy of war with an analysis of what is happening on the ground. The voice and agency of communities living in the thrall of conflict is frequently missing from analysis and policy.

Our research is based on 'the view from the village', which is both its strength and its weakness. On the one hand, we may have been able, at least partially, to penetrate the 'mud curtain'.[9] This has provided insights

---

[9] Dupree 1980. Dupree coined the phrase 'the mud curtain' to describe how Afghan

into how a community has adapted to and responded to war and new forms of political economy. On the other hand, the focus on one individual village means that one should be wary of drawing wider conclusions, particularly in Afghanistan where every valley has its own unique history and microclimate. However, we still feel that it is possible to map out some tentative conclusions which are pertinent to the emerging discourse on the political economy of conflict:

1. There has been a systemic change in the economy of Badakhshan

Based on the evidence of Deh Dehi, the drug economy clearly provides many livelihoods and incomes in the context of an enduring conflict. The shift from wheat to opium cultivation and from the livestock trade to the opium trade has been a remarkably rapid transition and a large number of people now have an important stake in this economy; from the poor farmer, to the opium trader and shopkeeper, to the commander who controls and taxes the trade. Their involvement in this economy is perfectly rational, given the lack of alternatives and the lucrative nature of the opium trade.

2. The growth of the opium economy is linked to processes of globalization and the collapse of the nation state

This systemic shift in the local political economy is symbiotically linked to the processes of globalization and the collapse of the nation state. The collapse of the Afghan state has created a power vacuum that has been filled at the local level by commanders. At the same time the decline of superpower patronage has meant two things. First, controls on non-state entities have declined. Second, these non-state entities have increasingly had to generate their own resources to service their military activities and maintain their patronage networks. These processes have coincided with the erosion of state authority in Tajikistan, the rise of Central Asian mafia networks and the increased porosity of the border with Tajikistan. All these factors have enabled Afghan drug barons to link into and profit from the global drugs trade. As Duffield notes, warlords may act locally but they think globally.

---

villagers managed to protect themselves from the incursions of the state.

3. This is not just a transitional phase: 'normal service will not be resumed shortly'

Afghanistan is in many ways the archetypal intra-state conflict, characterized by its longevity, socially divisive nature and its external support and trade networks. The opium economy in Badakhshan is a classic example of the growth of parallel or cross-border trade in zones of instability. Duffield characterizes cross-border trade as follows:

- It is a mercantilistic activity which is largely uninterested in long-term productive investment.
- It is involved with controlling and apportioning wealth.
- Profit depends on maintaining differences and discrete forms of control.
- The dynamics of cross-border trade are likely to encourage informal protectionism. In many respects it has illiberal, quasi-feudal tendencies.

These points all clearly characterize the opium trade in Afghanistan. An important point to make here is that peace would disrupt the systems of production and exchange that provide such warlords and their followers with livelihoods. Peace is not in their interests, nor is it a viable option.

4. Implications for policy-makers: the need for coherence

Although there is a growing body of writing on the political economy and functions of conflict systems, there is limited evidence that this has been absorbed into mainstream analysis and policy. As Dufffield notes, policy and thinking still appears to be based on a 'break-down' model of conflict which assumes that war is somehow irrational and chaotic. This is particularly the case in Afghanistan. Kaplan's (1994) apocalyptic vision of the 'coming anarchy' is frequently invoked with regard to Afghanistan. Similarly, media coverage of the Taliban reinforces the view that the country has descended into barbarism.

While most policy-makers and practitioners involved with Afghanistan have a more nuanced analysis of the problem than Kaplan or the tabloid press, important gaps in understanding are manifest at different levels and locations within the aid system; whether it is UN diplomats frustrated at their inability to get warring factions round the negotiating table to iron out their differences, or the UNDCP official wondering why poor Afghan farmers will not switch from growing the poppy to improved wheat, there is a lack of analysis of the incentives systems and structures which support violence and the war economy.

We still hear a familiar refrain from the international community of the need for the 'set piece response' of calling a cease fire, forming a broad-based government[10] and holding elections. This would be accompanied by a 'developmental fix' of social reconstruction assistance. How this peace package will address the interests of the non-state entities is not clear, since they have little interest in or need for a unitary Afghan state.

5. Action has got ahead of understanding

As mentioned at the beginning of this paper, in many respects action has got ahead of understanding. There are a number of 'black holes' in our understanding and analysis. These include an understanding of the coping strategies of the perpetrators of violence as well as those of the victims. We have limited knowledge for example about the operation of parallel and grey economies and the political economy of warlordism. This paper would have benefited from additional information and direct interviews with commanders in Afghanistan and the drugs mafia in Central Asia; these are areas about which very little is known or written, yet they are critical to our understanding of contemporary conflict.

In the aid world more of a premium is put on doing than on knowing or understanding (Duffield 1998). This is partly because careers in aid work tend to be broad (emergency services in Nicaragua last year, monitoring in Kosovo this year, refugee camps in Pakistan next year) rather than deep (learning a language, knowing the history, having long-term personal networks). Interestingly (and at the risk of being politically incorrect), the first fine-grained studies of Afghans living on what is now the Afghan–Pakistan border were conducted by British colonialists. The British army

---

[10] As one aid donor caustically remarked, 'we don't need a broad-based government, just a broad-minded one!'

offered higher salaries to those officers who could learn local languages and culture; in the nineteenth century this incentive led to social descriptions, collections of folk tales and proverbs and numerous grammars and dictionaries.[11]

A key conclusion of our work in north-eastern Afghanistan is that action has got ahead of understanding and more detailed contextual analysis is important for both improved understanding and policy.

Bibliography

Berdal, Mats and Keen, David (1997) Violence and Economic Agendas in Civil Wars: Some Policy Implications. *Millennium: Journal of International Studies* 26(3): 795.

Duffield, Mark (1998) *Aid Policy and Post Modern Conflict: A Critical Review.* Occasional paper 19. Birmingham, School of Public Policy, University of Birmingham.

Duffield, Mark (1999a) Globalisation and War Economies: Promoting Order or the Return of History? Draft paper prepared for the Fletcher Forum of World Affairs issue on the Geography of Confidence: Environments, Populations and Boundaries, Feb. (8pp.).

Duffield, Mark (1999b) Reading Development as Security: Post-Nation State Conflict and Reconstructing Normality. Draft paper presented at the conference on NGOs in a Global Future, University of Birmingham.

Dupree, Louis (1980) *Afghanistan.* Princeton, Princeton University Press.

Glatzer, Bernt (1998) Is Afghanistan on the Brink of Ethnic and Tribal Disintegration? In: William Maley (ed.) *Fundamentalism Reborn? Afghanistan and the Taliban.* Lahore, Vanguard Books:167-181.

Goodhand, Jonathan, and Hulme, David (1999) From War to Complex Political Emergencies: Understanding Conflict and Peace-Building in the New World Disorder. *Third World Quarterly* 20(1): 13-26.

---

[11] Grima 1992. A similar point is made by Duffield (1998: 94).

Grima, Benedicte (1992) *The Performance of Emotion Among Paxtun Women.* Oxford, Oxford University Press.

Johnson, C. (1998) *Afghanistan: A Land in Shadow.* Oxford, Oxfam.

Jones, B. (1999) A Partnership Perspective on: 'Doing Development in Complex Political Emergencies: Perils and Possibilities'. Paper presented at NGOs and the Global Future conference in Birmingham, Jan.

Kapila, M., Templer, G., and Winter, E. (1995) *Review of British Aid to Afghanistan.* London, ODI, June.

Kaplan, Robert (1994) The Coming Anarchy, *The Atlantic Monthly* 273(2): 44-76.

Keen, David (1997) The Political Economy of War. In: F. Stewart (ed.) *The Social and Economic Costs of Conflict in Developing Countries.* London, ESCOR, DFID.

Keen, David (1998) The Economic Functions of Violence in Civil Wars. *Adelphi Paper, 320.* London, International Institute of Strategic Studies: 1-88.

Ostrom, K. (1997) *Understanding the Economy of Afghanistan: An Exploratory Study.* London, SIDA, Jan.

Putnam, R. with Leonard, R. and Nanett, R. Y. (1993) *Making Democracy Work: Civic Traditions in Modern Italy.* Princetown, Princeton University Press.

Richards, Paul (1996) *Fighting for the Rain Forest: War, Youth and Resources in Sierra Leone.* Oxford, James Currey.

Roy, Olivier (1986) *Islam and the Resistance in Afghanistan.* Cambridge, Cambridge University Press.

Roy, Olivier (1989) Afghanistan: Back to Tribalism or on to Lebanon? *Third World Quarterly* 11(4): 70-82.

Shahrani, M. Nazif (1998) The Future of the State and the Structure of Community Governance in Afghanistan. In: William Maley (ed.) *Fundamentalism Reborn? Afghanistan and the Taliban.* Lahore, Vanguard Books: 212-242.

Part V

Political Formation

Afghanistan's Road to Failure

Reinhard Schlagintweit

The subject of this volume, 'Country without State?', puts the focus on the actual condition of Afghanistan. It is a statement as well as a question. Is it true? There are many facts that confirm it, but there are others that cast doubt. Facts which at first sight seem unequivocal can be judged in different ways depending on the aspect from which they are seen.

What do we mean by 'Country without State'? Obviously one – extreme – form of this political phenomenon is a country in anarchy, a region without recognizable law and order. 'Country without State' can also point to a country with too little or very weak civil order. We may also give this label to a country which, while possessing a government and enjoying reasonable civic order, refuses to observe the conventional norms of state behaviour: to accept responsibility for the rule of law, to observe international regulations, to fight crime. When we look at these characteristics, we find two variables. An objective one is the availability or lack of governance and structure; if they are missing, there is not a state but chaos. The other variable is predominantly subjective: the observance or neglect of standards which are valid for the person or institution passing the judgement; if these standards are violated, the country is considered a threat to peace and stability.

In Afghanistan we find elements of both characteristics. Today Afghanistan is neither an anarchy nor a totally criminal state. However, the enduring civil war and the primitive form of its administration has created a state of near chaos. International order has been overthrown. Universally accepted rules for governance are being neglected, measured both by the yardstick of the international community and by the needs and expectations of the Afghan population.

For the United States and other countries, Afghanistan is one of the 'rogue states'. They blame the country's leadership for neglecting fundamental rules of international behaviour; promoting a dangerous form of international terrorism; refusing to cooperate politically with the United Nations, and producing 50 per cent of the world's and 80 per cent of heroin consumed in Europe. To a large extent these reproaches are justified. They relate to forms of behaviour which are typical of the postmodern phenomenon of the weak, failing state.

The verdict that Afghanistan is not a state in our meaning of the word is mainly based on the shortcomings of its administration and the lack of normal standards of care for its population. I intend to discuss here mainly the internal aspects of the Taliban's deficiencies.

1. The Deficiency of the Rule of the Taliban

Even if we take into consideration the ravages of twenty years of war, the Taliban's indifference to the needs of their subjects cannot be condoned. The simplest social services are missing. The educational system has collapsed and is being reactivated only in the most rudimentary manner. Hospitals and health services are decaying. Doctors, teachers and officials get no pay, or receive just a pittance. Ministries more often than not are empty and lack qualified personnel; offers of humanitarian assistance are being handled arbitrarily or impeded. The authorities do not seem to have any regard for the people's need for basic supplies and services. Legal – and illegal – revenues are mainly used for armed struggle, probably not only in Afghanistan itself.

Minorities suffer badly. They are displaced, starved, resettled or in other ways suppressed. In some cases, armed conflict might have caused these violations of basic rights. But when the fighting ended, the Taliban did not try to heal wounds inflicted by battle or to reconcile the ethnic and religious groups they had fought. After having conquered virtually the whole country, they continued to behave like a party still fighting for power, not like a victorious movement. Nor did the Taliban consider plans for the reconstruction of the country's infrastructure and administration or for its economic development.

Serious observers conclude that the Taliban tended to ignore the state level altogether. They seemed to lack the political will and the maturity necessary for ruling a country. Nobody listened to the grievances of the people, defined their interests and helped them to solve their problems.

2. 'State' Criteria

It is nevertheless questionable if all this really is sufficient to justify the charge that Afghanistan is a country 'without a state'. Recently I discussed this question with a former Afghan politician. He had spent some time in Pol-e-Charki prison and views present-day conditions in Afghanistan very critically. He objected to the assumption that Afghanistan is not a state. In his view the Taliban's rule complied with the essential components of state required by traditional Islamic law: a legal order which is somehow being enforced; a currency and a tax system; and a ruler who exercises power.

This argument must be taken seriously. These are convictions held by many Afghans inside and outside the country. They highlight the cultural differences that separate us in the West from many serious Muslims. From our point of view, Afghanistan may fit into the category of 'failed state'. But according to traditional standards, the Taliban had good reasons to consider their rule as legitimate and demand loyalty and recognition

Another argument can also help us to pass a less sweeping verdict: where the Taliban were victorious, they restored law and order, often for the first time in years. It is true that in many cases conquest was accompanied by shocking cruelties, particularly in the Hazarajat, in Mazar-i Sharif, in Shomali; that is why in parts of the country the Taliban were and still are considered an occupation force. But the majority of people under their rule profited from the return of stable conditions. The pacification of the country allowed farmers to till their land. According to the UNHCR four million refugees returned. The supply of goods greatly improved. So did protection against arbitrary violence and looting. A great number of people had good reasons to prefer the 'weak state' situation to the anarchy that prevailed during the first years of the civil war.

This is true also for the city of Kabul. There, minorities were still being discriminated against, women were not permitted to move about freely, to work or to earn a living. But the times of lawlessness, of violence, of arbitrary destruction prevalent during the power struggle between post-communist warlords belonged to the past.

3. The Lack of Alternatives

We tend to complain about the shortcomings of the Taliban's governance, the de facto government of nine-tenths of the country. But the question needs to be answered: is there an alternative to the Taliban? It is not difficult to condemn a bad state of affairs and to wish that things were better. It is a different matter, however, to discover whether this state can be changed and, if so, whether an alternative really would be preferable.

Under the circumstances at the middle of the year 2001 there seemed to be three theoretical possibilities for a different rule in Afghanistan.

Improved Model of the Taliban

Out of their ranks emerges a more progressive leader or a moderate group, splits the movement and becomes its leader. The new leadership rises to power, replaces the present *shura* and introduces a better, more enlightened policy.

There has never been convincing evidence that such a change could happen. Occasional reports suggested that inside the Taliban movement less radical forces were to be found – reasonable governors and ministers, a Kabul group more open to the UN's efforts for peacemaking. But those trends have not developed a political profile. The Taliban never were a disciplined, tightly structured movement; but the authority of their leader, Mullah 'Omar, always seemed uncontested. There was no reason for assuming that the Taliban possessed a reservoir of rationality, modernity and responsibility from which a new national leadership could emerge.

Reinvigorated Opposition

If the parties of the Northern Alliance and the groups abroad had agreed on common strategies and common goals they could have been a much more formidable military power and a convincing partner for negotiations. This never happened.

A preferred option is the return of the monarchy with either the former king or a younger member of the royal family as an integrating force. This alternative has often been discussed. The old king and the institution of monarchy still enjoy a certain amount of popularity with the Afghan population. But on the political level the monarchy has no real chance. It has never been promoted with great energy, and it does not appeal to a significant majority of the Afghan parties inside and outside the country. Many groups oppose it because of the royal family's overtures to the Soviet Union in the 1960s and 1970s. During recent years this solution has become even more unlikely, since many groups, particularly the Taliban, would for religious as well as political reasons never accept a king as head of state.

Military Victory of the Anti-Taliban Coalition

The Northern Alliance is being supported by powerful allies: Iran, Russia, Uzbekistan. Until 1996 they ruled large parts of the country, but since then it has become less thinkable that they could profit from weaknesses of the Taliban and conquer Kabul and the majority of the provinces. One can never exclude a sudden implosion. But would the Alliance be able to survive a victory? This is very unlikely.

Moreover, would this coalition really be an improvement to the *shura* of Mullah 'Omar? Doubts have to do with the dimension which the ethnic element in inter-Afghan fighting has assumed in the last ten years. Observers who worked in Afghanistan in 1992, when the civil war had just started, were already convinced that the country's disintegration into ethnically defined areas had become inevitable. None of the political rivals was prepared to accept any political solution but exclusive power for himself and his own ethnically defined group (Schetter 2001). In the meantime, ethnic dissent has multiplied. The various groups are increasingly driven by fears based on experience and will not tolerate rule by any other ethnicity. All efforts by the United Nations to find a road to peace have so far been wrecked by those obstacles.

Even today, after twenty years of devastating war, there is no indication that the Afghan parties are seriously ready for compromise. Nor that, once in possession of power, they would be better able to administer

Afghanistan. I am not optimistic that the new efforts presently undertaken to convene a *loya jirga* will succeed. A durable rule by the northern coalition must remain a utopia. This is also true for the – hypothetically – best answer to the patchwork composition of this multi-ethnic state, a federation. As a consequence we have to accept that the present character of the Afghan state has a high degree of socio-political inevitability.

4. The Lack of an Elite

When in 1994 the Taliban started to clean up the fiefdoms of local warlords or to integrate them, they were hailed as a saving force. Their radical kind of Islam and the prospect of a broadly based, unified rule met the wishes of the population and the expectations of foreign countries. They all hoped that the Taliban would end the civil war.

The Taliban would not have been able quickly to pacify large parts of the country had they only been the product of chance or the Pakistani ISI. I do not want to minimize the contribution of Pakistan's 'services' to the Taliban's conquests. Their support was no doubt an important factor. However, victorious movements like this cannot be fabricated and, particularly in Afghanistan, cannot for a long time manipulated from the outside. The Taliban represented values and traditions characteristic of the actual conditions in the country. The weaknesses and deficiencies of their rule did not seem to be the result of bad faith on the part of any particular power group. It is more likely that they represented the impotence of the country as a whole.

The Taliban did not offer valid answers to the needs and challenges of Afghanistan, therefore they are in all likelihood a transitory phenomenon. However, provisional arrangements in other parts of the world teach us that temporary solutions can be very persistent. We have seen how difficult it is to find alternatives to the Taliban rule. For this reason we cannot exclude the possibility that the political and social conditions which they inherited or created will for an extended period of time dominate the fate of Afghanistan.

One of the main reasons responsible for this state of affairs is the absence of a political and cultural elite. Afghanistan is a country without an elite. Practically the whole of its civil society lives abroad. In several waves –

1974, 1978, during the Soviet occupation and even in the 1990s – nearly all academics, intellectuals, high officials and leading businessmen left Kabul, the city where most of them lived. The great families in the provinces and many tribal chiefs followed. This was more than a blood-letting, this was a bleeding to death, the complete loss of that part of the population which normally produces political, administrative, cultural and economic leaders. Unless political and economic conditions improve decisively I doubt that even 10 or 20 per cent of those several hundred thousand well-trained Afghans living in Western or Asian countries will return and help to rebuild their home country. They will at best be available if and when the changes which only they could bring about have already occurred.

The socio-political upheavals that took place in Iran more than twenty years ago differ significantly from what happened in Afghanistan in those decades; yet it is rewarding to compare the changes that Iran underwent with the transformation of Afghan society in the 1980s. In Iran the Revolution of 1979 eliminated from power and influence a ruling class which during the reign of the Shah had adopted a Western lifestyle and acquired great wealth. At the same time a new middle class of well trained and able professionals began to appear. They were the avant-garde of the revolution. It was to their representatives that the Islamic Republic awarded the key positions of the administration, the economy and the educational system, albeit under the control of the Shi'ite clergy.

It is true that the clergy 'hijacked' the revolution, as the American expert Robin Wright (2000: 14) put it. From a sociological point of view, however, the revolution had replaced a class of leaders which had become alienated from the population with new forces from the young bourgeoisie. They represented the technicians, experts and students in the country, and they were culturally and socially close to the mass of the population.

A little later, Afghanistan, too, underwent a kind of social revolution. The country also exchanged its elite. But Afghanistan never had much of a middle class, and their members did not make the revolution; they did not even stay in the country. They were either killed or sought refuge abroad. They did not significantly participate in the war against the Soviet Union, and they did not return from exile. More than two decades of armed conflict prevented the formation of a new middle class or a civil society of the kind that had emerged in neighbouring Iran.

In present-day Afghanistan there is no elite. But there is a new establishment The people who belong to it come from the lower strata of the population. They won the war of liberation and the civil war; they represent the large majority of the Afghans living in the countryside: village dwellers, the tribes, and a group which most resembles what could today be called an elite, the rural clergy.

5. Rule of a Periphery

These social changes have led to a significant shift in the balance between rural and urban Afghanistan. The relationship between those social and cultural poles had always been precarious. Today the city has lost out. The periphery dominates the country. Nobody stops the village from forcing its values upon the city. In the eyes of village people the city stands for decadence and moral corruption, for secularism, emancipation of women, Westernization, communism.

These developments have occurred in a country which always held to a very orthodox form of Islam. Now the influence of religion has increased even further. All the leaders of the resistance, for a long time supported by the West, were Islamists, some even clerics. Islam was the ideology which defeated communism. With the Taliban a very special kind of religious orthodoxy took hold of Afghanistan. Hikmatyar and Massoud, both clear-cut Islamists, were well educated. They were prepared to reconcile Islam at least with the technical and administrative elements of modernity. The political parties they created were supposed to take over the state and lead the nation. The Taliban brought a very different kind of Islam. Their Islam corresponds with the traditions of tribes and villages. Politics, nation, not to mention political parties, are alien to them. This transnational fundamentalism is part of an apolitical or antipolitical ideology that tends to make the state weak and to neglect its normal functions. And they belong to the Pashtu tradition which has always been hostile to any curtailment of the freedom of the tribes.

The victory of the Taliban was another victory of anti-modern forces in Afghanistan. Fifty years before, these forces had stopped Amanullah's attempts to become the Afghan Atatürk. The second chance to modernize the economy came with East-West competition in aid programmes during the 1960s and 1970s. But aid had little effect on the life of the overwhelming majority of the population. The improvements did not trickle down to peasants and tribesmen. Even the communists aimed at modernity. We easily forget that the revolution of 1978 pursued, among others, goals which we would call progressive and applaud if the Taliban or any of the present Afghan groups adopted them: social justice, empowerment for women, educational reforms. None of them has put them into practice in the areas under their control.

6. Early Roots of State Failure

I come back to my subject 'Country without a State'. The term generally used by English-language scholars is more precise: 'failed state' or 'failing state'. This term means that a society is no longer able to form institutions capable of carrying out the essential mandate of a state administration: to protect its members and to care for their needs. In a failing state, the groups holding power are unable or unwilling to cope with the problems of the population and to provide security for them.

The number of states that fail is growing. Until a few years ago, colonialism and the East-West conflict offered systems of order that gave countries with a weak identity and incompetent institutions a supporting framework and guaranteed their existence. This framework provided material support if needed, and put pressure on smaller states to correct, or at least adapt, their policies. Stabilizing its elements secured the stability of the system. Since 1990 this 'order' has disappeared; it has become history. Many countries of the Third and Fourth World, left alone, increasingly succumb to centrifugal forces and develop symptoms of weakness. Neighbours that no longer share the discipline of an ideological and military system take advantage of political vacuums and interfere. Population growth and globalization exacerbate economic problems. Criminal businesses like drug trafficking, uncontrolled exploitation of natural resources and smuggling, become important instruments of fragmented, irresponsible political power. The list of countries where the state is abandoning its functions stretches from Somalia to Pakistan. It includes most successor states of the Soviet Union, particularly in Central Asia. Afghanistan belongs to the avant-garde.

Yet it is not easy to find a clear answer to the question of whether in Afghanistan the state has really failed. Obviously there are still elements of statehood, both in the traditional Islamic sense of the word, which not only the Taliban, but all Afghans and many of their friends claim, and also in our own understanding of it. Afghanistan has a glorious history, rich cultural and religious traditions, and the successful war of liberation has created a national pride which protects its identity. Even the Taliban whose ideology has moved far away from concepts like state and nation as points of their ideological orientation professed to maintain, to rule and to represent Afghanistan in its national borders. Moreover examples like the speed and effectiveness which which the Taliban halted opium production, and the extent of their control prove that, in a pre-modern way, the country is being ruled and governed.

National myths may be strong in the minds and aspirations of Afghan leaders; but they were not strong enough to steer their deeds. Afghanistan has not completely failed as a state. But elementary functions and structures are missing. For decades, the state has been progressively decaying. It is failing.

Afghanistan's failure is the result of political catastrophes. Nature and geography long ago turned it into an underdeveloped country – not only economically, but also in the political field. More than twenty years of war, first against the Soviet Union, then between internal groups, completed the wholesale destruction of its resources. Again and again, its leaders proved unable to lead the country through difficult times. The monarchy failed; the royal family was too weak, took the wrong decisions and put personal ambition above national interest. This was jointly responsible for the catastrophe of the Afghan–Soviet War. The war parties did not reach peace and unity. Their failure is mainly due to the fact that each tried to secure a dominant role in a post-war state for their ethnic group, and enlisted the military help of outside powers for this purpose. The Taliban missed their great chance to unite Afghanistan because they used a transnational form of Islam as their political ideology and put it above national goals and national responsibilities.

7. When Peace Can Return?

In view of its structural deficiencies it is difficult to see where Afghanistan can find the energies and qualities needed to cope with the main issues confronting it: to reconcile the ethnic groups, establish security for all, restructure the political life, rehabilitate the economy. Each of these tasks would absorb the energies of a strong, qualified government enjoying the full support of the international community. The Afghan groups claiming power lack all this. Therefore, it is not only difficult, it seems impossible to envisage a reversal of the process of state failure. For a long time Afghanistan will be a country, if not without state, at least with not many state elements. Outside pressure, isolation and threats, aimed at improving governance, have not yielded the slightest results. Under present conditions, pressure rather works in the opposite direction, strengthening reactionary trends and impeding communication and development. Outside action could at best weaken and delegitimate a regime. It will never replace it by an accepted, viable alternative able to exert the 'legitimate monopoly of power', to use Max Weber's famous criterion for a state.

Many years will pass before our hopes and expectations for a healthy state of Afghanistan come true. Even the most urgent developments will take much longer than one would like to think. There will be setbacks and unforeseen detours. On this difficult path, Afghanistan needs help. For a long time, a cornerstone of European foreign policy has been its belief in the constructive power of dialogue and the positive value of aid.

We would feel proud if this volume made a modest contribution to friendly, effective assistance to Afghanistan and its people. It is possible to do something for the country and its people, even in present circumstances, but only if we develop a better comprehension of the causes and roots of their plight. This means placing Afghanistan's present performance in the context of its political and social history without condoning violations of basic human rights or support of criminal action.

Bibliography

Schetter, Conrad (2001) Ethnizität und Ethnische Konflikte. Ph.D. Diss. University of Bonn.

Wright, Robin (2000) *The Last Great Revolution*. New York, Knopf.

Tribe and State in Afghanistan after 1992

Ahmed Rashid

Until the communist coup in 1978 Afghanistan had maintained a loose federal arrangement between a centralized state and semi-autonomous ethnic regions and the Pashtun tribal belt. The breakdown of this arrangement as the communist regime attempted to centralize all aspects of state power was one of the catalysts for the uprising against the regime that began well before the Soviet invasion of Afghanistan in 1979. In parallel with the communists, the Islamicist Pashtun Mujahidin who were backed by Pakistan in the 1980s strove to impose a centralized state system in which tribal and ethnic autonomy was not recognized as a principle of governance. Since the emergence of the Taliban in 1994, this process of centralization has continued, making it more difficult for the Taliban to rule over the increasing amount of territory they have conquered.

The jihad against the Soviet Union galvanized minority ethnic groups in a way never seen before in Afghanistan. These ethnic groups fought Soviet forces, organized themselves and were the beneficiaries of considerable foreign aid, which led to a reassertion of their ethnic rights and demands once Kabul fell to the Mujahidin in 1992. This new reality was not accepted by the Taliban, who rely heavily on Pashtun support. The Pashtun tribes make up the largest Afghan ethnic group but still comprise only 40 per cent of the estimated twenty million population.

The Taliban leadership is almost exclusively drawn from the three most backward and conservative southern Pashtun provinces of Kandahar, Hilmand and Uruzgan and includes largely those from the Durrani section of the Pashtun tribes. Moreover they are even more narrowly defined, by non-Pashtun and Ghiljai Pashtun alike, as the 'Kandahari' group. Taliban leader Mullah Muhammad 'Omar's decision to rule from Kandahar rather than Kabul only accentuates the Taliban's highly localized power base.

There is little space given to Ghiljai Pashtuns in the Taliban military and political *shuras* and even less to non-Pashtuns. For example, the Taliban *shuras* that govern Herat in the west and Mazar-i Sharif in the north are almost entirely dominated by the Kandahari group, even though the populations of these areas are predominantly non-Pashtun. Such a Pashtunification of the non-Pashtun regions was not attempted by the former monarchy, the communists or the Mujahidin.

This ethnic and local bias has affected the Taliban's ability to gain legitimacy in the eyes of many Afghans, despite their capture of Kabul (in 1996) and other cities in the north. The Taliban's refusal, as they continue their war to conquer the rest of Afghanistan, to absorb the non-Pashtun ethnic groups and leaders has meant that territorial expansion has done nothing to extend their political power. In keeping with their Deobandi Islamic traditions, the Taliban are opposed to tribal and ethnic formulations of power but this makes it even harder for them to legitimize their rule because, on the surface at least, they are trying to do away with the historical and traditional patterns of exercising state power that have evolved in Afghanistan since the advent of the Durrani Pashtun dynasty in the mid-eighteenth century. In practice, as they try to keep control of the Ghiljai Pashtun belt in eastern Afghanistan, they have had to rely on traditional Ghiljai *jirgas* and tribal elders to keep the peace. This conflict between theory and practice only increases tensions within the Taliban and between the Taliban and the people. Increasingly the Taliban have used the Ghiljai Pashtuns as a manpower resource for their army, but refused to give prominent Ghiljai commanders from the jihad era a share in political and military power and decision making.

Moreover, by formalizing the drugs and smuggling trade, which now makes up 100 per cent of Taliban income for their war effort, they have helped strengthen a new disruptive elite of drug smugglers, traders, truckers and transporters who have no historical political legitimacy but have the necessary funds to buy support. The Taliban leaders and their families have themselves become heavily involved in the drugs and smuggling trade, further undermining their credibility as pure, incorruptible Muslims.

The new trader-transporter elite has forged strong economic links to criminal groups involved in the same trade in Pakistan, Turkmenistan,

Uzbekistan and Iran. This creates a vested interest amongst all these groups to keep the war going and the Taliban in control. This mafia is clearly undermining the traditional social and state system, leaving it without legitimate elements to adjudicate legal and developmental issues within the population. The situation in the non-Pashtun areas controlled by the Taliban is even worse, with hardly any representation from genuine local political elites.

At the same time within the Pashtun belt, the return of Pashtun refugees from Pakistan, particularly to Ghiljai areas, has created new tensions between the tribes and the Taliban as the returning refugees seek to get their old lands, water sources and other facilities back from the conquering Taliban, who have often handed over these resources to their followers. The Taliban administration lacks the legitimacy to adjudicate these issues. In the last few months there have been major disputes between the Taliban and the Ghiljai tribes in Afghan provinces adjoining Pakistan.

The Deobandi interpretation of Islam as practised by the Taliban has also undermined traditional systems of authority, legitimacy and other spiritual unifiers of the Afghan nations such as their strong belief in Sufism. The harsh and primitive interpretation of Islam by the Taliban is far from the original spirit or aim of Deobandism. Moreover Deobandism was never a strong Islamic sect in the Pashtun belt, let alone in the rest of Afghanistan. As it was imported from Pakistani *madaris* in the North West Frontier and Baluchistan provinces, it gives the Taliban the image of being manipulated by outsiders – especially when Pakistani Deobandi leaders such Maulanas Sami al-Haqq and Fazlur Rehman claim to have virtually invented the Taliban.

Taliban Deobandism is virulently anti-Shia, thus alienating the Hazara population; it is virulently anti-Sufi, thus alienating those who follow traditional practices of Islam in the rural areas; and it contrasts with the long-standing Afghan tolerance and moderation towards non-Muslims such as Sikhs, Jews and Hindus who ran much of Afghanistan's economy and money markets previously. The Taliban have also diluted the meaning and content of jihad for many Afghans by calling their war against the Northern Alliance a jihad.

The Taliban's interpretation of Islam is also heavily influenced by *pashtunwali*, but it is a *pashtunwali* as interpreted by the most backward and conservative Pashtuns in the south. *Pashtunwali* varies considerably across the Pashtun belt and of course does not exist in the non-Pashtun belt. These differences are not accepted by the Taliban. Their ethnic intolerance is thus exacerbated by their insistence that their code of Islamic–*pashtunwali* behaviour is adopted by all the other ethnic groups in Afghanistan.

The Taliban's failure to put together a coherent government concerned with public welfare, economic development and job creation – even in the south which has been under their control for more than six years now – is a part of the warlord culture that has evolved in Afghanistan since 1992. The former government of President Burhan al-Din Rabbani can equally be accused of leaving public welfare almost entirely to the UN and NGO aid agencies. However, as the Taliban control over 80 per cent of Afghan territory, this lack of governance, at a time of worsening economic crisis and when a drop in international donor aid and Taliban social restrictions have debilitated Western aid agencies, has made the Taliban look even more ineffective than the Rabbani government.

The overriding fear is that, as they lack a government, a party or a coherent strategy, the only way the Taliban can keep their movement together is to continue the war – first against the Northern Alliance and then, by extending sanctuary to Islamic militants and rebel groups from Pakistan, Iran, Central Asia, the Middle East and Kashmir, to extend that war into the neighbouring region. The Taliban leadership have to appear to be constantly under threat either at home or from their neighbours in order to maintain what is now an increasingly fragile unity and control.

There have been increasing signs that public discontent within the Pashtun belt against the Taliban is growing. The drought, the economic hardship and the isolation from the rest of the world community have to some extent galvanized public and tribal unrest. The key task for peace initiatives, the international community and the Afghans themselves will be how this public discontent with the Taliban and the continuation of the civil war will be mobilized to eventually bring peace to Afghanistan.

Perceptions of State and Organisation of the Northern Alliance

Michael Pohly

> 'We might divide the world into two, one part characterized by stable democracies and the other home to nominal nation-states that are not democracies. We might also take into account that in the first-mentioned half of the world there is peace while the other is ravaged by war. Given this situation we need not hesitate to envision two or even more international systems. The occidental part of this international system consists of democratic nation-states that differentiate between religion and politics. Their borders correspond to a sovereignty that is the product of a longer period of growth. These states do not define themselves in ethnic categories but in terms of citizenship. The other part consists of nominal nation-states that are sovereign in a formal sense but are undemocratic. Their population consists of ethnic groups thrown together without constituting a national community.' Tibi (1995: 62)

Tibi's differentiation between nation-states and nominal nation-states applies to Afghanistan in a limited sense only. Afghanistan does have territorial borders that are being respected by most neighbour states. Even though there is a question mark with regard to Pakistan. The border between these two states follows the Durand Line, which has been in dispute ever since it was drawn. Initially it was a matter of concern for the Pashtun tribes of the south-east whose territory was divided by the Durand Line. Traditionally Pashtuns consider themselves as Afghans. In fact, the words Afghan and Pashtun used to be synonyms. In the meantime Afghanistan has passed through 22 years of civil war. Pakistani Islamists no longer hesitate to suggest that Afghanistan should become an 'autonomous province' of Pakistan.[1] Islamabad's commitment to the dominant one among the contending parties in the Afghan civil war

---

[1] See A. Abdullah and K. Hassan in *Dawn*, Aug. 10, 2000: 'A few words about the fusion of the two brotherly countries. The idea of Afghanistan forming an autonomous province of Pakistan is not an unfamiliar or impracticable one. The letter *alif* in the Urdu (or A in English) word Pakistan stands for Afghans... Let the Afghans give the idea a calm and cool consideration in the larger interest of Muslim unity. There is plenty of commonality between Pakistan and Afghanistan in respect of their religion, culture, race, history, geography, etc.'

indicates that the unofficial annexation of Afghanistan is making headway. In fact, it seems to have progressed more than what is apparent.

How could Afghanistan possibly counteract? The United Nations continues to recognize the government of President Rabbani, but he controls only a minor portion of the territory, approximately 15-20 per cent. Besides, he has no authority outside the territory his government controls militarily. There is no functioning state or government machinery, not even a semblance of it. Taking this situation as our premise we find ourselves right at the heart of the publication topic 'Afghanistan – Country without a State'. The question is, who in Afghanistan wants a state, and if so, what type of state?

The Taliban have given a clear answer to this question. They want the religious, anti-democratic state ruled by the *shari'at*. In that state the people are not sovereign. The individual has no rights, only obligations toward the *umma* (community of believers).

What about the Northern Alliance, which is a heterogeneous coalition held together only by their opposition to the Taliban?

To be brief: The Alliance does not give a clear answer. It is in no position to answer the question because that would require a consensus. Attempts at reaching such a consensus would cause the breaking away of one or the other faction, and this would result in a weakening of the Alliance's military position. A brief look at the organization of the Alliance and its constituents will explain why this is so.

1. Organisation

The National Islamic Unity Front for the Liberation of Afghanistan (Jabha-i Muttahid-i Islami-i Nijat-i Afghanistan), henceforth called the Northern Alliance is a military alliance forged out of expediency. Its territory of operation is in the north, in parts of the central massif, and in the north-east of Afghanistan. This heterogeneous coalition of seven parties, which are ethnically and religiously disparate, is essentially a coalition of the country's minorities.[2]

---

[2] As for the different members of the Alliance see Pohly (1998: 45-84)

Perception of State and Organisation of the Northern Alliance

Over a longer period the political business of the coalition was taken care off by the militia of General Dostum, because it had more foreign support than the others and constituted the strongest military force in the Alliance. Dostum's militia/party is called the National Islamic Movement of Afghanistan (Jumbish-i Milli-i Islami Afghanistan). It lost this position because of internal power struggles, a lack of political acumen, and also because of competition between the foreign supporters. Ever since, Ahmad Shah Massoud has played the leading role. A Tajik from the Panjsher Valley region, he no longer has competitors. He is chairman of the Shura-i Nizar and also military chief of the Islamic Association (Jam'iyat-i Islami), which is headed by (former) President Burhan al-Din Rabbani, who is likewise a Tajik. Another constituent of the Alliance is the Islamic Unity of Afghanistan (Wahdat-i Islami-i Afghanistan), which regards itself as a united front of the Hazara. The Hazara, who are predominantly Shi'ite, are led by Khalili and Akbari.

The main Hazara region is the central massif. In Kabul they are about one third of the population and in Mazar-i Sharif roughly twenty percent. Iran acts as their protector and the patron of Wahdat. There is another Shi'ite faction in the Alliance, called the Revolutionary Movement of Afghanistan (Harakat-i Inqilabi Afghanistan), led by Shaikh Asif Muhsini (sometimes called Ayatullah). Isma'ilis, led by (General) Sayyid Ja'far Nadiri, inhabit primarily Badakhshan, both on the Afghan and the Tajik side of the border. Like the Shi'ite Hazaras, the Isma'ilis are a religious minority. Another religious minority are the Wahhabis, with their Islamic Front of Afghanistan (Jabha-i Islami-i Afghanistan), headed by Abd al-Rabb Rasul Sayyaf, a Pashtun. Another constituent is the Islamic Party (Hizb-i Islami) of Gulbuddin Hikmatyar. He too is a Pashtun. Prior to the Taliban he used to be Pakistan's man in Afghanistan and, as such, a fierce opponent of the other Alliance members.

Presently Massoud towers above the other leaders. Like Hikmatyar, Sayyaf, Akbari, Khalili, and Muhsini he is one of the so-called jihad fighters, resistance fighters who sought to introduce Islamism, availing themselves of the Soviet occupation (1979-89) as an opportunity to implement their ideology by force of arms and with international assistance, especially from Pakistan. Their favourite method was to indoctrinate Afghans in the refugee camps and the provinces under their control.

Quite early in this struggle differences of opinion developed between Massoud and some of his comrades in the Islamist camp, as well as with the Pakistani mentors. This caused Massoud to distance himself from Pakistan, even though he received much assistance from there, at least initially. Most of the support for his party, however, came from Saudi Arabia. After the fall of Kabul in 1992, Massoud changed fronts and obtained support from Iran and India, partly even from Russia. Presently most of the finances for the Alliance are contributed by Sayyaf. Ideologically there is but little difference between Sayyaf and Rabbani, they are competitors within one and the same Islamist framework. Sayyaf is a high-calibre demagogue. Although Sayyaf and Massoud do not trust each another, they co-operate well, even though this works more to the advantage of Massoud than Sayyaf. This co-operation ensures that the Islamists, who are strongly represented in the Jam'iyat-i Islami, stay in line, while at the same time diminishing the role of Rabbani, who lacks Sayyaf's demagogy. Sayyaf's financial contribution provides Massoud with some leverage in his dealings with Iran and Russia – he does not have to go cap in hand.

There is little doubt that Massoud is popular among Afghans, more than any other resistance leader. Besides, he is a brilliant military tactician. His military prowess is the main reason for the support he enjoys, although that support is no longer as unconditional as it used to be during the Soviet occupation. It is not only his opponents who accuse him of being power-hungry, this opinion is shared even by some of his aides. They have also noted his inability to think and act beyond a limited variety of tactical choices. Besides, he cannot tolerate strong personalities next to him. Finally, there is the lack of a political concept. He has under his command Tajiks, Uzbeks, Hazaras (from his own Panjsher region) and individual Pashtuns. His most important rivals have either been eliminated or neutralized, such as Hikmatyar, Dostum, Rasul Pahlawan, and Isma'il Khan of Herat. Massoud succeeded in gaining the loyalty of even those commanders who are members of neither the Jam'iyat-i Islami nor the Shura-i Nizar, and some of those are important military leaders. Although they constitute a kind of second line, they form the backbone of the

Perception of State and Organisation of the Northern Alliance

Northern Alliance. One such commander is Anwari of the Harakat-i Islami, who has replaced Muhsini with a council of eight persons. Other examples are Qasimi of Wahdat (Akbari faction) and 'Irfani (Khalili faction). The latter two listen more to Iran than to their local party leaders. Zabayun, Hikmatyar's representative in Afghanistan, works hand in hand with Massoud, and so does Humayun Jarir, who was Hikmatyar's representative in the Cyprus talks. Neither of them hesitates to differ with Hikmatyar's positions. Haji Qadir, a former governor of Jalalabad and a prominent businessman, used to belong to the Hizb-i Islami of Yunus Khalis. Massoud won him over for the Northern Alliance. Although he had a poor record as a governor, Haji Qadir is a successful businessman. A son of his escaped from the Taliban prison in Kandahar, together with Isma'il Khan, the famous Mujahidin commander of Herat. Haji Qadir's influence in eastern Afghanistan is somewhat curtailed by Hazrat-i 'Ali, a successful military commander in Kunar. But Massoud has him too on his side.

2. Political Profile

Politically, the Northern Alliance unites radical Islamists and anti-democrats, such as Sayyaf, Hikmatyar, Khalili and Akbari, with moderate Islamists such as Rabbani and Muhsini, and also with apolitical intellectuals and the field commanders, who are indispensable for the conduct of the war, as well as former cadres of Parcham, one of the two factions of the defunct Communist Party.

The religious spectrum comprises Sunnis, Shi'ites, Isma'ilis and Wahhabis. On occasion they accuse each other of heresy.

Ethnically speaking, Tajiks are the numerically dominant group. Followed by Uzbeks, Hazaras, Turkmens and Pashtuns. Every now and then a clash occurs between these different factions. In August 2000, disgruntled Sunni Hazaras withdrew and allowed the Taliban to march on Taluqan. Such dissension has a history. While Rabbani was still President in Kabul, Pashtuns allied with his government clashed with the Hazaras.

The most important foreign backers of the struggle against the Taliban are Iran and Russia. In the period from 1992-94 Iran changed its priorities in this respect, putting less emphasis on religious legitimization and giving greater importance to the common cultural heritage of the region. Present-day Afghanistan corresponds largely to the ancient east Iranian province of Khurasan. The change of emphasis noticeable here is partly due to those Afghan Shi'ite groups who rejected Khomeinist tutelage. In part it is due to developments in Iran, with new governments attempting to pursue a more pragmatic course. But it is also due to Pakistani attempts to manipulate history so as to make Afghanistan look like a part of Pakistan, in the most natural way.

Both Iran and Russia are keen on uniting the Northern Alliance under Massoud's command. The military defeats of Dostum, Malik and also Wahdat make this look like an attainable objective.

Apart from personal rivalries between Massoud, Rabbani, Dostum, Isma'il Khan and Khalili, as well as between Dostum and Malik, or between Malik and Isma'il Khan, ethnic and religious conflicts raise their head every now and then. Recently Iran began to gather such former representatives of the Khalq faction as had escaped the purges carried out by the Taliban. Tehran's aim is to have those remnants of Khalq incorporated into the Northern Alliance, which has already absorbed elements of the Parcham faction, Khalq's bitter rival. Thus this Iranian attempt is likely to ignite new conflicts. Looked at both from a strategic and a tactical point of view the Iranian move appears certainly sound, and yet it scarcely stands a chance, because it is not realistic. Among Pashtuns the Khalq faction is the strongest organized force even today. Should the Iranians succeed at bringing this faction together with the Northern Alliance, the latter would gain the necessary influence among Pashtuns in order to pose a real challenge to the Taliban.

Iran and Russia share a common objective: Afraid that Uzbekistan and the other northern neighbors of Afghanistan might be destabilized, they want to evict the Taliban from northern Afghanistan. Moscow's announcement that Chechen training camps in Mazar-i Sharif will be bombed are more than threats. Russia has not abdicated its role as a superpower, and it claims for itself the same privileges as the United States. The Russians believe that they have as much right to bombard Afghanistan as the Americans. Secretary of State Madeleine Albright's visit to the southern republics of the former Soviet Union and President Clinton's subsequent visit to Moscow demonstrate a change of policy with regard to the region. The understanding reached in Moscow with regard to combating international terrorism is an unmistakable declaration of war against the Taliban and their Pakistani mentors. The winner of this new agreement is Massoud. Since spring 2000, Massoud has not had to pay for the weapons delivered from Russia and Iran.

3. Political Demands

In 1998 the Northern Alliance announced that it intended to convene a Grand Assembly in order to form a transitional government which would prepare a Constitutional Assembly. This announcement was made against the background of diverse peace initiatives such as the 'Six plus Two Talks', the OIC, UNO, the Cyprus and the Rome Initiative. The future government was to emerge from free and fair elections. The state would be national. But would it also be secular?

Afghanistan is to become home to democracy and human rights for men and women. In order to achieve this goal, ethnic, political and religious discrimination is to be eliminated, with the help of Islamic law and the respective UN resolutions, as long as those are not opposed to Islam.

The aim is to implement jihad and introduce the *shari'at*, to defend the territorial integrity and protect its independence. Here some more quotes from the 'Decisions of the Second Meeting in Cyprus':

> Principles:
>
> In order to achieve lasting peace and to create the conditions for stability of the political and social systems as well as to realize the common weal the following principles are inalienable. They correspond to the essentials of Islam, to Afghan traditions, the Charter of the United Nations and the Declaration of Human Rights. These principles are:
>
> Political power derives its legitimacy from the people by way of elections.
>
> Rights and freedoms of the population are to be realized by the law and to be guaranteed.
>
> The personal and social security of the citizen is to be ensured.
>
> The independence, integrity and national sovereignty of the country is to be maintained.
>
> The national unity, solidarity and the sentiment of belonging together is to be fostered and strengthened among the various segments of the Afghan people.
>
> Every form of discrimination on the basis of sex, religion, ethnic or tribal affiliation, and language is to be totally rejected.
>
> Before the law all citizens are equal.

I quote these decisions of the Cyprus Meeting because we are dealing here with a process to which the delegates committed themselves on behalf of the Northern Alliance.

These declarations of intent are a resolute rejection of Taliban ideas. They also show that 'all wishes and hopes' have been taken into account. And yet, a political discussion has not even started. Just like similar statements by the Northern Alliance, the Declaration of Cyprus has the disadvantage of being replete with contradictions. A few examples may suffice to demonstrate this and to highlight the disastrous lack of clear conceptions.

Implementing the objectives of jihad means to establish a religious state in which the *shari'at* is the law. Such a demand rules out the establishment of a nation-state based on a separation of religion and state. Large parts of the *shari'at* law are irreconcilable with the UN Declaration of Human Rights, for instance the physical inviolability of the individual in case of certain transgressions. Religious law limits the citizen's basic rights. What will happen if a political group demands the abrogation of the *shari'at*? Will they be confronted with a fatal *fatwa*, as happened in Egypt? Will those who raised the demand become outlaws?

As already mentioned, in an Islamic State the individual has obligations towards the community. There are no rights for the individual. Do equal rights exist there – irrespective of sex, origin or religion?

The phase during which Rabbani exercised government authority in Kabul did not look promising for a democratic future, and the same must be said about the rule of the various other groups in the territories under their control.

4. The Lack of State

Recapitulating the historical development of Afghanistan, we see that the state, the product of this development, was the result of an arrangement by colonial powers. It served their purposes as a buffer state. State authority rarely reached beyond the larger towns. The political elite controlling the resources consisted mainly of Pashtuns. In the 1960s a compromise was reached that led to a Constitution which granted other ethnic groups a share of power. The compromise, however, was never implemented, and once the parliament was dissolved, the ethnic balance was jeopardized. In 1973 the compromise arrangement received another blow when Prince Daoud overthrew his cousin, King Zahir, and proclaimed an Afghan Republic. Whatever civil rights existed were limited even more, although this remained primarily an urban issue. The countryside had in any case barely been touched by state institutions. The coup of April 1978 meant the final end of the consensus achieved in the 1960s. The military take-over on behalf of a pro-Soviet party provoked a conflict involving the rural areas. The result was spontaneous uprisings and a growing civil war.

At that point of history, many Afghan political leaders were still hoping to be able to lead a war of 'national liberation' (rather than a jihad or 'holy war'). Prof. Qayyum Rahbar, chairman of NUFA (National United Front of Afghanistan) saw a chance for the peoples of Afghanistan to become one nation through the welding effect of the civil war which united all of them on a common platform, resulting in full participation of all the ethnic groups in a just manner. However, Qayyum's dream was brought to naught by the Soviet invasion and the West's choice of the Islamists as their party in Afghanistan, a choice essentially made for the West by Pakistanis and Saudis. The result is that today there remain but few vestiges of state structures. State institutions have almost all been undone. Their place has been taken by various versions of Islamism that treat Afghanistan as a playground for their antidemocratic utopianism, of which the Taliban are the most extreme expression.

The secular nation-state of Afghanistan was a fiction. Being a foreign institution it could not exert itself against competing loyalties, including claims to unity that transcend the country, such as Pan-Islamism etc., and along with those claims corresponding identities – identities that belong to the realm of ideals promoted by the conditions of the Cold War. But the establishment of a nation-state with a functioning central authority was also thwarted by more basic identities, such as those of tribal federations, not necessarily tied to state mechanisms.

The Afghan nation-state lacked the required historical experience. Its sovereignty was nominal. The infrastructure was still in the process of being created. There were ethnic groups with their own identity transmitted as cultural norms, and they fought with one another for power. Once this ethnic multiplicity became politicized each one began to reach out for dominance over the state. A lack of consensus and a dearth of political culture prevented the emergence of rules of competition. But such rules were required to diffuse ethnic conflicts over power and resources. The consequences for Afghanistan are there for everyone to see.

5. Resumé

In view of the Afghan disaster it is difficult to answer the question raised at the beginning. If we scrutinize the first and second tier of the Northern Alliance's leadership we do not come across a proponent who could guarantee change toward a civil state in the Western European sense. In the past neither the former Communists nor the Islamists and *jihadis* have demonstrated a commitment to democracy. The men around Massoud do not have the caliber to enforce democracy and the concept of a nation-state that would proffer an alternative to the Taliban's project of a theocracy. In the past it was they, the Islamists, who demanded a rejuvenation of 'islamic values', drawing a dividing line between themselves and the West. The Soviet occupation of Afghanistan led to a war of ideologies, and this war did not only eliminate the autochthonous resistance but also Western values. It rather looks as if Massoud had learned to make tactical use of concepts such as human rights and democracy in order not to lose international support, from the United Nations for instance.

Bassam Tibi calls the conflict between secular nation-state and religious state a War of Civilizations. The worst solutions in this war are the semi-solutions. Those behind the various peace initiatives, such as the Northern Alliance with the Cyprus Initiative, need to clarify what really differentiates them from the Taliban.

Bibliography

Abdulla A. and Hassan K. (2000) n.T. *Dawn*. August 10, 2000.

Pohly, Michael (1998) Die Nordallianz. In: Citha D. Maass and Johannes Reissner (eds.) *Afghanistan und Zentralasien. Entwicklungsdynamik, Konflikte und Konfliktpotential*. Teil B: Hintergrundanalyse. Ebenhausen: 45-84.

Tibi, Bassam (1995) *Krieg der Zivilisationen: Politik und Religion zwischen Vernunft und Fundamentalismus*, Hamburg: Heyne

The Taliban
and International Standards of Governance

Citha D. Maass

1. Introduction: Recognition Controversy

How does one deal with a pariah regime in the international community? How is it possible to address and communicate with the regime without conceding formal recognition? How can mutually binding agreements on basic humanitarian aid projects be negotiated? These questions raise practical problems for diplomats and UN aid workers on the one hand and, on the other, reveal a certain degree of political hypocrisy mixed with frustration and helplessness.

Hypocrisy is certainly involved because the decision to classify a regime as 'legitimate' or 'illegal' depends on one's political perspective. Militant groups branded by one conflict party as 'terrorists' are praised as 'freedom fighters' by another conflict party. Today's pariah regime may turn into tomorrow's legitimate national representative if this volte-face suits the revised interests of the major international powers.

In the case of the Afghanistan conflict, the emergence of the Taliban revived the controversy. Since the Taliban have laid claim to the Afghan seat in the UN General Assembly, basically the debate has focused on two issues: the internal dimension (can the Taliban justify their claim by their own performance?) and the external dimension (whose interests in the international community will be served by a formal recognition of the Taliban?). The Taliban's struggle for military supremacy and political recognition adds another case study to the long list of violent take-overs whose successful outcome ultimately hinges on the crucial issue of international recognition. Violent take-overs can range from a highly personalized coup d'état to a large-scale liberation war. Within this broad category of militant take-overs, the Taliban-based controversy puts the Afghan case into a special subcategory for two reasons:

In the course of the long and complex war history, too many Afghan claimants to national supremacy have discredited themselves. As a consequence, criteria and procedural traditions for installing a new leadership as the legitimate national government lost their credibility or lacked broad national consensus.

The highly externalized character of the Afghan conflict poses a further problem: too many external actors have a stake in the conflict. They pursue divergent interests, causing a rather diffuse pattern of cross-cutting interests. Their commitment to push their Afghan clients into a meaningful political dialogue may not be strong enough, but their potential to sabotage consensus-building in mediation initiatives, including the recognition issue, is definitely big enough.

Basically, both developments tend to prolong the war, discouraging external actors from altering the status quo. This does not work in favour of the Taliban's claim, raising the question of how the Taliban intend to establish it.

In methodical terms, the analysis focuses on the Taliban as a political power group, but not as an ideological phenomenon. Therefore, it is asked whether or not they are politically capable of ruling a state. Less relevant is which version of an Islamic state the Taliban intend to install in Afghanistan.

2. Methodical Limitations

Uncertain State of Information

It is well-known that systematic research has not been possible in Afghanistan for a long time. Thus, only an uncertain and fragmentary database is available. Under normal conditions, one would use primary sources such as official declarations in order to analyse a regime's perceptions. However, the decrees issued by Mullah 'Omar or the Kabul shura cannot be considered as very useful for learning about the Taliban's conceptual intentions.

This can be illustrated by one of the decrees issued in spring 2000. According to the decree, it is forbidden to use leather for tailoring shirt or coat collars. The order is justified on the grounds that the animals may not have been slaughtered in the stipulated Muslim manner. To a Western mind, this example is rather unusual for 'official' announcements. Yet it is rather typical for the style of Taliban decrees, as confirmed by a general observation made by a UN official. The official has been regularly interacting with the Taliban and opined in May 2000 that during the previous year Mullah 'Omar's office had not announced anything worth being taken seriously. Thus, the Afghan public did not pay much attention to the decrees either.

Highly Externalized Decision Making in Domestic Conflict

A sound analysis is also impeded by the fact that all parties to the conflict maintain close linkages with external actors. In the case of the Taliban, Pakistan's far-reaching involvement is well-known. The pattern of linkages, dependencies and mutual blackmailing is even more intricate because it is not only the ISI (Inter-Services Intelligence) which has supported the Taliban but also various other groups in Pakistan. Since these groups politically compete with each other, it can be assumed that the Taliban play one group off against another one. In addition, non-Pakistani Islamist groups also exercise their influence on the Taliban top leadership. These organizations operate from their headquarters in Saudi Arabia or the Gulf countries or the Middle East.

In view of these interdependencies, it is difficult to identify the Taliban's own share in the decision making. They should not be discarded simply as puppets of the ISI, as functioning at the whim of the transport and drug mafia, or as forming the ideological arm of Islamist parties like the JUI (Jamiat-e Ulema Islam). They certainly incorporate all these roles, yet they constitute more than the sum of all the components.

However – and this has to be emphasized – on top of everything else they represent the claim to power by the Pashtun ethnic majority, even if they vehemently deny this. Again, it is difficult to determine their role because they do not fit into the pattern of traditional Pashtun rivalries. On the contrary, they intend to break even the little power that had been left to traditional Pashtun tribal leaders and also deny the exiled king any symbolic or mediatory role. Even if it remains uncertain what role the Taliban actually play in the infighting between the various Pashtun lobbies, it is not appropriate to dismiss the Taliban's role merely as the one of a 'Pashtun client regime dependent on Pakistan'. Although the Pakistani mentors assume that a Taliban government will not revive the controversial demand of a 'Greater Pashtunistan', they should not take this for granted.

Recently, a new tag has been added to the dubious image of the Taliban. Inside Afghanistan, the term 'Kandaharis' is increasingly being used for the Taliban, in particular for their leadership. According to my information, an average Afghan or Pashtun refers to 'those Kandaharis' in a derogatory manner if he wants to distance himself from the hardliners in Mullah 'Omar's inner circle.

This can be interpreted in two different ways. First, without a value judgement, the term 'Kandaharis' is obviously still equated with 'Pashtuns' in general. Second, a note of disrespect can be heard. If the second interpretation is correct, it can be interpreted as a first indication that the Taliban have already crossed the zenith of their power extension and all-Afghan acceptance. If this is true, the Taliban's image is suffering, with them no longer being perceived as idealistic fighters for a 'pure Islam'.

It cannot be ruled out that the might of the Taliban has begun to decline. Such a process may ultimately result in a change of roles, slowly eroding the influence of the Taliban and ultimately reducing them to one among several other power groups within the two broad Pashtun tribal confederations. The hidden loss of power might be exposed if a third alternative emerges. It could function as a catalyst for transforming latent dissatisfaction with the Taliban into open resistance.

To summarize this point, one can state that several different and competing influences can be distinguished, yet still hardly any concrete information has become available on how the inner circle of the Taliban functions and how it actually makes decisions.

3. Character of a 'Secret Society'

For both researchers and politicians, it is frustrating to realize that the Taliban behave like a 'secret society' as Ahmed Rashid has rightly said (2000). If one compares the Taliban with ethnic separatist movements in India and in South Asian states, one becomes aware of the differences. For the other movements in South Asia, details about the leadership structure, power relations within the movement, the process of decision making, different ideological wings, financial networks and international linkages can be specified. By contrast, knowledge about the Taliban remains vague.

The Taliban are extremely adverse to transparency and media contacts. They are also conspicuous for their lack of ideological programmes and media-based dissemination of their political aims. Such a strategy strongly deviates from a general reliance on TV as the most efficient propaganda means. One wonders whether it is, in fact, only for religious reasons that taking photos and making films have been forbidden by the Taliban, or whether it is basically a clever tactic to deny the international public access to visual information in order to keep world interest in the domestic affairs of Afghanistan as low as possible.

Who benefits most if the war in Afghanistan has been internationally forgotten? Quite obviously the Taliban and their Pakistani mentors, because under such circumstances they can consolidate their control in secrecy. In our media-oriented world, donations for humanitarian purposes can most efficiently be raised by broadcasting dramatic TV pictures of disaster victims. By contrast, donor fatigue will easily set in if appropriate pictures are missing. If no UN and NGO representatives work in Afghanistan, no information about the actual methods of Taliban control and their human rights violations can be reported to the international public. It can be doubted whether Mullah 'Omar has forbidden reproductions of human beings only for reasons of his personal shyness and obscure interpretations of the Koran.

Taking the above-mentioned methodical restrictions into account, the question arises about the role the Taliban play in the current phase of the conflict.

4. Defining the Terms

To start with, the terms 'law and order force' and 'nascent national government' need to be elaborated. The overall category in which the Taliban take-over has to be classified is the one of a violent change of power. In the case of militant usurpations, the question of how the new rulers seek legitimacy and recognition is particularly relevant.

The Danish scholar Asta Olesen has described (1995) the mechanisms by which in the past Afghan kings and political leaders sought to legitimize their rule internally. The external dimension is raised in modern international politics, namely whether or not the new rulers will be recognized by other states. Will the new regime be ostracized as a 'pariah' in the international system or accepted as new representative of the state?

The differences between the terms 'law and order force' and 'nascent national government' need to be clarified. The term 'law and order force' refers to a situation most aptly described as the 'security of a graveyard', brought about by the new authorities. As a short form the term 'regime' can be used, meaning that the new authorities have not been recognized as a legitimate government. By contrast, the term 'nascent national government' is meant to indicate the potential enabling the new rulers to mature into a legitimate and capable government. After the violent take-over, the new rulers have not yet overcome the last obstacle in their power struggle. However, they have good chances of being recognized officially as the new government by internal or external actors, be it by their own people or their defeated military opponents or the international community. In this case, the term 'nascent government' refers to a 'government in the making'.

Yet, what sounds so logical in scientific terms is not so easy to define in real politics, which is often determined by power interests. One soon realizes that cynicism and hypocrisy are strongly involved.

5. The Issue of Recognition in International Law and the Global Power System

The question of how to classify the Taliban, and the related question of whether or not they might be capable of reconstructing a war-torn state, would not have arisen at all if they had been recognized by the USA shortly after their take-over of the capital Kabul in September 1996. In such a case, all attempts of scientific classification would have been irrelevant because power interests had already decided the issue. Nevertheless, it is worthwhile to ask which norms of international law can be applied to a violent transition of power and how political reality responds to it.

In terms of international law the case is absolutely clear. Only states, but not governments are recognized. The transition from regime A to regime B is not relevant according to the international law, but only the continued existence of the state. The norms of international law are only applicable if regime A and regime B formally split the state territory and announce two independent states.

Resorting to the principle of only recognizing states offers a convenient diplomatic pretext for those external actors who want to avoid a decision. Their diplomats gain enough time to probe the new power constellation. If their government realizes that its own interests or those of its allies are better served by the new regime, then an actual co-operation with the new regime will not be long in coming. In this case, it does not matter at all whether or not the new authorities are capable or incompetent to govern a state.

Such an attitude of 'wait and see' shifts the decision to the political level. Considerations of power and self-interest ultimately determine the decision, not primarily criteria of legitimacy and internationally accepted basic norms. A simple act of administration executes the political decision. The government keeps its embassy functioning, the diplomatic envoy of the new authorities is accredited. It is generally seen as final proof that the violent transfer of power has actually been successful if the new delegation is accredited by the United Nations. When the new representatives take over the UN seat, their government has been de facto accepted by the international system.

Power and interest become involved as soon as an external lobbyist starts to promote the de facto recognition of the new regime. If the lobbyist is not efficient enough and fails to convince major international powers, the prospects will drastically diminish over time. This can be illustrated by the example of the US reluctance to recognize the Taliban. If at all, the Taliban had a small chance of gaining US support (with UNOCAL sponsoring) only in the first months after their take-over of Kabul in September 1996 and before their defeat in Mazar-i Sharif in May 1997. One of the reasons for their failure to gain this, though not the sole one, was international shock about the Taliban behaviour. They committed such outrageous violations of human rights in the first hours and days after their capture of Kabul that Western governments saw basic international norms offended.

Washington's attitude towards human rights violations has obviously changed if one compares its reaction to the situation in Pakistan in the early 1980s with that in Afghanistan in the late 1990s. The decisive factor explaining the different attitudes is the change in US global interests and in the international balance of power, but not good or bad performance of the other government (Pakistan) or the concerned regime (Afghanistan). In the early 1980s, at the height of the Cold War and during the fierce fight against Soviet occupation of Afghanistan, Washington shut its eyes to the situation in Pakistan. Since Pakistan was a strategic ally, Washington ignored the fact that the military dictator Zia ul-Haq gave new prominence to Islamic law (shari'at) which legalized radical punishments like chopping off the hands of thieves and public whipping. By contrast, in 1996 Washington used the human rights violations committed by the Taliban as a pretext to delay recognition. The US administration took this decision because it feared that its silence might undermine its internal image and its international reputation as a global leader.

In the case of the omitted recognition in September 1996, Washington's self-interests decided the matter. However, in late May 1997 the situation was more complex. When the Taliban initially succeeded in capturing Mazar-i Sharif, the strategically important stronghold of the Northern Alliance, they were formally recognized by Pakistan. Saudi Arabia and the United Arab Emirates (UAE), both on good terms with Pakistan, immediately followed suit because they expected strategic, economic and religious–ideological advantages from a Taliban-ruled Afghanistan.

It is worth examining in more detail why Pakistan's diplomatic campaign in favour of the Taliban was premature. It failed for different reasons:
- internal military balance of power: the unexpected defeat of the Taliban within less than five days of their capture of Mazar-i Sharif

in late May 1997 shattered their own hopes and those of their Pakistani mentors of gaining international de facto recognition;
- adherence to international human rights standards: the reservations about the Taliban's human rights record, dating back to their seizure of Kabul, were reconfirmed by the large-scale massacres committed by the Taliban in Mazar-i Sharif;
- international clout: Pakistan, even in co-operation with the influential Saudi Arabia, did not possess sufficient international influence to lobby successfully for their client's recognition.

Pakistan's weakness as a lobbyist, resulting from its relatively insignificant role in the global power hierarchy, could have been compensated by an internal Afghan factor. Had the Taliban succeeded in controlling Mazar-i Sharif and in further advancing into the Northern Alliance's heartland, Pakistan's chances of winning international acceptance for the Kabul regime would have significantly improved. In such a case, the factor of 'internal military dominance' might have provided Pakistan with a sufficiently strong argument to make the major global powers aware that their interests would be best served by recognizing the dominant military faction in Afghanistan.

This did not happen, as two negative factors reinforced each other: no clear internal dominance of the regime and an insufficient capacity by the external lobbyist to mobilize international acceptance. Pakistan's premature initiative turned out to be counterproductive because at this juncture the Taliban have fewer chances to be recognized than ever before. Thus, according to the above-mentioned definition, they have to be classified as a 'regime', being no more than a 'law and order force'. Internationally, they are ostracized as a 'pariah'.

6. Internal Criterion of Legitimacy: State-Building Capacity

So far the argument has shown that the quest for international recognition is basically determined by external criteria. Even if the rules of the global power game set this priority, one should not entirely dismiss internal criteria.

The most significant internal factor has already been referred to in the definition of the term 'nascent government': whether the new regime has the potential to rule the state better than the defeated government. In general, transfer of power implies that the previous government has been ruined by mismanagement and the old leadership has considerably discredited itself. When the new regime takes over power, it deliberately uses this argument for propagandist purposes, trying to project itself as the 'better' government.

There is a wide range of different criteria for a 'better' government. At one end of the spectrum figure purely pragmatic criteria like combating corruption and consolidating state deficits, while ideological criteria like installing a 'true and pure Islamic system' can be found at the opposite end.

Since the end of the cold war, the term 'good governance' has been introduced. Such a concept with specific criteria has, however, hardly been applicable to a particular situation in a war-destroyed country. Instead, the decisive criterion in such a specific situation is the capability to reconstruct the state with its basic institutions, its primary economic functions and indispensable state authority and, at the same time, reunite the fragmented society. Corresponding to the term 'nation-building', such a qualification can be called 'state-building capacity'. If one wants to specify the appropriate criteria, scientific literature does not give an answer. Obviously, not enough research has been done on this topic.

Therefore, criteria have to be deduced from the actual situation and from the most urgent needs in Afghanistan:

- earnest determination by the regime to stop fighting and redirect mental and financial resources to rebuilding the destroyed country;
- basic willingness to integrate appropriately the previous opponents in the war into the state and society in order to prevent the risk of subversive and long-drawn out guerrilla warfare;
- well-aimed and co-ordinated efforts to overcome the emotional gap, the deep-rooted violations, hatred and revenge in the fragmented society by a state-sponsored process of national reconciliation;
- capability to restore at least the most rudimentary functions of an administration;

- willingness and knowledge to start a planning process to develop reconstruction concepts;
- co-ordination and promotion of economic revival.

This list could be further specified. These criteria already demonstrate that measures are required which by far exceed the basic task of restoring 'law and order'. What is needed, most of all, is an awareness – even in a rudimentary form – that planning and co-ordination are absolutely necessary for reconstructing the country.

A small example may illustrate this. In May 2000, I interviewed the Taliban Deputy Minister for Planning in Kabul. He read out a list indicating which sectors of the main overland roads would be repaired next. The way he went down the list made me feel that I only had to tick the sector whose repair should be financed by the German government. When I finally asked him according to which criteria the Taliban had determined the priorities for repairing the roads sector by sector, he looked at me without comprehension. Even when I rephrased my questions and insisted on an answer, it was to no avail. The Taliban minister was not able to follow my argument that scarce financial resources should force the Taliban to design a framework and a list of priorities before they actually started working on the roads.

Many more examples of this type could be mentioned. From my talks with several Taliban authorities in May 2000, I have to conclude that the Taliban have not at all entered into a learning process. From the capture of Kabul until 1998, I received the standard reply that the first tasks of the Taliban are: to gain (military) control of the entire territory, to disarm their enemies and to bring security (meaning physical security). Only if and when these tasks have been accomplished, will the Taliban authorities think of building the state. How this state would look and what its ideological nature would be was, however, never described. Instead, the slogan was repeated again and again that 'the holy Koran is our constitution' – again an empty standard phrase.

At the time of writing, in summer 2000, I have not found any indications that the Taliban have understood how necessary it is to plan a concept for reconstruction. Therefore, I am convinced that the Taliban lack the basic requirements of a 'state-building capacity', i.e. to realize mentally that a rudimentary planning procedure is needed. Saying this, I do not mean that the Taliban may not be able to develop administrative and conceptual skills needed for implementing a programme. Instead, I doubt very much whether the Taliban leadership has any interest at all in civil planning – as opposed to military logistics and co-ordination.

As long as the Taliban still consider a military victory as a realistic option and continue to concentrate all their capacities and resources on this sole task, they cannot fulfil the preconditions for a 'nascent government' and do not have the potential for maturing into a future government. Thus, according to internal criteria as well, they have to be classified merely as a 'law and order force', exercising their control by despotism and intimidation.

Bibliography

Olesen, Asta (1995) *Islam and Politics in Afghanistan*. Richmond, VA, Curzon Press (Nordic Institute of Asian Studies, Monograph Series, 67).

Rashid, Ahmed (2000) *Taliban: Islam, Oil and the New Great Game in Central Asia*. London and New York, I.B. Tauris.

Part VI

International Dimensions

Afghanistan
– The Perspective of International Law

Hermann-Josef Blanke

'Afghanistan – Country without State?': The question raised in the title of this book may seem to be inspired by international law. Since the end of the Cold War, attention has tended to move away from a focus on geopolitical issues towards inner-state conflicts. The notion of a 'failed state' nowadays lies in the centre of scholarly interest, as the then UN Secretary-General Boutros Boutros Ghali highlighted on the occasion of the United Nations Congress on Public International Law in 1995. In his view, a 'failed state' could be characterized by 'the collapse of state institutions, especially the police and judiciary, with resulting paralysis of government', a 'breakdown of law and order', as well as 'general banditry and chaos'. In the context of a 'failed state', international interventions would emphasize the 'promotion of national reconciliation and the re-establishment of effective government' (Boutros Ghali 1995: 9). From the standpoint of public international law, the phenomenon of a 'failed state' must be located between state sovereignty and the right to self-determination of peoples, both being fundamental principles of the modern international legal order. The principle of state sovereignty and equality of states is not only founded in Article 2 (1) of the UN Charter, it is, moreover, the very basis of the constitutional system of the international community. The right to self-determination reflects that sovereignty today is not an end in itself, but is to serve the people and stands for human rights. The connecting link between these two principles on the one hand and the issue of 'failed states' on the other, is that lifting the sovereignty veil of a state can be particularly justified when the fundamental values of humankind and human rights are at stake due to despotic misuse of state power and the collapse of governmental power, i.e. a 'breakdown of government' (Thürer 1996: 9-14 et seq.).

In a first step, I will proceed by introducing the concept of a 'failed state' in a factual sense. I will then go on to apply this concept to the present situation in Afghanistan. The analysis primarily draws on reports issued by the UN Secretary-General on the situation in Afghanistan and the repercussions on international peace, on the reports of the Special Rapporteur of the UN Human Rights Commission[1], as well as the pertinent resolutions of both the General Assembly and the Security Council.

When we discuss 'failed states' we tend to think of Somalia, ruled by 'warlords' since 1991, of genocide and massacres in Rwanda, or of the Congo, which has been practically 'ungovernable' since the foundation of that state. These cases are all Third-World countries and have the following elements in common (Thürer 1996: 13):

- a geographical-territorial aspect: cases of 'failed states' are commonly characterized by inner-state, endogenous problems, which, however, in some cases may also have cross-border implications;
- a complete breakdown of state regulatory power;
- the absence of a reliable partner for negotiation which could be influenced and/or controlled from outside.

When applying these criteria in the Afghan context, the justification for using a question mark in the heading to this book becomes evident. In a resolution of 29 February 2000 the UN General Assembly correctly spoke of 'the intensification of armed hostilities in Afghanistan and the complex nature of the conflict, including its ethnic, religious and political aspects'[2], the mass killings and systematic human rights violations against civilians and prisoners of war[3], reports of rape and cruel treatment[4], the continued displacement of millions of Afghan refugees[5] and reports of attacks on and

---

[1] Interim report on the situation of human rights in Afghanistan, prepared by the Special Rapporteur of the Commission on Human Rights, Document A/54/422 of 30 September 1999

[2] See General Assembly Resolution A/RES/54/185 of 29 February 2000 ('Question of human rights in Afghanistan'), para. 5 *lit.* c.

[3] *Ibid.* para. 2 and 13.

[4] *Ibid.* para. 13.

[5] *Ibid.* para. 5 *lit.* d.

looting of cultural artefacts in Afghanistan.⁶ The serious and continuing violation of fundamental rights to life, liberty, security of person, freedom from torture and from other forms of cruel, inhuman or degrading treatment or punishment, freedom of opinion, expression, religious persuasion, association and movement, and demonstrations, as well as the permanent violation of the rights of women and girls⁷ are undoubtedly a consequence of the internal conflict in Afghanistan. At the same time, ever since the military invasion by the Soviet Union in 1979 the internal, in particular the ethnic-religious aspects of this conflict⁸ are closely intertwined with external interference and intervention.⁹ Thus, we can hardly speak of a prevailing 'endogenous' problem, which is, however, characteristic of a 'failed state'. The resolutions of the Security Council and of the General Assembly view external interference mainly as supply of weapons and military training, or the support of either side of the warring parties by third states.¹⁰

Conversely, the regime of the radical Muslim group Taliban troubles all the neighbouring states. Not only countries like Uzbekistan, Tajikistan and Kirgizstan feel threatened by the Taliban, also the regime in the Islamic

---

⁶ *Ibid.* para. 16.

⁷ See General Assembly Resolution A/RES/53/165 of 25 February 1999 ('Situation of human rights in Afghanistan'), paras. 4, 6 *lit.* b, 12 *lit.* c, d, e, f, g; see also Interim report on the situation of human rights in Afghanistan, prepared by the Special Rapporteur of the Commission on Human Rights, Document A/54/422 of 30 September 1999, paras 46 *et seq.*

⁸ General Assembly Resolution A/RES/53/165, para. 6 *lit.* c.

⁹ *Ibid.*, para. 9: 'The General Assembly [...] Urges all States [...] to refrain from interfering in [the] internal affairs [of Afghanistan]'; see also General Assembly Resolution A/RES/52/211 of 19 December 1997, Part B, preambular para. 15: 'The General Assembly [...] Stressing the importance of non-intervention and non-interference in the internal affairs of Afghanistan, and deeply concerned at all forms of continued support which have caused or may cause the prolongation of the conflict [...]'; see also Security Council Resolution 1214 (1998) of 8 December 1998, preambular para. 8.

¹⁰ General Assembly Resolution A/RES/54/185, para. 7; Security Council Resolution 1214 (1998), para. 3; see also Interim report on the situation of human rights in Afghanistan, prepared by the Special Rapporteur of the Commission on Human Rights, para. 35 *lit.* a, mentioning the 'basic goal of ending the externally supported military conflict' in the context of safeguarding human rights.

Republic of Iran, which itself has strong roots in the Islamic faith. Even a country as large and powerful as the People's Republic of China shows concern. In a small land strip called Vakhan, Afghanistan shares a tiny border with China, perhaps more precisely with the autonomous region of Xinjiang, which belongs to the People's Republic, but is inhabited mainly by a Muslim population, the Uigur. Through this slim piece of land, not only Taliban Islamic propaganda reaches the Uigur, but, moreover, the Taliban directly support Uigur opposition in many ways. Apparently, the government in Beijing views the situation with such seriousness that it decided to contact the Taliban in the matter. Beijing also aims at stopping the flourishing drug traffic between Afghanistan and the Chinese province. Afghanistan today lies in the middle of Central Asia, the area of the ancient Silk Road, which has nowadays become a 'drugs road'. It is today the largest producer of opium in the world.[11] From there, drugs are shipped to the East and, via Russia, the Caucasus and Turkey, to the West. In this respect, the Special Rapporteur of the Commission on Human Rights relies on the reports of the UN international drug control programme according to which 63,500 hectares of opium poppy are being cultivated in Afghanistan, having a potential annual output in raw opium of 3,200 tonnes. However, the Rapporteur also mentions the attempts of the Taliban to destroy these drugs.[12]

The thereby illustrated thesis of equally important endogenous and exogenous factors to the conflict may, however, have to be modified to a certain extent due to the Security Council resolution of 15 October 1999. In that resolution, the Security Council demanded that the Taliban turn over the terrorist Osama Bin Ladin[13] and strongly condemned 'the continuing use of Afghan territory, especially areas controlled by the Taliban, for the sheltering and training of terrorists and planning of terrorist acts [...]'.[14]

---

[11] See Interim report on the situation of human rights in Afghanistan, prepared by the Special Rapporteur of the Commission on Human Rights, para. 44.

[12] *Ibid.*

[13] Security Council Resolution 1267 (1999) of 15 October 1999, para. 2.

[14] *Ibid.* preambular paragraph 5; see also Security Council Resolution 1214 (1998), preambular para. 13 and para. 13.

This aspect touches upon another inner-state dimension of the Afghan tragedy, which, however, does not fundamentally change the analysis.

The international community's interest in effectively combating terrorism leads to a second criterion defining the notion of a 'failed state'. From the perspective of a national constitution the collapse of a state's regulatory power has been mentioned. This denotes the very core of a state, which sociologist Max Weber, who was born in Erfurt in 1864 and taught sociology in Munich from 1919 onwards, called the *Gewaltmonopol, i.e.* the state's monopoly to resort to the use of force (Weber 1966: 27 et seq.). Nevertheless, *Gewaltmonopol* and state terrorism are not necessarily antagonistic as the case of the Libyan revolutionary leader Moamar Al-Gaddhafi underlines. State terrorism is merely characteristic of the abuse of the *Gewaltmonopol* but not of its disappearance. The yardstick used for the competence of the modern state to use within its territory physical force and to confine the use of force to state organs, is, also in Afghanistan, the situation of human rights which are of a universal character. The report of the UN Special Rapporteur for the second half of 1999 highlights mass executions by the Taliban after recapturing the area of Bayman, an area in the centre of the highlands of Afghanistan called Hazarajat.[15] Thus, the General Assembly urged that the perpetrators be brought to trial.[16] However, the institutions required to follow this appeal do not exist in the country (Ermacora 1995: para 50). This lack of institution-building is not only due to the state of war but is firmly rooted in the political ideology of the Taliban, which rejects every attempt of effective control of their power and does not provide for any checks and balances. It was, therefore, not without good reason that in November 1998, the UN Secretary-General suggested to establish within the United Nations Special Mission to Afghanistan (UNSMA) a 'civil affairs unit', 'with the primary objective of monitoring the situation, promoting respect for minimum humanitarian standards and deterring massive and systematic violations of human rights

---

[15] See Interim report on the situation of human rights in Afghanistan, prepared by the Special Rapporteur of the Commission on Human Rights, paras 11 *et seq.*, 19 *et seq.*

[16] See General Assembly A/RES/54/185 at para. 8 *lit.* e).

and humanitarian law in the future'.[17] Similarly, the report of the UN Commission on Human Rights directly links the issue of institution-building with the protection of human rights. It argues: 'Institution- and capacity-building must advance human rights [...]'.[18] From the viewpoint of international law, the rule of the Taliban, who are in control of 97 per cent of the Afghan territory, must nonetheless be considered 'state power'. The fact of grave violations of humanitarian minimum standards does not alter this assessment. The 'government' by the so-called 'Islamic Emirate of Afghanistan' (IEA), the leader Amirul Mominin as well as the President of the Council of the 'Islamic Emirate of Afghanistan' Mullah Mohammed Rabbani must, according to the formal criteria of international law, be termed as an 'effective' government capable of acting with a perspective of some permanence (Ipsen 1999: para 22, 23). When the German Federal Constitutional Court (*Bundesverfassungsgericht*) had to render judgment on the issue of whether or not there was political persecution in the sense of 'statehood' or 'quasi-statehood' (Article 16a of the German Constitution – *Grundgesetz*) in Afghanistan, it held decisive, whether or not political persecution in fact took place within a system of governance which showed a certain degree of stability in the sense of an overarching peaceful order at least on a core territory.[19] The allegedly continuing preparation of a state constitution by the Taliban may serve as an interesting indicator in this context. The Taliban themselves maintain that they have not only brought 'peace, security and territorial integrity' to the country but also 'law and order'.[20] Moreover, the military structure of the Taliban increasingly resembles those of regular armed forces. It does not have much in common any more with the former 'classic' combat units of the Mujahedin of the times of war against the Soviet invaders.[21] However, this progressive

---

[17] See Security Council Resolution 1214 (1998), para. 7.

[18] See Interim report on the situation of human rights in Afghanistan, prepared by the Special Rapporteur of the Commission on Human Rights, para. 60(5).

[19] BVerfG, 2 BvR 260/98 judgement of 10 August 2000, at 17, with reference to the judgement BVerfGE 80, 315 [334 *et seq.*].

[20] See Interim report on the situation of human rights in Afghanistan, prepared by the Special Rapporteur of the Commission on Human Rights, para. 36.

[21] See Human Rights Watch, Report on the Situation in Afghanistan (New York, 13 July 2001).

Afghanistan – The Perspective of International Law

consolidation of state power does not alter the fact that the Taliban continue to struggle for international recognition.[22] It nevertheless has to be stressed that it remains difficult to assess the *quality* of the *Gewaltmonopol* from the outsider's perspective of an international lawyer.

Even if it cannot be said that the perceived lack of institution-building in today's Afghanistan has as yet crossed the rubicon of a 'breakdown of government' and, therefore, to a 'failed state' in the sense of international law, the archimedic point of statehood is constantly being highlighted in other subjects of this book. Contributions like 'The View of the State by Afghans Abroad', the 'Loya Jirga – An Efficient Political Tool?', 'Tribe and State' and 'Governance and State Authority' obviously have close connections to the demand of 'modernity' for a unity of decision and effect of the state (*staatliche Entscheidungs- und Wirkungseinheit*). The same is true for the relationship of 'Religious Orthodoxy and the Maintenance of Afghanistan's Performative Traditions' or the issue of 'Educational Politics' and women's rights. State power, the monopoly of resort to the use of force, as well as the legitimacy of a state's use of force have in the context of this book turned out to be the 'litmus test' for the statehood of Afghanistan. May these aspects become the points of crystallization of the statehood in the future!

In relation to Islam and religious orthodoxy, it must be stressed that from a perspective of Western political and constitutional thought, the absence of theocratic-fundamentalistic forms of religion is seen as an absolute precondition of democracy. For these religious forms will otherwise destroy the very basis of any democratic development of political will, i.e. the individual judgment and decision of each and every citizen. They will replace democratic decision-making by an authoritative statement of the will of God and its direct implementation (Böckenförde 1996: N6). The political order of civil society, which accepts religious freedom as a fundamental constitutional principle and a human right, does no longer include religious matters and religious beliefs, as was the case with the idea of *polis*. Neither does it view religion as its necessary foundation, or utilize religion when searching for legitimacy. Rather, religion is independent

---

[22] See Interim report on the situation of human rights in Afghanistan, prepared by the Special Rapporteur of the Commission on Human Rights, para. 36.

from that order. The secularization of state and religion stands as an prime achievement of modernity and is widely recognized as an opportunity for religious freedom (Böckenförde 1999: 259 and Bielefeldt 19XX: 31, 35). Yet, in this respect, the chasm between the modern Western-type constitutional state and the fundamentalistic Islamic state appears insurmountable.

The third aspect of a failed state, the absence of a reliable negotiating partner that is open to influence and control from the outside, does not have to be treated in any depth here. For such a state is essentially not considered as disappeared as long as no new state has emerged on that territory on the basis of self-determination of the people concerned. It, thus, has to be noted, in particular with a view to the title of this publication, that even a 'failure of state' does not lead to the loss of statehood in the sense of legal personality from the international legal standpoint. A 'Country without State', therefore, remains, at least from a legal standpoint, a case so exceptional, that it would hardly be conceivable in reality. In terms of legal dogma, a 'failed state' continues to enjoy a legal personality, although it may have lost factual capacity of action (Ipsen 1999: para 5,9). Accordingly, both the Security Council and the General Assembly continue to assert in their respective Resolutions, the 'sovereignty, independence, territorial integrity and national unity of Afghanistan'.[23] Moreover, they urge the parties to the conflict to respect the international treaties which were ratified by Afghanistan. These are namely the Geneva Convention relative to the Protection of Civilian Persons in Time of War of 12 August 1949, of which the fiftieth anniversary was celebrated only last year, the 'Convention on the Prevention and Punishment of the Crime of Genocide', the 'International Covenant on Civil and Political Rights', as well as the 'Convention against Torture and Other Cruel, Inhuman or Degrading Treatment or Punishment' and others.[24] The General Assembly has

---

[23] See the second prambular paragraph of Security Council Resolution 1267 (1999): 'The Security Council [...] Reaffirming its strong commitment to the sovereignty, independence, territorial integrity and national unity of Afghanistan [...]'; General Assembly Resolution A/RES/54/185, para. 7: 'The General Assembly [...] Urges all States to respect the sovereignty, independence, territorial integrity and national unity of Afghanistan [...]'.

[24] See the third point of consideration of General Assembly Resolution A/RES/53/165

repeatedly called on the warring parties to co-operate with the Secretary-General of the United Nations and the High-Commissioner for Human Rights, with a view to stopping the mass killings of prisoners of war and civilians and to investigate crimes of rape and cruel treatment in Afghanistan.[25] Although a non-state party to an armed conflict will also profit from Article 3 of the four Geneva Conventions containing basic provisions aiming at protection 'in the case of armed conflict not of an international character'; the calls and demands of the Resolutions only make sense if the international community continues to consider Afghanistan as capable of acting, be it through the Afghan factions of the Taliban or the 'United Front', i.e. the Northern Alliance as *state* parties to the conflict. Thus, what was said above on the *Gewaltmonopol* and state power is thereby confirmed.

From a legal perspective it can, thus, be stated that, albeit amputated to some degree, the statehood of Afghanistan is, even after twenty years of war, still considered a fully fledged subject of international law. The title of this book must, therefore, be understood not from a narrow legal perspective but rather in a wider political sense, comprising historical, sociological as well as geopolitical elements. The crucial issue for the future will be the exercise of effective and common good-oriented state power, currently divided and fragmented between the Taliban and the Northern Alliance. Whether or not political attempts in that direction will eventually succeed, will depend on the pacification of Afghanistan and the creation of a stable and lasting peaceful order including the whole region. The implementation of the Tashkent Declaration on Fundamental Principles for a Peaceful Settlement of the Afghan Conflict of 19 July 1999 will undoubtedly have to play an outstanding role in this context.[26] This Declaration is essentially founded on the notion of the full exercise of the right to self determination of the Afghan people, an axiom of international law which was already mentioned above. A political solution to the conflict will only be possible with the participation of all Afghan parties and factions, as well as all parts of Afghan society. The same is true for a

---

and A/RES/54/185.

[25] See General Assembly Resolution A/RES/54/185, para. 13.

[26] See United Nations, General Assembly/Security Council, Document A/54/174-S/1999/812, annex.

constitutional consensus.[27] The institution of the *loya jirga* has played an important role in this context in the past. National conciliation and the creation of effective state power have to be the central aims of the re-construction of Afghanistan in the framework of 'peace-building'.[28] In this context, therefore, parallels to the situation of a 'failed state' clearly exist. These attempts must be embedded in a framework of international co-operation and support for re-construction with close co-operation with the United Nations. The latter could thereby strengthen their role in world politics by developing an intelligent concept of crisis prevention and resolution, as well as the reconstruction of society and law.

Postscript, October 2001

Due to international developments following the terrorist attacks on the United States of America on 11 September 2001, and the American counterstrike, which began on 7 October 2001 and is supported by NATO Member States on the basis of Article 5 of the North Atlantic Treaty ('Enduring Freedom'), the rule of the Taliban seems to be in progressive dissolution. However, it would appear premature to speculate on the structural features of an Afghan state to come after the demise of the Taliban.

---

[27] See General Assembly Resolution A/RES/52/211, para. 8; Interim report on the situation of human rights in Afghanistan, prepared by the Special Rapporteur of the Commission on Human Rights, para. 58.

[28] See for 'Peace-building' Thürer, *op. cit.*, who calls these measures 'Chapter 4' of the UN Charter.

Afghanistan – The Perspective of International Law

Bibliography

Bielefeldt H. (1998) *Philosophie der Menschenrechte*. Darmstadt, Wissenschaftliche Buchgesellschaft.

Böckenförde E.-W. (1996) Das Unwahrscheinliche wollen. *Frankfurter Allgemeine Zeitung* (2 May 1996) 102: N6.

Böckenförde E.-W. (1999) *Staat, Nation, Europa*. Frankfurt am Main, Suhrkamp.

Ermacora Felix (1995) Final Report on the Situation of Human Rights in Afghanistan. New York, United Nations, Economic and Social Council E/CN.4/1995/64.

Ipsen K. (1999) *Völkerrecht*. München, C.H. Beck.

Thürer D. (1996) Der Wegfall effektiver Staatsgewalt: 'The Failed State'. In: D. Thürer, M. Herdegen amd G. Hohloch (eds.) *Der Wegfall effektiver Staatsgewalt: 'The Failed State'*, 34 Berichte der Deutschen Gesellschaft für Völkerrecht. Heidelberg, Müller.

Weber M. (1966) *Staatssoziologie*. Berlin, Duncker & Humblot.

Human Rights Watch (2001) *Report on the Situation in Afghanistan*. New York .

United Nations, General Assembly/Security Council, Document A/54/174-S/1999/812.

United Nations, Interim Report on the Situation of Human Rights in Afghanistan, prepared by the Special Rapporteur of the Commission on Human Rights, Document A/54/422 of 30 September 1999..

United Nations, General Assembly Resolution A/RES/54/185 of 29 February 2000 ('Question of human rights in Afghanistan').

United Nations, General Assembly Resolution A/RES/53/165 of 25 February 1999 ('Situation of human rights in Afghanistan').

United Nations, United Nations, General Assembly Resolution A/RES/52/211 of 19 December 1997.

United Nations, Security Council Resolution 1214 (1998) of 8 December 1998.

United Nations, Security Council Resolution 1267 (1999) of 15 October 1999.

United Nations, Boutros Ghali, Boutros (1995) Concluding Statement by the Secretary-General of the United Nations Congress on Public International Law. Documents of the United Nations Congress on Public International Law – Towards the Twenty-First Century. International Law as a Language for International Relations (13 – 17 March 1995, New York).

The Role
of Outside Actors in the Afghanistan Conflict

Amin Saikal

The strategic landscape of the Afghanistan conflict is changing. After nearly a decade of disentanglement from the conflict following the withdrawal of Soviet occupying forces from Afghanistan, major power interests are once again on the rise in the war-torn country. The United States and Russia, which engaged in a proxy war for the soul of Afghanistan in the 1980s, have finally found common ground in their opposition to what has been created in the intervening period: the Pakistan-backed ultra-orthodox Islamic Taliban militia. In a summit in early June 2000, the two powers agreed on the need to contain the Taliban as a perceived source of support for the spread of 'Islamic militancy' and 'international terrorism'. This was a development which also resonated well with India, Iran, the Central Asian republics, China and the European Union, all of which have grown apprehensive of the Taliban for varying reasons. Since then an unprecedented degree of strategic discussion and co-operation has developed between Washington, Moscow and New Delhi, and through the latter two with Tehran in opposition to the Taliban. By implication, Pakistan has faced greater isolation than ever before, given its persistent refusal to abandon its sponsorship of the Taliban. This development, if carried forward prudently, has the potential to change the dynamics of the Afghan conflict towards a viable resolution, and at the same time help save Pakistan from becoming a menace both to itself and to the region. It could also help the United States to generate an appropriate strategy to play a constructive role in fostering stability and security in South, Central and West Asia.

Troubled by its protracted military engagement to pacify Islamic opposition to its rule of Chechnya and by the growing Islamic activism in its former Soviet Central Asian republics, Russia has increasingly grown wary of the Taliban. It has castigated the militia for aiding cross-border Islamic militancy into the former Soviet Central Asian republics, and for providing assistance to what it has called the 'Chechen Islamic rebels'. It has been profoundly perturbed by recurrent bursts of Islamic opposition activity in Uzbekistan and Tajikistan, which in August 2000 was also manifested in a reportedly Taliban-supported protracted armed attack by an Islamic group, made up of Uzbek, Tajik and Chechen elements, on parts of Kirgizstan bordering Tajikistan. The attack resulted in a major military confrontation at the cost of many lives. It alarmed not only the Kirghiz government and its Central Asian counterparts but also Moscow, which has assumed responsibility for the security of the borders of Central Asian states with Afghanistan. Russia has also been especially incensed at the reception that the Taliban have given to the Chechen Islamic fighters, allowing them to open a mission in Kabul and use Afghanistan as a conduit for their anti-Russian resistance in Chechnya.

While beefing up its border guard defences along the Central Asian states' borders with Afghanistan, Moscow has repeatedly threatened military actions, if necessary, against Taliban positions in Afghanistan, and supported tougher UN sanctions against the Taliban. In November 1999, it worked closely with the United States in securing UN Security Council Resolution 1267 to impose limited sanctions, and then again a year later, pursuant to Security Council Resolution 1333, to impose a more comprehensive regime of sanctions, including an arms embargo against the Taliban.

As a corollary, it has become more receptive towards the anti-Taliban forces in northern Afghanistan, led by Commander Ahmad Shah Massoud, representing the ousted government of Burhan al-Din Rabbani, which still occupies Afghanistan's seat in the United Nations General Assembly. This has been especially so since the Taliban's capture, with direct Pakistani military and Arab mercenary participation in the fighting, of the city of Taliqan in August 2000. Russia has reportedly sold some new arms to Massoud's forces, including four helicopters with India's financial help.

Although publicly at odds with Russia's handling of Chechnya, Washington has increasingly come to appreciate Moscow's concern about the Taliban. This comes against the backdrop of a topsy-turvy approach by Washington to the Taliban phenomenon. When in 1994, Pakistan, or more specifically its then Interior Minister, Nasirullah Babar as well as its military

The Role of Outside Actors

intelligence (the ISI), generated the Taliban (some claim with help from the CIA), Washington was quite content to remain conspicuously silent about the development. It turned a blind eye to the militia's extremist ideological disposition and medievalist practices. It appeared to have been persuaded by Islamabad's argument that the Taliban would serve its interests as both an anti-Iranian Sunni factor and a stabilizing force in opening up Afghanistan as a viable corridor through which the US and its allies could find profitable access to the resources and markets of the newly independent Central Asian republics. This was an argument which was also embraced by Saudi Arabia and the United Arab Emirates (UAE) – the only two other countries apart from Pakistan that have recognized the Taliban as a government. In this, Riyadh was motivated by its regional Sunni sectarian rivalry with Shi'ite Iran, and Abu Dhabi was influenced by the bargaining leverage that the Taliban could provide it against Iran in its territorial dispute with the latter over the Islands of Abu Musa, and the Greater and Lesser Tunbs in the Gulf. A combination of Washington's silence and the Saudi and UAE provision of ample funding proved instrumental in enabling the Taliban to secure rapid territorial expansion in Afghanistan, forcing the Rabbani–Massoud Islamic government out of Kabul to the north by September 1996 and gaining control over much of Afghanistan two years later.

It was only in 1998 that Washington felt impelled to change course. With a number of experienced personnel assuming senior positions in the State Department, especially Under Secretary of State Thomas Pickering, it found itself with little choice but to voice criticism of the Taliban. It shunned not only the Taliban's prejudicial version of Islam, discriminating against women, Shia Muslims and non-Pashtun ethnic minorities in Afghanistan, but also its tolerance of narcotic production and drug trafficking, and support of Islamic extremists. The situation dramatically changed with the August 1998 bombing of American embassies in Nairobi and Dar es Salaam. Washington accused the multi-millionaire Saudi dissident, Osama Bin Ladin, who had once been side by side with the US in opposing the Soviet occupation of Afghanistan, of masterminding the bombing. It launched a cruise missile attack on Bin Ladin's camps in Afghanistan and demanded his extradition. However, the Taliban's refusal to budge on their protection of Bin Ladin brought the chickens home to roost for both Washington and Riyadh. The latter froze relations with the Taliban, and the former has been trying ever since, though in vain, to persuade Pakistan to use its leverage with the Taliban to secure Bin Ladin's hand-over. For a brief period in September–October 1999 it appeared that Washington was making some progress over the matter with Prime Minister Nawaz Sharif, who for the first time publicly accused the Taliban of supporting sectarian violence and fuelling Islamic extremism in Pakistan. However, within days of speaking out, the Prime Minister was deposed by a coup, led by General Pervez Musharraf – a development which brought to power the very forces, that is the military and the ISI, that had been the real movers of Pakistan's Afghanistan and Kashmir policies since the early 1980s.

Indeed, initially, General Musharraf likened himself to the founder of modern Turkey, the nationalist-reformist Mustafa Kemal Ataturk, and expressed support for the formation of a broad-based government and a peaceful settlement of the conflict in Afghanistan. He also indicated to President Bill Clinton during the latter's brief stop-over in Pakistan in early 2000 that he would seek to use Pakistan's influence with the Taliban to advance the Bin Ladin issue. However, by May 2000 he had modified his position. While seeking to deflect growing criticism of his inability to address Pakistan's deep-seated social and economic ills and to return the country to a democratic rule sooner rather than later – some of the very factors on which he had drawn to justify his military takeover – General Musharraf was increasingly swayed by the influence of the military and growing militant Islamic forces that have swept Pakistan itself. These are of course the very two constituencies which have effectively interacted with the Taliban to serve as organic sources of nourishment for each other. Musharraf consequently backed away from his original promise to pressure the Taliban, greatly to Washington's annoyance. It is clear to Washington that neither Bin Ladin and his associates, who included many from the Arab world, nor the Taliban hosting them would have been able to carry out off-shore operations without Pakistan's consent, for Pakistan is the only outlet which they have to the outside world. Washington's impatience was echoed in the State Department's annual Human Rights Report for 1999. It not only accused the Taliban of supporting 'international terrorism', but also named Pakistan as the country where 'Kashmiri terrorists' receive support, justifying the imposition of its own and the UN's limited sanctions against the Taliban, and also putting Pakistan on notice for similar actions. A further attempt by Thomas Pickering, who visited Pakistan in late May, to iron out differences with Islamabad yielded very little.

To the contrary, Pakistan's military leadership finally dropped some of Pakistan's past pretence of non-interference in Afghanistan. In a BBC interview on 2 August 2000, General Musharraf made it clear that it was in Pakistan's national security interests to support the Taliban as a cross-border force dominated by ethnic Pashtuns, who populate both sides of the long Afghan–Pakistan border. This was a view which had been floated by his Foreign Minister Abdul Satar two years earlier. With regard to Bin Ladin, he urged the United States to enter direct dialogue with the Taliban – a stand upon which Pakistan has often insisted as a way of gaining broader international recognition for the militia. He had earlier also warned that any airstrike by Russia against the Taliban targets could only benefit the anti-Taliban forces and escalate the war in Afghanistan. In so doing, General Musharraf confirmed what had been suspected for a long time by many analysts to be Pakistan's policy of exploiting Afghanistan's mosaic composition to promote cross-border ethnic clientism as a means of achieving wider regional interests.

The net effect of this policy, begun under Pakistan's former military ruler General Zia ul-Haq (1977–88), has been to promote the political supremacy of the Pashtuns as a historically dominant force in Afghanistan. It has thus pitched the country's Pashtuns against its non-Pashtuns, transforming the Afghan conflict into an ethnic one. Pakistan's aim has been to secure a client government in Kabul as a reward for its help to the Afghan Islamic resistance to the Soviet occupation, but for four major purposes. The first is to secure a 'strategic depth' against its arch-enemy, India, in Afghanistan. The second is to put a permanent end to the long-standing Afghan–Pakistan border dispute and Afghanistan's past support for the creation of a Pashtunistan entity out of the North West Frontier and Baluchistan provinces of Pakistan. The third, since the independence of the Central Asian republics, is to ensure some clout for Pakistan as an important player in the region. The fourth is to provide an 'Islamic venture' for Pakistan's own Islamic militants to divert them away from causing too many domestic problems.

Another development that has now made the Taliban less relevant to the advancement of US interests is the militia's anti-Iranian character. Originally, as relations between the United States and Iran were highly antagonistic, with Washington standing determined to contain Iran, and as Iran's relations with America's GCC allies, especially Saudi Arabia, were grounded in regional rivalries, the Taliban could easily appeal to Washington and its Gulf allies. However, this factor is no longer a major point of consideration. Since the rise to power of President Muhammad Khatami in mid-1997 and his push to reform the Iranian Islamic system in order to generate an 'Islamic democracy' and 'Islamic civil society', with principles of 'civilizational dialogue' and co-operation underlining Iran's foreign relations, the situation has changed. While US–Iranian diplomatic ties still remain ruptured, a steady thaw in other areas between the two sides is in progress. If the current trends continue, and the US drops its sanctions against Iran, the need for a restoration of ties between the sides is a reality that neither side may be able to ignore for too long. In conjunction with this, Iranian–Saudi relations have also registered a marked improvement in the last few years. The two regional rivals have leaned increasingly towards wider bilateral understanding and security co-operation. Although Iranian–UAE relations continue to be tense because of their territorial disputes, Iran is no longer viewed as a major threat to any of the GCC countries.

This is equally true of Iran's position in Central Asia. Tehran's close ties with Russia, which has emerged as Iran's principal arms supplier, its constructive role in mediating a settlement between the ruling secularist and Islamist forces in Tajikistan, and its restraint from siding with Islamic opposition forces in other states in the region, have proved to be quite reassuring to the regional leaderships, as well as to Moscow and, for that matter, to Washington.

Meanwhile, Khatami's Islamic reforms have successfully revealed the Islamic extremism practised by the Taliban and in many parts of Pakistan in the worst light possible. Although for reasons of domestic and regional political expediency, the Khatami government has at times tried to open dialogue with the Taliban, in principle it cannot approve of either their brand of Islamic extremism or Pakistan's intrusion into Afghanistan. In the final analysis, the Khatami leadership can establish formal ties with the

The Role of Outside Actors

Taliban only when the militia has changed its medievalist behaviour, reached a settlement with the opposition, including the 15 per cent Shi'ite segment of the Afghan population, and demonstrated independence from Islamabad. The prospects do not appear to be bright for the realization of any of these objectives in the foreseeable future.

Given the fact that for the United States Iran is a much bigger strategic and economic prize than Pakistan, there are compelling reasons for Washington not to pursue its past anti-Iranian policies. It is now in the interest of the United States to underline two important points: its opposition to the Taliban's brand of Islam and Pakistan's continued nourishment of the militia; and its support for Khatami's reforms as the best means of improving prospects for a US–Iranian *rapprochement*.

In addition, a move in this direction could also inject more vitality into US–Indian relations. A shift in American policy for closer ties with India has already gathered pace. This has been underlined not only by President Clinton's successful visit to India in early 2000 and the US's repeated urging of Pakistan to refrain from inflaming the Kashmir dispute, but also by an agreement between the US and India to co-operate in the area of 'international terrorism'. This agreement essentially reflected America's concern over Pakistan's involvement in causing the Kargil war of 1999, its continued support for the Taliban, and the links between the Taliban and Kashmiri Islamic nationalists fighting for independence from India. A point that New Delhi may have successfully driven home to the Americans is its claim that Pakistan's intelligence was fully behind the Kashmiri militants' hijacking of the Indian Airlines passenger plane in late December 1999, and the Taliban's complicity in that incident.

While the Indian, Iranian, Russian and Central Asian common opposition to Pakistan's involvement in Afghanistan has already led to close co-operation among these actors, any further steps by Washington to tighten the *cordon sanitaire* around Pakistan could prove to be instrumental in accelerating three major developments.

The first is that it could result in wider policy co-ordination (although with only indirect participation of Iran, as long as there are no formal relations between Tehran and Washington) to secure a viable resolution to the Afghan conflict. At present, there is a serious power imbalance on the ground in Afghanistan. The Taliban are substantially advantaged by Pakistan's full and unwavering military support, steady flow of human support from Pakistan's religious groups and schools, and Bin Ladin's wealth and personal fighters, as well as by the revenue that the militia generates from illicit dealings, including heroin production and drug trafficking. The opposition continues to remain under-resourced. Although the opposition, which is made up of various northern-based groups, has achieved a greater degree of unity of purpose and action in recent times, it still lacks sufficient resources to overcome some acute logistical and defensive problems. This has deterred it from expanding its territorial control beyond a few north-eastern provinces and providing more than limited support to local uprisings elsewhere in the country. As long as this remains the case, and the regional and international actors remain ambivalent towards Pakistan, the Taliban and their Pakistani backers will have little incentive to settle for a negotiated settlement of the Afghan conflict and the United Nations will have little leverage to play a meaningful role. For that matter, any peace efforts mounted from outside, whether they are by the former king Zahir Shah to convene a *loya jirga* (the traditional Grand Assembly) or by the Organization of Islamic Conference (OIC) to promote a settlement, are unlikely to produce any meaningful result.

Washington seems to have finally recognized this disparity as hampering the process of achieving a negotiated settlement; and has recently taken a few limited steps which attest to this recognition. It has permitted the Afghan opposition loyal to Commander Massoud to open an office in Washington on behalf of the Rabbani government. Although this office is not a replacement for the Afghan embassy which was closed down two years ago because of a dispute between its staff over whether it should represent the Taliban or the Rabbani government, it has signalled a change in the US attitude. Washington has also ventured into a dialogue with the Massoud side in an attempt to assess the opposition's defensive capacity, and some US legislators have strongly argued for aid to Massoud's forces. Furthermore, a mission representing the Head of the European Union, led by the French General Morillon, paid a 'goodwill visit' to Massoud in the Panjsher Valley in mid-2000, and this led to the President of the EU inviting Massoud on an official visit to Brussels and publicly condemning

Pakistan's support of the Taliban. There are also signs of the EU's willingness to co-ordinate policy with the US, Russia and India to boost the international standing of the opposition to the Taliban.

Meanwhile, despite former Russian president Boris Yeltsin's criticism of the American cruise missile attack on Afghanistan, his successor, Vladimir Putin, has actively sought to co-ordinate efforts to increase international pressure on the Taliban and their Pakistani backers. Moscow will be pleased to see a close monitoring of the implementation of the UN sanctions against the Taliban, which would be mandatory for Pakistan to observe, and could easily paralyse the militia's war machine.

These are very limited steps and have not as yet led to a noticeable change in the balance of forces on the ground in Afghanistan, but they have provided a needed measure of psychological boost to the opposition. If the objective is to inject some balance in the fighting capacities of the Taliban and the opposition, then a lot more needs to be done. The higher the cost of the war for the Taliban and Pakistan the greater the chances of their opting for a negotiated settlement, as the Soviets did after their airforce took a heavy toll in the wake of America's supply of Stinger missiles to the Afghan Islamic resistance forces, the Mujahidin, from 1986. Whatever assistance is provided to the opposition, it must of course be proportionate to the need for opening the way for a negotiated settlement rather than prolonging the bloodshed in Afghanistan.

The second development is that, despite Musharraf's claim that the Taliban are a security imperative for Pakistan, a negotiated settlement of the Afghan conflict, with the objective of creating a broad-based, representative national government, may well be the only way out of the mess in which Pakistan has placed itself. Given Pakistan's virtual economic bankruptcy and its problems of law and order, corruption, social fragmentation, sectarian violence and massive human rights violations, which have already buttoned down even Musharraf's military rule, the cost of its involvement in the Afghan conflict is something it can do without. The widespread religious militancy and associated social and political difficulties and international isolation that it has generated for Pakistan call for the problem to be settled promptly. All the costs cannot justify the need for a 'strategic depth' – something which now in relation to a nuclearized Pakistan and India is worth very little. There seems to be a view in the

Pakistani leadership that a backdown from supporting the Taliban could require Pakistan to pay a very high price in terms of a domestic backlash. The point is that if Pakistan's involvement in Afghanistan is not retrenched soon, the costs of containing its effects on Pakistan may prove to be even higher. There is no sound logic behind Pakistan's involvement and it must take care not to make the same mistakes that other adventurers into Afghanistan have made before it.

The third development is to help America in nurturing a post-Cold-War strategy that could assist it in improving its standing in the region without too much risk of getting involved in any direct military conflict. The US shortsightedly and insensitively disentangled itself from Afghanistan following the Soviet pullout. It had done this once before, in the mid-1950s, when it turned down Afghanistan's repeated requests for economic and military aid for the post-Second World War modernization of the country. The price that it ultimately paid for that refusal was to counter the Soviet invasion of the country two and half decades later. Its neglect of post-communist Afghanistan has now landed it with the terrible problems of 'international terrorism' and regional instability. These problems have not only ensured the perpetuation of bloodshed and destruction in Afghanistan, but also now threaten the very existence of America's foremost former regional ally in the fight against communism. Pakistan has now dangerously turned into a nuclearized but virtually rogue actor. It was this development that finally prompted Washington in early November 2000 to claim openly that the US and Russia had information that Pakistan was engaged in direct military involvement in Afghanistan and that Pakistan's support of the Taliban could prove very costly for Pakistan itself. Washington's dilemmas in dealing with this actor cannot be underestimated. To apply effective pressure on it could move it into one of two directions: it could either jolt its leadership out of its present destabilizing dispositionary mode, and force it on a constructive path of behaviour, or burden it to the point of Pakistan imploding and disintegrating. However, given Pakistan's prevailing national circumstances and past responses to outside pressure, its leadership may realize the first scenario rather than let the second one happen.

In either case, the US needs to develop a sound strategy towards South, Central and West Asia. A serious move to bring about a resolution of the

The Role of Outside Actors

Afghan conflict, with support from Russia, Iran, India and Central Asia, is most likely to benefit not only the cause of long-term stability, but also America's wider interests in the region. A failure to do so may occasion America to regret the passing of a valuable opportunity. In the present climate of regional changes and America's own geostrategic requirements, the prospects for a settlement of the Afghan conflict are not quite as dim as they might perhaps seem. However, the achievement of a settlement will very much depend on how responsibly and promptly the US provides the needed leadership and to what extent the receptive regional actors are prepared to act.

The Failure of UN Mediation in Afghanistan

Anwar-ul-Haq Ahady

Since the Soviet invasion in December 1979 there have been two rounds of mediations by the UN regarding the conflict in Afghanistan. The first round culminated in the Geneva Accords of 1988 which provided the basis for the withdrawal of Soviet forces from Afghanistan. Despite serious obstacles during the first few years, that round of mediations constitutes a spectacular case of UN success (Harrison and Cordovez 1994; Rubin 1995). The second round of mediations began after the completion of the withdrawal of Soviet forces in 1989. Unfortunately, this round of UN mediation in Afghanistan has failed to achieve its objectives.

Here I would like first to discuss the factors that have a bearing on the success of mediation in general; then I would like to analyse the failure of the second round of UN mediations in Afghanistan; finally I would like to present some recommendations regarding the UN peace-making efforts in Afghanistan.

Mediation is a weak form of conflict management. Empirical research has established that the effectiveness of mediation in conflict settlement is considerably less than either military and economic intervention or their combination (Regan 1996). Despite its relative ineffectiveness, mediation has received a great deal of scholarly attention in the past three decades. The literature on conflict management identifies a large number of factors that influence the chances of mediation success (Kleiboer 1996). In this paper I will confine my remarks to a brief discussion of only those variables that have a clear bearing on UN mediation in Afghanistan.

Scholars of conflict resolution have classified the variables that influence the chances of mediation success into four categories: (1) the nature of the dispute, (2) the attributes of the disputants, (3) the attributes of the mediator and (4) the strategy of mediation (Kleiboer 1996). As far as the nature of the dispute is concerned, empirical research has established that when the issue of contention is the transfer of sovereignty from one group to another, or changing the ideology of the ruling elites, the chances of successful mediation diminishes significantly. Similarly, conflicts with a high level of intensity and large number of fatalities are very resistant to mediation (Regan 1996).

The distribution of power between the disputants is extremely important in determining the success of mediation. Generally, disputants are rational actors and pursue their self-interest. They accept mediation if it serves their interest. When the perceived distribution of power favours one party, that disputant prefers to pursue a strategy of military victory instead of a negotiated settlement. Unless outside intervention can change the cost–benefit calculus of the disputants, more powerful disputants are not likely to accept mediation.

The distribution of power is closely related to another concept which is very useful in the analysis of mediation: the ripeness of a conflict for mediation. Many scholars believe that a conflict is ripe for resolution when:

(1) a mutually hurting stalemate, marked by a recent or impending catastrophe, exists;

(2) the efforts of both parties to impose unilateral solutions are blocked and bilateral solutions become conceivable, leading antagonists to believe that there is a workable alternative to combat; and

(3) power relations have changed in such a way that a party that previously had the upper hand in the conflict starts slipping and the underdog starts rising (Kleiboer 1996: 363).

Thus, unequal distribution of power between the disputants prevents a conflict from becoming ripe for resolution and hinders the success of mediation.

In contrast, the chances of successful mediation increase when various parties in a conflict accept the identity and legitimacy of the disputants. Good relations between the disputants in the past also increase the likelihood of successful mediation.

Obviously mediators are very important in the success of mediation. Among mediators' attributes, leverage is the most important variable. Of course, leverage depends on the amount and quality of tangible and intangible resources available to the mediator. It is the use of leverage that enables a mediator to change the calculus of cost–benefit for the disputants. When on its own a conflict is not ripe for resolution, leverage can alter the position of the disputants and help the chances of successful mediation (Zartman 2000). Although the impartiality of the mediator is usually helpful, impartiality cannot compete with leverage. Of course, the status of the mediator also helps the success of mediation.

The strategy that a mediator pursues also influences the outcome of mediation. Generally, there are three types of strategies available for a mediator: facilitation, formulation and manipulation. Needless to say, facilitation is the most passive and manipulation the most active strategy. A facilitator communicates messages between disputants and arranges for their meetings. A formulator, in addition to serving as a communication link between disputants, suggests ideas for resolving the conflict. A manipulator uses his/her leverage to push the disputants towards a settlement (Touval and Zartman 1985: 10–12). Empirical research has established that the chances of success for mediation are much greater when a mediator pursues an activist strategy of manipulation (Regan 1996: 348; Zartman 2000: 264). However, the strategy of manipulation is not appropriate for every mediator. A strategy of manipulation without leverage simply does not make sense.

The international environment is also very important for the success of mediation. The resolution of many regional conflicts in the late 1980s and early 1990s became possible after substantial improvement in Soviet–American relations. Indeed, the success of the first round of UN mediation regarding Afghanistan was also due to this change.

Thus, to conclude this section on the general discussion of variables that influence the outcome of mediation, I would say that conflicts that are characterized by great intensity, ideological animosity, struggle for sovereignty and uneven distribution of power between the disputants are very resistant to mediation. Only very competent mediators who enjoy great leverage, pursue an activist strategy of mediation and are lucky enough to have a conducive international environment can succeed in their mission.

Now I would like to discuss the failure of UN mediation in Afghanistan in the light of the above theoretical discussion. Once again, this discussion will have to be rather brief and conceptual. Whether one measures the intensity of conflict in terms of human fatalities or destruction of property, the conflict in Afghanistan has been very intense throughout. Thousands of people were killed in the fighting between the communists and the Mujahidin in the period between the withdrawal of Soviet forces and the collapse of the communist regime (1989–92). Similarly, in the struggle for power between the various Mujahidin groups, about 80 per cent of Kabul was destroyed, thousands of people killed and hundreds of thousands of people were displaced. The same is true about the fighting between the Taliban and their opponents. Similarly, in each phase of the conflict, sovereignty remained the major issue of contention. As discussed earlier, conflicts where sovereignty and ideology are the main issues of contention and where large numbers of people have been killed are very resistant to mediation. In this regard, the difficulties of UN mediation in Afghanistan are pretty much in accordance with the findings of mediation research.

The conflict in Afghanistan has also been characterized by actual or perceived unequal distribution of power among the disputants. After the Soviet withdrawal, even though Dr Najibullah's government enjoyed a tremendous amount of military capability, the Mujahidin believed that, without strong backing from the Soviets, Najibullah's military power was bound to decline. In contrast, they believed that their military victory was inevitable (Ahady 1991). Even when Najibullah's government showed staying power and the Mujahidin suffered a few major military setbacks, no mutually hurting military stalemate prevailed in Afghanistan. Thus, the Mujahidin had little incentive to accept a negotiated settlement. After the collapse of Najibullah's regime, some groups among the Mujahidin were of the opinion that they enjoyed military superiority over their Mujahidin competitors. Consequently they wanted a more prominent role for themselves. When their military power proved to be a lot less, a military stalemate prevailed. However, once again, the stalemate was not hurting all factions. Consequently, the warring factions had no incentive to support a mediated solution. With the rise of the Taliban, the military and political balance of power has dramatically changed in favour of the Taliban. With over 90 per cent of the country under their control and most of their opponents defeated, without foreign pressure, it simply does not make sense for the Taliban to accept mediation. They hope that they will prevail militarily and rule the country as they wish.

Furthermore, UN mediators in Afghanistan had very little leverage over the disputants. They could not reward those who were willing to co-operate with the UN or punish those who objected to UN mediation. Consequently, UN mediators had to follow a low-profile mediation strategy of facilitation. However, given the intensity of the conflict and the uneven distribution of power, only an activist mediation strategy, backed by adequate resources, could change the cost–benefit calculus of the disputants and strengthen the chances of successful mediation.

Thus, the failure of UN mediation in Afghanistan is in accordance with the expectation of theoretical and empirical research on mediation. Of course, from the policy point of view, what the UN can do to enhance the success chances of its mediation in Afghanistan is the most important question. Let me once again very briefly share my thoughts with you on this matter.

I still believe that the UN is more suitable than any other organization or state to be in charge of peace-making efforts in Afghanistan. I believe it is important to realize that, on their own, the disputants in the conflict in Afghanistan are not likely to accept a negotiated settlement. The existing balance of power in Afghanistan does not favour a mediated solution. Without strong pressure, the disputants in Afghanistan are not likely to reach an agreement about peace. The success of UN mediation in Afghanistan requires strong leverage. Unfortunately, thus far the UN has committed negligible resources to its peace-making efforts in Afghanistan. UN mediators in Afghanistan have received a very limited mandate from the General Assembly and the Secretary General. With the existing minimal level of leverage, no UN mediator can succeed.

I believe that the international community, through the UN, should commit a large amount of resources to peace-making in Afghanistan. Once the UN has built leverage in Afghanistan, it should pressure all those disputants that are currently opposed to a mediated settlement.

I also believe that the UN ought to develop a comprehensive peace plan for Afghanistan. The lack of a comprehensive peace plan increases uncertainty and suspicion even among the supporters of a UN-organized political solution. Although the position that the Afghans themselves should determine the framework of a peace agreement sounds morally and political correct, in reality it is an exercise in escapism. If the Afghans could agree among themselves about peace, they would not need activist mediation by the UN. The people of Afghanistan need and desire a just peace. Because in the past two decades military power has become the major determinant of political power, unfortunately, the will of the overwhelming majority of the people does not count. To change this unjust violent situation, we need strong international pressure in support of a just and comprehensive peace plan.

A comprehensive peace plan must address the domestic as well as the foreign dimensions of the Afghan conflict. Although it would be premature to present a detailed comprehensive peace plan here, I would like to identify some substantial issues that peace-makers in Afghanistan should take into consideration.

1. Contrary to the position of the Islamist resistance organizations and the Taliban, Islam is not an issue of contention in Afghanistan. Practically all political groups and the people accept the dominant role of Islam in the socio-political life of Afghanistan. Some groups use Islam to camouflage their own drive for power. The UN ought to be aware of this.

2. Although Afghanistan is a multi-ethnic society, the overwhelming majority of the people accepts the Afghan identity of the country, the state and the nation. All Afghan citizens – regardless of their ethnic, tribal, sectarian and linguistic backgrounds – should enjoy legal and political equality and equality of opportunity in socio-economic matters. Some Afghan groups emphasize ethnic conflict and advocate federalism based on ethnicity as a solution to the problem. I am a democrat and I support the decentralization of power when it really helps the people. But federalism based on ethnicity hinders national integration; it is impractical; and it could easily lead to national disintegration in the future. Therefore, I would like to draw the attention of the UN officials and our friends in the West to the pitfalls of ethnicity-based federalism. The objective of peace-makers should be equal rights for all citizens of Afghanistan and not ethnicity-based federalism.

The Failure of UN Mediation

3. The real issue of contention is the principle of sovereignty. The communists insisted on the sovereignty of the communist party; the Mujahidin wanted an oligarchy of resistance organizations to rule the country; and the Taliban insist on the sovereignty of the clergy. None of them concede the principle of sovereignty of the people. I believe that no peace plan should sacrifice the principle of the sovereignty of the people to appease the warlords. Fortunately, the UN has consistently advocated the right of all the people to participate in the political process, including the election of national leaders. The UN should continue its insistence on the right of all people to participate in the political process.

4. In the past few years, two types of political struggles have been going on simultaneously in Afghanistan. One struggle is the war between the warlords; the second struggle is the efforts of the people to regain their rights that have been violated by the warlords. Unfortunately, UN mediations have been focused on the reconciliation of the warring factions. The UN should not confine its mediation efforts to the Taliban and the United Front. They are not the only disputants in the Afghan conflict. The UN should also have systematic contacts with non-combatant groups.

5. Although in the long run it is important to insist on the observance of the principle of sovereignty of the people and its corollaries, in the short run, in the interest of realism, some concessions to the warlords might be necessary. However, the duration of these privileges should e rather short (a few years) and specified in advance.

6. To achieve a just peace, it is important to mobilize the people and build a democratic alternative in Afghanistan. Although this is primarily a task for the Afghan democrats, the UN and the West can encourage the development of such an alternative. On this point, I disagree with Professor Saikal's recommendation. In order to put pressure on the Taliban to accept a negotiated settlement, Professor Saikal advocates international support for the Northern Alliance or the United Front. Historically, however, the Northern Alliance is part of the problem. It was the Northern Alliance that totally disregarded the UN-negotiated agreement with Dr Najibullah and, instead of allowing an orderly transfer of power, caused the violent overthrow

of Dr Najibullah's regime in 1992. Because the Northern Alliance played a major role in the initiation of the civil war that began in 1992, it is highly unlikely that it will be accepted as a national alternative by the people. Furthermore, the values and the history of the Northern Alliance do not make it a credible candidate for championing the cause of the rights of the people. All members of the Northern Alliance, at various times, have systematically violated the rights of the people. The Taliban's violation of human rights and women's rights should not make the Northern Alliance look like a champion of democracy. The international community should exert pressure on all warring factions by supporting a democratic alternative to both the Taliban and the Northern Alliance. Once again I disagree with Professor Saikal, who dismisses the former king Zahir Shah as an alternative. The former king enjoys a tremendous amount of support among the people and a significant degree of international credibility. If Zahir Shah's supporters manage his initiative with competence, the former king can become a viable alternative.

7. In the past two years the UN Security Council has shown significant interest in Afghanistan. However, this interest is limited to the organization's concern about international terrorism and drug production and trafficking. Although both of these issues are grave matters and deserve the attention of the UN, I believe that international terrorism and drug production are only the consequences of a more fundamental problem. The primary problem in Afghanistan is the absence of a government that enjoys national and international support and observes international norms. Once such a responsible government is established, the problems of terrorism and drug production can be dealt with much more effectively. Thus, the UN ought to be primarily concerned with peace-making in Afghanistan.

8. We all know that foreign interference, especially by regional powers, is a major cause of the continuation of the civil war in Afghanistan. I think it is time for the UN to identify those foreign powers that fuel the war in Afghanistan and pressure them to accept a mediated solution for the conflict.

9. A comprehensive peace plan will remain a useless document unless it is backed by resources. The UN must be willing and able to mobilize political and economic resources to create strong leverage. The UN must make it clear to the Afghan disputants that, without observance of international norms and acceptance of the principle of the sovereignty of the people, no Afghan group, regardless of military success, will receive international recognition and financial aid. Regarding this matter, consistency in UN policy and behaviour is very important. The UN must reward those Afghan groups that advocate the political resolution of the conflict and punish those who insist on military means.

As I mentioned above, these points do not constitute the outline of a comprehensive peace plan. Rather, I think it might be useful to take these points into consideration in peace-making efforts. Of course, some of my recommendations can be easily dismissed by policy-makers as unrealistic. The more realistic practitioners can argue that the Afghan conflict is not important enough for the UN to allocate a large amount of resources to its resolution. Without the allocation of adequate resources, the UN mediators are not going to have adequate leverage to manipulate Afghan disputants. Consequently, any call for a comprehensive peace plan and activist mediation strategy is useless.

Given the current power distribution in Afghanistan and the limited interest of the UN in Afghanistan, I admit that my call for an activist mediation strategy, backed by leverage, is rather unrealistic. However, if we confine our policy options to existing realities, we may as well conclude that there is nothing that the UN can do. Unless we are willing to go beyond the current realities, with all due respect to the celebrated UN mediators, I am afraid UN mediation in Afghanistan will continue to be an exercise in futility. The status quo has been very painful for the people of Afghanistan for a long time and is beginning to bother the international community too. Quite often changing the existing realities is the objective of public policy. I believe the UN has the capacity to bring about positive change in Afghanistan. I strongly urge the UN to change its profile in Afghanistan because its ineffective low profile of the past ten years is not helping the people of Afghanistan.

Bibliography

Ahady, Anwar-ul-Haq (1991) Conflict in Post-Soviet-Occupation Afghanistan. *Journal of Contemporary Asia*. 21(4): 513-528.

Cordovez, Diego and Harrison, Selig S. (1995) *Out of Afghanistan: The Inside Story of the Soviet Withdrawal*. New York, Oxford University Press.

Keleiboer, Marieke (1996) Understaing Success and Failure of International Mediation. *Journal of Conflict Resolution* 40(2): 360-389.

Regan, Patrick M. (1996) Conditions for Successful Third-Party Intervention in Intrastate Conflicts. *Journal of Conflict Resolution* 40(2): 336

Rubin, Barmett R. (1995) *The Search for Peace in Afghanistan*. New Haven, Yale University Press.

Touval, Sadia and William Zartman (1985) International Mediation: Conflict Resolution and Power Politics. *Journal of Social Issues* 41(Summer): 27-45.

Zartman, William (2000) Mediating Conflicts of Need, Greed, and Creed. *Orbis* 44(2): 255-266.

Biographical Notes

Anwar-ul-Haq Ahady is professor of Political Science at Providence College. He obtained his PhD from Northwestern University, and has published widely on Middle Eastern and West Asian security issues.

Heike Bill completed her MA in Iranian Studies at the University of Bamberg. After further research at the South Asia Institute in Heidelberg on provincial administrative and fiscal system in Mughal India, she currently works as gender consultant for Deutsche Welthungerhilfe in Afghanistan.

Rolf Bindemann obtained his MA in anthropology at the Freie Universität Berlin. He is the author of the book *Religion und Politik bei den schiitischen Hazara* (Religion and Policy of the Shi'ite Hazaras).

Hermann-Josef Blanke is professor for International Law at the University of Erfurt. He is also director of the board of the Mediothek for Afghanistan.

Sigmar-W. Breckle is professor for Biology at the University of Bielefeld. He is the former director of the board of the Arbeitsgemeinschaft Afghanistan.

Jonathan Goodhand worked an aid worker in Afghanistan with NGO relief and development programmes. He has published articles on conflict, aid and NGOs in a number of international journals. He is currently a lecturer in Development Practice in the Department of Development Studies at the School of Oriental and African Studies, London.

Ahmad Sultan Karimi is a political scientist. He is director of the board of the Mediothek for Afghanistan.

Max Klimburg is art historian and lecturer at the Institute of Cultural and Social Anthropology at the University of Vienna. Besides numerous articles he is the author of the books *Afghanistan: das Land im historischen Spannungsfeld Mittelasiens* (Afghanistan: The Historical Cross-Roads in Middle Asia) and *The Kafirs of the Hindu Kush*.

Biographical Notes

Bruce Koepke is a research scholar at the Centre for Arab and Islamic Studies, The Australian National University, Canberra. He is currently completing a doctoral dissertation on impact of ultra-conservative Islam on cultural practices in Badakhshan, Afghanistan.

Citha Maass is on the permanent staff of the Stiftung Wissenschaft und Politik, Berlin. She has written numerous articles about the political situation in Afghanistan and South Asia.

Rameen Javid Moshref obtained his MA in Near Eastern Studies at the University of New York. He is the founder of the Afghan Communicator Magazine and has served as its Editor-in-Chief.

Christine Noelle-Karimi obtained her PhD at the department of Near Eastern Studies at U.C. Berkeley. Currently she is visiting professor at the Department Iranian Studies at the University of Bamberg. She is the author of the book *The Interaction between State and Tribe in 19th Century Afghanistan* as well as numerous articles on the field of Middle Eastern historiy and politics.

Angela Parvanta is a PhD candidate at the Department of Iranian Studies at the University of Bamberg. She works on the development of language nationalism in Afghanistan.

Michael Pohly obtained a PhD from the department of Iranian Studies t the Freie Universität Berlin, where he is assistant professor since 1999. He is the author of the book *Krieg und Widerstand in Afghanistan* (War and Resistance in Afghanistan) and the co-author of the recent published book *Osama bin Ladin und der internationale Terrorismus* (Osama bin Ladin and the International Terrorism).

Ahmed Rashid is a graduate of Cambridge University. He is a journalist based in Lahore. He is the correspondence on Pakistan, Afghanistan and Central Asia for the 'Far Eastern Economic Review' and the 'Daily Telegraph'. Besides various articles about the political situation in Afghanistan, Rashid is the author of the books *Taliban: Islam, Oil and the New Great Game in Central Asia* and *The Resurgence of Central Asia: Islam or Nationalism?*.

Biographical Notes

Amin Saikal is Professor of Political Science and Director of the Centre for Middle Eastern and Central Asian Studies at the Australian National University, Canberra. He is the author of *The Rise and Fall of the Shah* and has written extensively on current political developments in the Middle East.

Conrad Schetter holds a PhD in Geography. He is employed at the Zentrum für Entwicklungsforschung (Center for Development Research), University of Bonn. Besides numerous articles he is the author of the forthcoming book *Ethnizität und ethnische Konflikte in Afghanistan* (Ethnicity and Ethnic Conflicts in Afghanistan) and the Co-publisher of the book *Afghanistan in Geschichte und Gegenwart* (Afghanistan in Past and Present).

Reinhard Schlagintweit obtained a MA in Law from the University of Munich. Between 1952 and 1993 he was on the permanent staff of the German Federal Foreign Office (e.g. ambassador to Saudi Arabia, director general of the department Asia, Africa, Latin America). Since 1993 he is the chairman of the German National Committee for UNICEF.

Michael von der Schulenburg obtained a master in Economics from the Ecole Nationale d'Administration, Paris. From 1978 until 2000 he was on the permanent staff of the UN. Besides other appointments he was Chief of Mission of UNOCHA (United Nation Office for Humanitarian and Economic Assistance to Afghanistan), the United Nation Resident Coordinator in Teheran and Director for Operation and Analysis of the UNDCP (United Nations Drug Control Program). Since December 2000 he is the director for Management and Finance at the OSCE in Vienna.

Peter Schwittek worked as a lecturer of mathematics at Kabul University from 1973 to 1977. During the war against the Soviet Union and thereafter he visited different parts of Afghanistan in order to monitor humanitarian programs. Since 1998 he has been head of the office COFAA (Caritas Organization for Aid to Afghanistan) in Kabul.

IKO - Verlag für Interkulturelle Kommunikation
Holger Ehling Publishing
Edition Hipparchia
Frankfurt am Main · London

Frankfurt am Main	**Internet:www.iko-verlag.de**	**London**
Postfach 90 04 21, D-60444 Frankfurt	Verkehrs-Nr.: 10896	4T Leroy House
Assenheimer Str. 17, D-60489 Frankfurt	VAT-Nr.: DE 111876148	436 Essex Road
Tel.: +49-(0)69-78 48 08	Auslieferung: Order@KNO-VA.de	London N1 3QP, UK
Fax: +49-(0)69-78 96 575		Phone: +44-(0) 20 -76881688
e-mail: ikoverlag@t-online.de		e-mail: Holger@Ehling.com

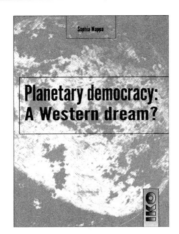

2001, 96 S., € 14,00, ISBN 3-88939-620-8

Sophia Mappa argues in her book that the values on which the Western democratic model is founded - as the individual and a specific form of state power - are far from being shared by the whole planet. In most of the other countries the group has priority over the individual and exclusive, occult and arbitrary power prevails over plurality and the law.

Currently, the dominant universalist discourse and its associated policies deny the existence of those fundamental cultural differences. Their eclipse, however, can lead scientists and politicians into untenable positions and, eventually, prevent them from asking the essential questions, analyzing their implications and acting in consequence.

Bestellen Sie bitte über den Buchhandel oder direkt beim Verlag. Gern senden wir Ihnen unser Titelverzeichnis zu.